SAVING BYZANTIUM

SAVING BYZANTIUM
THE STRUGGLE TO SALVAGE AN EMPIRE

LAURA BOLICK

For Isaac and Oliver

First published 2026

Amberley Publishing
The Hill, Stroud
Gloucestershire, GL5 4EP

www.amberley-books.com

Copyright © Laura Bolick, 2026

The right of Laura Bolick to be identified as the Author of this work has been asserted in accordance with the Copyright, Designs and Patents Act 1988.

ISBN 978 1 3981 2219 2 (hardback)
ISBN 978 1 3981 2220 8 (ebook)

All rights reserved. No part of this book may be reprinted or reproduced or utilised in any form or by any electronic, mechanical or other means, now known or hereafter invented, including photocopying and recording, or in any information storage or retrieval system, without the permission in writing from the Publishers.

British Library Cataloguing in Publication Data.
A catalogue record for this book is available from the British Library.

1 2 3 4 5 6 7 8 9 10

Typesetting by SJmagic DESIGN SERVICES, India.
Printed in the UK.

Appointed GPSR EU Representative:
Easy Access System Europe Oü, 16879218
Address: Mustamäe tee 50, 10621, Tallinn, Estonia
Contact Details: gpsr.requests@easproject.com, +358 40 500 3575

CONTENTS

Illustrations	7
Acknowledgements	9
Chronology of Main Events	12
Prologue	18
Introduction: From Witness to Historian	22
1 The Champions of Byzantium: Isidore and Bessarion	39
2 Emperor John VIII, Sultan Murad II and the Byzantine Empire in the Fifteenth Century	53
3 Salvation through Spiritual Union	66
4 Saving Byzantium as the Pope's Man	82
5 Greek Hawks in the Sacred College	102
6 The Battle for Constantinople	117
7 A Crusade for Constantinople	135

8	Byzantium at the Crossroads	156
9	Championing Byzantium: The Legacy	175
10	Reinventing the Empire	190
	Epilogue	205

Dramatis Personae	210
Appendix: A Brief Survey of the Byzantine Empire	229
Glossary	248
Notes	266
Bibliography	280
Index	308

ILLUSTRATIONS

1. Cristoforo Buondelmonti, *Chart of Constantinople*
2. Frans Hogenberg, *Byzantium Nunc Constantinopolis*, from *Civitates Orbis Terrarum*
3. Artist unknown, *Portrait of Cardinal Isidore*
4. Artist unknown, *Isidore, Metropolitan of Kiev and Rus, Cardinal, Patriarch of Constantinople, Archbishop of Cyprus*
5. Gentile Bellini, *Cardinal Bessarion and Two Members of the Scuola della Carità in Prayer with the Bessarion Reliquary*
6. Artist unknown, *Portrait of Cardinal Johannes Bessarion*
7. Bernardino Pinturicchio, *Pope Eugenius IV* (detail) from the fresco cycle of the Piccolomini Library
8. Bull of the Union of the Greek and Latin Churches
9. Peter Paul Rubens, *Portrait of Pope Nicholas V*
10. Giovanni Paladino, *Medallion of Pope Pius II*
11. Artist unknown, *Portrait of Emperor John VIII*
12. Statue depicting *Constantine XI Palaeologus*
13. Benozzo Gozzoli, *Joseph, Patriarch of Constantinople* (detail) from The Adoration of the Magi

14. Islamic-Ottoman School, *The Fatih Sultan Mehmed II*
15. Artist unknown, *Siege of Constantinople*
16. Turkish School, *Miniature of the Siege of Constantinople*
17. Paolo Romano, *Tomb of Pope Pius II*
18. Shrine with the statue of St Andrew commemorating the arrival of the relic in Rome
19. Byzantine School, *Icon of Saint Demetrios*
20. Antoniazzo Romano, *Madonna and Child*
21. Artist unknown, *Reliquary of Cardinal Bessarion*

ACKNOWLEDGEMENTS

The seed for this book was planted in 2013 by my PhD Viva examiner, Professor Donal Cooper, who encouraged me to keep writing beyond the submission of my dissertation. Transforming my doctoral thesis into a book for the general reader has been a genuinely fun and rewarding journey, made possible thanks to the support, guidance and encouragement of many individuals and institutions. I am profoundly grateful to all those who have contributed to the completion of this book.

First and foremost, I owe a debt of gratitude to my family. My husband, Frank, has been a pillar of strength and patience throughout this undertaking. His unwavering commitment and understanding have been invaluable – not just in the moments of triumph, but in the many long days and late nights spent refining arguments, clarifying ideas and navigating inevitable setbacks. He has asked questions that I would never have considered, and I am indebted to his unorthodox way of thinking that has provoked much thought and invaluable revisions. His faith in me has never waned, even when my own confidence faltered.

Our sons, Oliver and Isaac, have also been a source of immense joy and grounding throughout this venture. Their excitement and exclamations of amazement at the sheer number of words in a book, have provided moments of much needed humour and light relief, renewing my enthusiasm and stamina whenever I felt I was flagging. And their patience – whether enduring my frequent absences when I was buried in research, or hearing me talk (perhaps too enthusiastically) about the subject matter – has been much appreciated.

Much credit is due to my parents, Robert and Ellen Bolick, whose keen insights, meticulous attention to detail, and steadfast backing have significantly enhanced the quality of this book. Their championing of my work has sustained my resolve, and their nuanced guidance was crucial in shaping the final manuscript for a broader audience. They challenged me to think in depth and to communicate clearly, leaving an indelible mark on this project.

The financial support of the A.G. Leventis Foundation and the Hellenic Society made a vital difference in bringing this book to life. Their funding for illustrations not only enriched the text but also helped bridge the gap between academic research and public engagement. I am deeply appreciative of their commitment to fostering historical scholarship and their recognition of the importance of visual storytelling in understanding the past.

A special thanks to my publisher, Alexander Stilwell at Amberley Publishing, for believing in this project from the start. His guidance and professionalism were integral to navigating the path to publication, while his team's dedication ensured that the book reached its audience in the best possible form. It has been a pleasure to work with such an enthusiastic and skilled group of individuals.

Over the course of writing this book I enjoyed some unexpected experiences, including a series of cat-sitting retreats

Acknowledgements

that became something of a parallel narrative to the evolution of the work. Each chapter of this book, in its own way, is tied to the memories of a particular feline companion – their soothing presence, or unhelpful, yet charming, habits of traipsing over my papers with muddy paws provided levity and comfort during an otherwise intense process.

This book would not have been possible without those kind souls who shared their expertise, offered critical insights, and provided moral support along the way. My colleagues and friends in the historical community have been sources of inspiration and encouragement throughout, whether through spirited debates, thoughtful critiques or simply shared enthusiasm for my endeavour. While too numerous to name individually, their contributions are deeply felt and greatly appreciated.

I would also like to thank the libraries, archives and institutions that granted me access to their collections and supported my research over the years. Their dedication to preserving history enabled this book to take shape. Particular thanks go to the librarians and archivists whose assistance in uncovering obscure references and clarifying sources proved invaluable again and again.

Finally, I want to acknowledge the countless acts of kindness, both large and small, that sustained me throughout this process: the friends who lent an ear during moments of doubt, the mentors who offered encouragement at critical junctures and the many cups of coffee shared in the company of those who believed in this work. Writing may be a solitary pursuit, but it is built on a foundation of community.

To all who have helped in the creation of this book, I offer my deepest thanks. Any errors or omissions are, of course, my own.

Dr Laura Bolick

CHRONOLOGY OF MAIN EVENTS

Rise of the Palaeologan Dynasty (1261–1354)

1259	Michael VIII Palaeologus becomes co-emperor of the Empire of Nicaea.
1261	Michael VIII recaptures Constantinople from the Latin Empire, re-establishing Byzantine rule.
1261–1282	Reign of Michael VIII Palaeologus, marked by diplomatic efforts and economic strain.
1282–1328	Reign of Andronikos II. Period of escalating Ottoman advances in Asia Minor.
1341–1347	Byzantine Civil War between the regents of the minor, John V Palaeologus and John VI Kantakouzenos.
1354	Ottomans capture Gallipoli, establishing their first foothold in Europe.

Ottoman Advances and the Loss of Thessalonica (1371–1424)

1371	Battle of Maritsa – Ottoman victory further extends their control in the Balkans, and Emperor

Chronology of Main Events

	John V Palaeologus becomes an Ottoman vassal after accepting Sultan Murad I's suzerainty.
1396	Crusade of Nicopolis – European coalition is defeated by Ottomans.
1402	Battle of Ankara – Tamerlane defeats the Ottomans, temporarily relieving the pressure on the Byzantines.
1422	Murad II besieges Constantinople unsuccessfully but occupies Thessalonica's surrounding lands, leaving the territory at risk.
1423	Thessalonica, still under Byzantine control, faces an Ottoman siege and is sold to Venice in 1423 to save it from the Turks.

Appeals to the West and Loss of Thessalonica (1424–1430)

1424	Emperor John VIII Palaeologus begins diplomatic efforts with the West, seeking aid against the Turks.
1428–1432	Despot Constantine Palaeologus (later Constantine XI) consolidates Byzantine control in the Morea, capturing Patras and reducing Frankish influence.
1430	Thessalonica falls to the Ottomans, a major loss for the Byzantines and Venice.

Council of Ferrara-Florence and Union of Churches (1438–1439)

1438	John VIII travels to Italy with Byzantine delegates to negotiate a union of the Orthodox and Roman Catholic Churches in exchange for western military aid.
6 Jul. 1439	The Decree of Union is signed at the Council of Florence, ostensibly uniting the eastern and western Churches.

Aftermath of the Union and the Battle of Varna (1439–1444)

1439–1440 Byzantine delegates return to Constantinople, where the Union faces widespread Orthodox resistance.

1440 A Mass is held in Hagia Sofia celebrating the Union, but public dissent continues.

1443 Pope Eugenius IV calls for a crusade against the Ottomans. A combined Hungarian, Polish and Wallachian force under John Hunyadi makes early gains.

10 Nov. 1444 The Crusade of Varna is defeated by Murad II in a decisive Ottoman victory, halting efforts to relieve the Byzantine Empire.

Ottoman Advances in the Morea (1446–1448)

1444–1446 Murad II leads a campaign against Despots Constantine and Thomas Palaeologus in the Peloponnese, defeating them and breaching the Hexamilion Wall.

23 Feb. 1447 Pope Eugenius IV dies; Nicholas V is elected on 6 March 1447.

1448 Concordat of Vienna between the Holy Roman Empire and papacy is signed, strengthening papal authority in Europe.

Succession of Byzantine and Ottoman Leadership (1448–1451)

1448 Death of Emperor John VIII; his brother Constantine XI becomes the last Byzantine emperor.

1448–1450 Emperor Constantine XI appeals to Pope Nicholas V for military aid and struggles to implement the Union in Constantinople to secure military support.

Chronology of Main Events

1449	Cardinal Isidore arrives in Constantinople, continuing his mission to promote the Union among the monks, priests and residents.
3 Feb. 1451	Death of Murad II; Mehmed II ascends to the Ottoman throne with a renewed ambition to capture Constantinople.

Final Defence Efforts and Fall of Constantinople (1451–1453)

1451	Mehmed II renews treaties with Serbia and Hungary to ensure temporary peace along the northern borders.
Apr. 1452	Mehmed completes the construction of Rumeli Hisarı, a fortress on the Bosphorus that gave the Ottomans control over the maritime access to Constantinople.
1452	Constantine XI makes one last appeal to Pope Nicholas V for military aid.
Dec. 1452	Cardinal Isidore, representing Rome, arrives in Constantinople to persuade the local clergy to implement the Decree of Union.
12 Dec. 1452	A Mass is held in Hagia Sofia to celebrate the Decree of Union, but widespread Orthodox resistance to the Union persists.
Apr. 1453	Mehmed II begins the final siege of Constantinople.
29 May 1453	Constantinople falls to Ottoman forces. Emperor Constantine XI dies in battle.

European and Papal Responses to the Fall of Constantinople (1453–1464)

1453	Cardinal Isidore, who took part in the battle and was captured, escapes to Crete.

1454	Pope Nicholas V announces a crusade to recapture Constantinople, but European states are unresponsive.
1454	Formation of the Italic League, a defensive alliance among Italian states to counter Ottoman expansion.
24 Mar. 1455	Nicholas V dies; Calixtus III is elected on 8 April 1455 and revives crusade preparations.
1456	Calixtus III organises a fleet and allocates funds to prepare a military campaign but ultimately achieves limited success.

Pius II's Congress of Mantua and Crusade Attempt (1458–1464)

6 Aug. 1458	Death of Calixtus III; Pope Pius II is elected on 19 August 1458.
1459	Pius II convenes the Congress of Mantua, aiming to rally European leaders for a crusade against the Ottomans.
1460	Fall of the Morea to Ottoman forces; Despot Thomas Palaeologus flees to Rome, effectively bringing to an end the Palaeologan family rule over the Byzantines.
1461	Ottoman forces capture Trebizond, the last Byzantine successor state, ruled by the Comnenus dynasty.
1463	Pius II declares a crusade and gathers forces at Ancona.
14 Aug. 1464	Pius II dies and the crusading plans collapse.

Ottoman Conquests and Renewed Papal Crusade Efforts (1464–1471)

Sep. 1464	Pope Paul II succeeds Pius II but focuses on papal and Italian issues, slowing crusade momentum.
1466	Despot Thomas Palaeologus dies in Rome, ending hopes for a Palaeologan restoration in Constantinople.
1470	Fall of Negroponte (Euboea) to the Ottomans consolidates their control in the Aegean.
26 Jul. 1471	Death of Pope Paul II; Sixtus IV is elected on 9 August 1471.

Final Ottoman Expansion into Southeast Europe (1499–1521)

1499–1503	First and Second Ottoman-Venetian Wars consolidate Ottoman dominance over the Venetian territory in Greece.
1517	Ottomans conquer the Mamluk Sultanate, gaining control of Egypt, Mecca and Medina.
1521	Belgrade falls to Sultan Suleiman the Magnificent, extending Ottoman control into Central Europe.

PROLOGUE

In the fifteenth century, the period with which this book is concerned, a series of crises rocked the citizens of an empire that was defined by a common religion, culture and governmental structure. This empire did not occupy a single land mass, but encompassed territories scattered throughout the Mediterranean, Asia Minor and the Balkans. While these citizens identified themselves as Romans (*Rhomaioi* in Greek), later historians have called them Byzantines and their empire, Byzantium. For the purposes of the discussion that follows, I will also refer to them as Byzantines, but their claim to be Romans of the Roman Empire is critical to understanding how and why those living through the events that this book explores dedicated their careers and, even lives, to saving the Empire. They recognised the existential threat, but they did not accept that collapse was inevitable.

This fundamental sentiment and the commitment it generated can be traced back to Constantine the Great, whose legacy would continue to be invoked by the Byzantines for over a millennium. The Roman Empire experienced a major crisis in the third century, which manifested itself in widespread uprisings in almost every corner of its territory. It had physically outgrown its administrative, military and cultural structures. Recognising the existential peril, the ruling emperor, Diocletian, presided over a fundamental set of reforms that divided the rule of the Empire into eastern and western jurisdictions and established a Tetrarchy of two Augusti and two Caesari. This solved the challenges arising from the unwieldy size of the territories, but it set the stage for intense rivalry and intrigue between leaders, igniting endless civil wars as opposing factions vied for the imperial positions.

Eventually, Constantine the Great prevailed over both jurisdictions as the single most powerful leader, allocating subordinate positions to family members. Under Constantine, the Empire's centre of gravity shifted to the east, where the population density and economic prosperity were greater than in the west. In the east, the Roman Empire was defined by its perpetuation of the Roman imperial political structures; the culture of the ancient Hellenes; and eventually, the mass adoption of Christianity.

Constantine inaugurated the city of Constantinople in 330. He chose the ancient Greek colony of Byzantium for the site of his capital, a superb location at the point of two continents and surrounded by three seas: the Bosporus, Marmora and Golden Horn. It was only accessible by land from one direction, making it easily defensible and ideally positioned to control multiple, major international trade routes. It is no surprise that Constantinople became known as New Rome.

For Roman citizens at the time, the transfer of the centre of power to Constantinople was just another incarnation of an ever-evolving empire. The Empire was defined by many nations bound together by their identity as Roman citizens, under the rule of emperors deemed to be Caesars. In practical terms, new political and administrative systems were continually evolving, and changes in the social and economic structures can be charted over the centuries. Power was highly centralised in the court and its extensive civil service. Over time, the Empire's cultural character became more Greek than Latin.

The division of imperial rule between the eastern and western territories became permanent. On paper, the Empire was a single entity ruled by two emperors who divided the responsibility of East and West between them, but the links between the two parts loosened gradually and they became increasingly hostile towards each other. The tribes of the Ostrogoths, Visigoths and Huns eventually wiped out the western Roman Empire. In 410, the Visigoth Alaric led his tribe into Rome, and they were succeeded by the Huns who initiated a period of plunder and chaos across Italy. Byzantium faced threats from these same groups but held its ground. This eastern part of the Empire struggled more with the perpetual defence of its frontiers against the Persians in Mesopotamia and the Germanic tribes on its northern borders.

Although they faced similar existential threats, the rate of separation between the two halves of the Empire accelerated as culture, religious practices and political circumstances evolved. Communication became increasingly difficult as Latin continued to be spoken in the West and Greek emerged as the dominant language in the East. The fifth century was also marked by ecumenical religious councils in which the seeds were sown for the antagonism between Rome and Constantinople over Church supremacy.

Over the next few centuries, the popes in Rome would turn away from the East and look for western allies as they struggled to preserve Christianity and the Roman imperial legacy in the West. Against this backdrop, Charlemagne (748–814) appeared on the scene, creating a centralised Frankish power that became the Holy Roman Empire. The pope established spiritual authority over the Holy Roman Empire in exchange for recognising Charlemagne's position by crowning him emperor in a ceremony in Rome in 800. The papal endorsement of a new 'empire' with its own emperor in the West was a blow to the prestige of Byzantium as the only legitimate Roman Empire. Increasingly, both easterners and westerners believed that just as there should be a single Christian Church, so there should be a single Roman Empire.

This gulf, encompassing geography, politics, religion, culture and language, was ultimately responsible for the weakness that gave opportunities to the enemies of Byzantium. Over the centuries the differences would wax and wane in intensity, interrupted by periodic attempts to find a common ground that would enable east and west Christendom to unite against external threats. None of these were successful. By the fifteenth century, western rulers were so absorbed in their own domestic challenges and so hostile to the Greeks that they were oblivious to the greater danger posed by the rise of Islam, as the Ottomans systematically dismantled the eastern empire that had acted as a buffer zone for the West.

Not everyone suffered from this tunnel vision, and it is the commitment and efforts of two of these men that are the subject of this book. They embodied those Greeks and westerners who recognised the gravity of the situation and who worked to forge the unity that they were convinced would be sufficient to save both Byzantium and ultimately all Christendom.

Introduction

FROM WITNESS TO HISTORIAN

Historians who study the late Byzantine Empire talk in terms of inevitable collapse and downfall. They have traditionally defined Byzantium as an empire that ended in 1453 with the loss of Constantinople to the Turks, an empire for which the writing was on the wall as early as the fourteenth century. This reductive approach overlooks the complexity of the Byzantine Empire in the fifteenth century. Constantinople held an unrivalled symbolic position as the epicentre, but it was only one satellite of several that made up the empire. In the west, the despotate of the Morea, centred around Mistra, had usurped the sacred city as the cultural hub of Byzantium. It was the empire's bread basket, and it continued to survive for several years after Constantinople's demise. In the east, Trebizond was part of the empire, but it was governed independently by the Comnenus family, the dynasty that had ruled Constantinople in the eleventh century. Constantinople's fall was a heavy blow to the Byzantine psyche, and it essentially spelled the end of the Palaeologan dynasty, but there were alternative rulers and dominions that had the potential to fill the vacuum.

The birth of the modern historical approach to the fifteenth century in Byzantium can be traced to the eighteenth century, when the historian Edward Gibbon flagged the fall of Constantinople as the end of the Roman Empire, an empire that had been long gone in the West but had flourished for centuries in the East. Gibbon placed little value on the Byzantine culture, identifying it as decadent and inferior in comparison to developments in the West and a contributory factor in the inevitable decline that he outlined. Gibbon and his peers wrote from the perspective of the post-Enlightenment, attributing Man's progress in culture to a linear development from the Roman classical world to its revival in the form of the Renaissance in the West. Any period or civilisation in between was dismissed under the description of the 'Dark Age'. Art historians have challenged this verdict, leading the campaign to reclaim a place for Byzantium's long-standing and significant contribution to the Renaissance and the development of more modern art styles. Their colleagues, however, who specialise in the political, military and social histories of the late Byzantine empire, have not taken the same revisionist stance, and the Gibbonesque approach to the inevitability of Byzantium's demise has, by and large, prevailed.

The Byzantines themselves identified as Romans (Rhomaioi) – they did not perceive Byzantium to be distinct from the Roman Empire. In his classic study, *The Fall of the Byzantine Empire*, Steven Runciman begins with a chapter called 'The Dying Empire', and he sets the tone of the universally accepted position with statements like, 'Byzantium, as any cool observer could see, was doomed.' Accounts of the period revel in apocalyptic statements reflected in chapter titles such as 'The Breakdown', 'The Remnant of Empire', 'The End of Byzantine Independence',

Saving Byzantium: The Struggle to Salvage an Empire

'A Last Appeal', 'The Final Fall'. In Warren Treadgold's survey history of Byzantium, he goes so far as to claim that no contemporaries '[in 1391] could reasonably have predicted that Byzantium would last two generations more'.

From where does this theory of linear demise come? Hindsight, undoubtedly, has played a role: the Byzantine Empire no longer exists, therefore there must be signs in its history that indicated its end. However, the pervasive sense of inevitability, of collapse that was obvious and unavoidable, owes a profound debt to the writings of four contemporary authors who attempted to situate the trauma of the fall of Constantinople in the context of a bigger history. These men were Doukas, George Sphrantzes, Laonikos Chalkokondyles and Michael Kritovoulos. Their personal circumstances and experiences informed their writing and their interpretation of recent events. Though only one of them, Sphrantzes, was in Constantinople when it fell, these writers were all personally affected by the trauma of the siege and its aftermath, and they needed to find a narrative that would explain the disaster. They identified ungodliness and decadence as the root causes for their loss to the Ottoman armies. Following the lead of these contemporary writers, historians have reshaped this tone of self-condemnation into a theory of inevitable demise.

Several problems arise from the profound influence of these particular Byzantine accounts on modern day historians. The motivations are very different. Today's historian has a more objective approach to history as the practice of harvesting knowledge to develop our understanding of a period. In contrast, the fifteenth-century Greek historians defined the practice entirely differently. They recorded and interpreted historical events as consequences of man's moral choices. History was an exercise in educating the future – by illustrating the virtues and vices of key figures, historians supplied their readers (present and future) with a set of actions to emulate or to avoid. Current and rising leaders would use their writings as a sort of moral code for behaviour and character (or would claim so to do). History was also a means of memorialising the actions of those whom the writers deemed to be heroes. Consider Michael Kritovoulos' stated motivation for writing his history of Mehmed II:

> Kritovoulos the Islander, originally of the inhabitants of Imbros, wrote this history in the belief that events so great and wonderful, occurring in our own times, should not remain unrecorded, but ought to be written up and handed down to subsequent generations so that brave deeds, well worth recording, certainly no less so than those of the old heroes, shall not disappear from the knowledge of men, being hidden by time. Thus those who live after us may not be greatly injured by being deprived of such a history and its lessons, and the authors of these deeds may have a fitting memorial for time to come of their heroism and valour, through this history and its portrait of these deeds.

As we will see, these writers made no secret of the agendas that motivated their compositions or the personal bias that defined their conclusions. Whether writing as an historian or as a chronicler, they all endeavoured to record for posterity the events that they had lived through, and they offered their opinions on what was happening to the world in which they lived. They brought baggage to their enterprise in the form of personal trauma, grievances and axes to grind. They wrote through a lens of religious and cultural bias that defined their times. All historians and commentators of current affairs draw conclusions informed by their environment about their subject matter. These Greek writers were not unusual in doing so. While future historians are equally handicapped by the influence of the times in which they live, they are better placed to identify biases of past writers. In reading the texts of the four Greeks, their apocalyptic views on the Byzantine Empire ring out loud and clear. Their background and context make clear why they held these bleak views, and the question arises whether historians from Gibbon onwards have taken their outlook at face value to inform their own conclusions about the Empire.

Doukas's Historia Turca-Byzantina

One of the most important sources that has inspired latter day historians is *Historia Turco-Byzantina*, written by Doukas (c.1400–c.1462). Very little is known about Doukas, other than he worked for the Genoese in New Phocaea and then for the ruling family on the island of Lesbos. In his official role he was tasked with diplomatic missions that took him to the Ottoman court at Adrianople. He was not in Constantinople when it fell but was still a resident of Lesbos when Mehmed II conquered the island in 1462.

Doukas wrote a history that purportedly spanned from the creation of Adam to the present day. In reality, he covered the millennia from Adam's birth to the Latin occupation of Constantinople in 1204 in the book's first few paragraphs. His narrative focused in depth on the actions of the Byzantine 'Romans' as they faced the rise of the Ottoman Turks in the period 1341–1462.

His conception of history was that every human conflict represented a clash between good and evil, in which any triumph of evil was the result of the interference of Fortune in history or wilful human corruption. Doukas believed that the Romans (both Greek and Latin) were sinners who had brought about their own demise through their immoral choices and behaviours.

He liberally quoted from *Lamentations* to drive home his message of divine retribution, 'Her oppressors are [*sic*] become the head, and her enemies have prospered; for the Lord has afflicted her because of the multitude of her sins.'

In his section on the fall of Constantinople, Doukas had no doubt that moral turpitude and sin were the causes. In a passage worthy of the anguished Prophet Jeremiah himself, he lamented:

> Shudder, O Sun! And you too, O Earth, heave a heavy sigh at the utter abandonment by God, the Just Judge, of our generation because of our sins! We are not worthy to raise our eyes to heaven. We must first bow down and touch our faces to the earth, and then we may cry out, 'Thou art just, O Lord, and righteous is Thy Judgment. We have sinned and we have committed iniquities and injustices against all nations. With true and righteous judgement Thou hast visited upon us our tribulations. But spare us, O Lord, we entreat Thee.'

His grandfather, Michael Doukas, was a court notable who rose against John V Palaeologus during the civil war of 1341–1347. He joined the opposition that supported a rival family's claim to the throne in Constantinople, conspiring to replace the Palaeologues with John VI Kantakouzenos. Doukas the grandson glorified his grandfather's participation, even though the uprising was a failure, and the majority of the rebels were executed. Michael Doukas was one of the fortunate few who escaped and he fled to Ephesus disguised as a monk with his family. In exile, he was warmly welcomed and sponsored by the Turkish ruler, Emir Isa. The family settled and cultivated close ties with the Turks. Doukas recorded that his grandfather did not want to return to Constantinople as he believed that its demise was inevitable.

This family history of opposition to the Palaeologues informed the Doukas's approach to the history that he composed. He attributed the suffering of the Byzantines to their submission to the usurper, Michael VIII Palaeologus, whose reign inaugurated the dynasty's control over the empire. Doukas traced the demise of Constantinople all the way back to the civil war that had ruined his family, claiming that the internal conflict gave the Ottomans the opportunity to take the Balkans and to turbocharge their ascent at the expense of the Byzantine state. In the chapters that described the run up to 1453, he made it clear that he despised the local Constantinopolitans and blamed their refusal to work with the Roman Catholic Church for the loss of the city.

Doukas clearly yoked together the Palaeologan dynasty, Constantinople as a city, and the Byzantine Empire. He believed that the latter was betrayed by the citizens and the imperial family. He perceived the unfolding of events through the lens of his family's hatred of the Palaeologan leaders and their belief that the inequity of these men had angered God sufficiently for Him to inflict punishment on the whole of Byzantium. Modern historians have been influenced by Doukas's biblical statements, which seem to support their thesis of the Empire's inevitable decline but may actually reflect a family grudge against the ruling dynasty.

They have overlooked the equally important theme of 'redemption' in Doukas's 'history', a redemption that will herald the restoration of the Greek nation, liberated by the West. For Doukas, the blows dealt to the Empire were merely symptoms of a phase, not the demise of an entire empire. The fall of Constantinople represented the loss of a Christian city to an infidel army, and it would unquestionably be rescued by other Christians and restored to its rightful owners.

Doukas even stated that this conviction is what drove him to write his history. He revealed in Chapter 42 that an oracle had foretold the destruction of the Palaeologans by the Ottomans but predicted that the Turks would be next to fall before the restoration of a true Hellenic nation:

> While still a youth I learned from old and venerable men that the end of the Ottoman tyranny would take place with the extinction of the Palaeologan dynasty... According to this prophecy, the end of the emperors and of the City was to occur first, followed by the cessation of the Ottoman reign... We, therefore, who have reached this point in these present days, and who have witnessed the consummation of the dreadful and terrible threat made against our nation, await as in a reverie the restoration.

George Sphrantzes, Chronicon

A contemporary of Doukas, George Sphrantzes was a Greek chronicler who had actually been in Constantinople when it fell. After serving Despot Thomas Palaeologus in the Morea, he was appointed to a diplomatic role under Emperor Manuel II. Through these strong ties with the Palaeologan family, he became a friend and confidant of Constantine XI.

He wrote his career memoirs covering the events of the period from 1413 to 1477 in a text that is known as the *Chronicon Minus*. Sphrantzes introduced his chronicle with a survey of the state of the Byzantine Empire and the rise of the Ottomans during his childhood. The subsequent sections describe the biographical and major political events that affected him. The *Chronicon Minus* was not technically a history, and until the 1930s historians believed that it was a set of notes for a larger text called the *Chronicon Maius*, which surveyed the Palaeologan dynasty up to 1477.

The *Chronicon Maius* was one of the key sources for historians who studied the Byzantine Empire in the fifteenth century.

That George Sprhantzes had been physically present in Constantinople during the siege gave this text particular weight in the eyes of latter-day scholars. As with Doukas, the *Chronicon Maius*'s treatment of the demise of a dynasty was interpreted by later historians as the fall of an empire.

The text was composed of four books and a prologue that outlined the reasons for writing and preserving the record that followed. In Book I the writer covered the origins of the Palaeologan dynasty and surveyed the history of the Ottomans. Book II is an account of Emperor John VIII's rule; Book III dealt with the reign of Constantine XI and described, in great detail, the siege and fall of Constantinople; and Book IV focused on the loss of the Morea to the Turks.

In Book III, the fall of Constantinople was unequivocally positioned as the death knell of an entire empire:

> ...thus the dynasty of the Palaeologoi reigned in the Queen of cities for 194 years, ten months and four days. Our empire was founded by Flavius Constantine and ended with Constantine Palaelogus. With our unfortunate City as its capital, the empire of the Romans lasted for more than 1,143 years, ten months and four days.

But was that actually the observation of George Sphrantzes, eyewitness to the fall of Constantinople? In 1932 a Greek scholar, J. B. Papadopoulos, raised questions about the authorship of the *Chronicon Maius* after preparing a new critical edition of the text. Further investigation revealed that the *Chronicon Minus* had been expanded in the sixteenth century by Makarios Melissenos, the Metropolitan of Monemvasia in the Morea. A notorious counterfeiter of Palaeologan documents, Melissenos was involved in an uprising against the Turks in the Morea. When this attempt to oust the Ottomans from the island failed, he fled to Naples where he joined the community of exiled Greeks who were involved in inciting rebellion against the Turks on the Greek mainland. He promoted himself by claiming to own this work by George Sphrantzes that he had forged.

Melissenos must have been a talented writer of fiction as well as forger if the following passages were not from the pen of George Sphrantzes:

> I was taken prisoner and suffered the evils of wretched slavery. Finally I was ransomed on September 1 1453 and departed for Mistra. My wife and children had passed into the possession of some elderly Turks, who did not treat them badly. Then they were sold to the sultan's Mir Ahor [Master of the Horse], who amassed a great fortune by selling many other beautiful noble ladies... My children's beauty and proper upbringing could not be concealed, thus, the sultan found out and bought my children from his Master of the Horse for many thousand aspers.

In the following months and years his children lost their lives:

> In the same month and year [December 1453], the most impious and pitiless sultan, with his own hand, took the life of my dearest son John, on the grounds that the child had conspired to murder him. Alas for me, his unfortunate and wretched father! My son was fourteen years and eight months less a day... In September 1455, my beautiful daughter Thamar died of an infectious disease in the sultan's seraglio. Alas for me, her wretched father! She was fourteen years and five months.

Forgery issues aside, the author's personal experiences should have given historians pause for thought before they adopted the narrative for future histories. Sphrantzes and his family suffered brutally in the aftermath of the Ottoman occupation of Constantinople. On a personal level, Sphrantzes experienced the fall of Constantinople as the end of his world. He lost his position as a highly placed and regarded Byzantine statesman. He lost his family. It was entirely credible that his 'history' of everything that happened before this catastrophic event would be interpreted through this lens. Those who survived the assault on the city but suffered far less did not describe the event in terms of the end of an empire. As we will see, the Greeks who were present at the siege, men like Isidore, spoke of a cataclysmic event that should and could be reversed. The loss of Constantinople was undoubtedly a devastating blow, but not the end of the story for many.

The *Chronicon Maius* concluded that it was the accumulation of Byzantine sins that brought about the end of its empire. There would have been little reason to suspect the text's authenticity, and many historians drew on it as a source for the narrative that they built around an empire on a trajectory to demise. After historians became aware that the *Chronicon Maius* had not been written by Sphrantzes then its use as a contemporary source should have altered. It could no longer be interpreted as evidence that Sphrantzes believed that the Empire was doomed when Constantinople was lost. The real writer, Melissenos, enjoyed the benefit of hindsight; his text was not an eyewitness account.

Laonikos Chalkokondyles, Demonstrations of Histories

The third writer whose assessment of recent history shaped the discourse of inevitable decline was Laonikos Chalkokondyles. He wrote the *Demonstrations of Histories*, which examined the rise of the Ottomans at the expense of the Byzantines from the fourteenth century up to the mid-1460s. The medieval historian, Dan Ioan Mureşan, describes Chalkokondyles as 'the historian of the Byzantine doom and Ottoman boom'. Of the four accounts which have inspired scholars of the period, this manuscript was the most immediately successful and enjoyed the widest dissemination in the years after it was composed. Around thirty copies were made in a very short time, and it was read in both the East and West, entering the historiographical canon of both spheres. Recent scholarship has proposed that the work was written in Constantinople under Ottoman occupation between 1460 and 1464 for the Greek speaking audience that had remained in the city.

Laonikos Chalkokondyles was probably born into a distinguished Athenian family around 1430. After his family was exiled from Athens for political reasons, he was raised in Mistra where his father held the role of ambassador for the Despot of the Morea, Constantine Palaeologus, later Emperor Constantine XI. In ten volumes, Chalkokondyles tried to paint himself as a neutral observer of Islam and Christianity. His assessment of Islam deviated from the traditional judgements of his peers. He described it as a culture, not a manifestation of barbarism. He began his historical survey with the pre-history of the Greeks and Turks, and the final three books are dedicated to twelve years of Sultan Mehmed II's reign. Chalkokondyles did not identify as a Roman but as a Greek, distinct from the imperial Roman self-identity of his peers, Doukas and Sphrantzes. He referred to Constantinople as Byzantium, rejecting the connection with Constantine the Great as the founder of the eastern Roman empire. For Chalkokondyles, the Empire was Constantinople, and the fall of the city equated to the fall of the Empire. He even ascribed this opinion to Mehmed II, quoting a speech that the Sultan allegedly made to the Janissaries prior to the assault, in which he demanded that they help him win an empire.

Chalkokondyles put forward the theory that the virtues of the Ottomans justified their victories. While he condemned the tyranny and cruelty of Mehmed II, he recognised the skills and achievements of the Turks:

> I am referring to the fall of the Greeks and the events surrounding the end of their realm, and to the rise of the Turks to great power, greater than that of any other power to date... I am going to provide a detailed account, as accurately as I have been able to ascertain it, of how these things happened, each in turn; that is, how the affairs of the Greeks were quickly ruined, destroyed by the Turks, and how the latter rose to greatness, continuously reaching new peaks of prosperity during this period.

While Chalkokondyles attributed the rise of the Turks to their superiority, he also blamed the demise of the Byzantines on historical retribution for the past crimes of the Greeks, going back as far as the destruction of Troy. This was a variation on the theme of downfall as punishment for sinfulness: 'That, then, is what happened regarding the Greeks of Byzantion [sic]. This calamity seems to be the greatest that ever took place throughout the world in its excess of suffering, similar to the fall of Troy; in fact, wholesale destruction was the penalty that the Greeks suffered for what they did to Troy.'

In his assessment of the fall of Constantinople as the end of an empire, Chalkokondyles spoke in terms of the end of a world, as catastrophic as the destruction of Troy. This was an event that had entered into the mythological canon, and he predicted that the same would happen to the Byzantine Empire. Despite his protestations of neutrality, he served a specific agenda with these claims. Chalkokondyles anticipated that the Greek empire would be restored to the Greek nation and governed by a Greek ruler once again in the future. For the writer, Constantinople's fall was the necessary prelude to the rebirth of the ancient Greek state. He anticipated the revival of the ancient glory of the Hellenes, not a restoration of an eastern Roman empire – harking back to a time when Athens was the epicentre of the classical Greek world.

Michael Kritovoulos, History of Mehmed the Conqueror

In the nineteenth century, a copy of a history of the years 1451–1467 in the reign of Mehmed II, from an entirely different perspective, was discovered in Istanbul's Library of Ahmed III at Topkapı Palace. Its author was Michael Kritovoulos, whom we met above. He dedicated its five volumes to the Sultan. Book I included an account of the siege of Constantinople, and the rest of the texts covered Mehmed's subsequent military campaigns in Byzantium, and his efforts to rebuild Constantinople. Apart from the sixteenth-century copy in the Topkapı Palace library, there is no evidence of any other copies or translations. A German scholar, Constantin Tischendorf, discovered the autograph text and published it in 1860. It became one of the main sources for historians of the period.

Kritovoulos celebrated the deeds of the Ottomans in his history. He advocated collaboration with the Turks as the only way to preserve the Greek nation, religion, language and culture. To support his theory, he dwelt on the heroism of Mehmed, and the strengths and virtues of the Ottomans. In his opinion, the Byzantines could never hope to defeat such a great leader as the Sultan:

But the greatest obstacle of all was the forces of the Romans [Byzantines], both on land and on sea, always opposing them and fighting them and giving them much resistance and many struggles. Still, none of these things checked their forward progress, or curbed their impetuosity and valour until, having overthrown and completely demolished all, they firmly held the rule. They showed everyone their great strength, being valorous men to the very end and never yielding anything, from the very start, of their plans and ideals. Whenever they conquered their enemies, they went forward against them a great distance. And when they were beaten, they did not fall back or give up their good hope, but because of their confidence in themselves and their hope for the future, they endured everything, even when it was unknown to the Fates; moreover they bore up valiantly under events, daring even beyond their powers, taking unbelievable risks, and keeping good hope even in the worst circumstances.

Kritovoulos began his narrative with the death of Sultan Murad I and the accession of his son, Mehmed II. He described the new Sultan's aspirations for global domination and drew parallels with Alexander the Great. The account of the Sultan's efforts to repopulate Constantinople and to stimulate the economy reflected one of the book's central themes: the transition of power from the Byzantine Greeks to the Ottoman Turks. In Kritovoulos's interpretation, the Sultan's Ottoman tribe was predestined to succeed the Byzantines. He set the Ottomans in the context of a classicizing, Hellenistic view of history; that great empires and ruling dynasties had a finite lifespan. In his timeline, the Assyrian Babylonians were succeeded by the Egyptians, the Medes, the Persians, the Greeks, then the Romans and now the Ottomans. The motif of destiny controlled by external forces comes across in the amount of time Kritovoulos spent describing various portents during the siege of Constantinople:

What disturbed them [the Constantinopolitans] no less were the inexplicable events happening just then, events which they took as divine portents—unusual and strange earthquakes and boilings of the earth, and from heaven thunders and forked lightnings and frightful thunderbolts and brightness seen in the sky, and fierce gales and floods of rain and torrents. Furthermore, there were irregular movements of unusual stars, their wandering courses, and again their disappearances, and still others again fixed in position but for long periods pouring out smoke. And many other such marvellous and unusual signs showed the Divine power presaging the future and suggesting a new order of things and a complete change. For pictures sweated in the churches, as did pillars, and statues of holy men. There were instances of supernatural possession or inspiration of men and women which boded no good, and the soothsayers prophesied many misfortunes. Old prophecies and oracles were recalled and repeated, and every sort of thing which is likely to happen under such circumstances, all took place, all pointing to no good. These all brought great terror and agony to people, totally confounded them, and gave no hope for the future.

Was this narrative of divinely instigated, inevitable collapse an objective assessment of the Byzantine Empire? Once again, the personal circumstances of the author dictated his interpretation. Kritovoulos, born around 1400, was the son of a notable family from Imbros. He wrote the *History of Mehmed the Conqueror* while employed in the Ottoman civil service. That it was intended for his patron is clear from Kritovoulos's dedication of the texts to the Sultan. As a young man, Kritovoulos had studied in Constantinople in the circle of the renowned scholar George-Gennadios Scholarios. Scholarios promoted collaboration with the Turks, and his influence can be detected in Kritovoulos's writings and actions. The Greek had played a political role in the negotiations to prevent the Ottomans besieging the northern Aegean islands. He used his good relationship with Mehmed's courtiers to secure the position of governor of Imbros after the island was finally confiscated by the Sultan. Furthermore, he was able to persuade Mehmed to transfer control of Imbros and Lemnos to the Byzantine despot, Demetrius Palaeologus. Demetrius was held in vassalage to Mehmed, and the islands were included in this arrangement.

The bleak outlook forged by the personal circumstances of these four writers whose 'histories' survived, has had a disproportionate impact on the outlook of later historians. This book reconsiders the years in the run up to the fall of Constantinople and its aftermath from the perspective of contemporaries who, without the personal tragedies or biases that informed the four writers of surviving 'histories' and without the benefit of hindsight, acted in the belief that the rise of the Ottoman Turks could be stalled, and that Byzantium could be preserved for generations to come. It demonstrates that this belief was realistic and that the actions of the Greeks to resist the Turks were not futile. The Byzantines had not buried their heads in the sand, nor were they oblivious to a looming existential threat. For them, defeat in 1453 was not inevitable and, more importantly, that defeat was not the final blow to the Empire's existence. Nowhere was this story more evident than in the careers of two prominent Byzantines; careers defined by the challenge that the Ottomans posed. These men embraced this challenge with a conviction motivated by the certainty that their cause was winnable. They were Iohannes Bessarion and Isidore of Kiev. Throughout the course of this book we see how they identified the dangers facing their religion, culture, way of life and territorial integrity, and what actions they took to avert those risks. By setting aside the historians' rhetoric that this Empire was doomed, we can question whether it could have been saved, and we can even question whether the territorial losses of the Byzantines should be judged as the loss of Byzantium as a conceptual entity.

I

THE CHAMPIONS OF BYZANTIUM: ISIDORE AND BESSARION

Isidore and Bessarion led remarkably parallel lives and became close acquaintances and colleagues despite an age gap of around thirteen years. Their similarities begin with the enigma that surrounds their very names, as well as the place and date of birth of both men. Late medieval and early renaissance Greeks set little store on a man's life before he entered the Church, so sources are scarce, verging on the non-existent, for both Bessarion and Isidore's early years. Their names may have been adopted after they became monks, so we cannot say for certain what their parents called them. Speculation drawn from calculations based on documented and dated events indicates that Isidore was probably born in 1390 and Bessarion in 1402 or 1403.

Surviving sources that account for Isidore's early years are frustratingly scarce. His career played out in Greece, Italy and the Slavic states, and we have access to a few texts written by local scribes from these areas. However, they are inconsistent and problematic. Muscovite Rus' writers speculated that the

Cardinal was born in Thessalonica, and they stressed his Greek roots or identified him as Greco-Slav. Greek sources favoured Constantinople or the Morea, possibly in Monemvasia, as his birthplace, and they also suggested that he came from noble lineage. Certainly, the depth and quality of his education along with the attention he received from the Palaeologan family implies that he had imperial connections. A modern scholar, Haris A. Kalligas, put forward the theory that Isidore may have had imperial blood: he was possibly an illegitimate child of Theodore I, Despot of the Morea, making him the nephew of Emperor Manuel II. Evidence for this, however, is circumstantial. The earliest surviving text connected to Isidore is Emperor Manuel II's funeral oration composed for the anniversary of the death of his brother Despot Theodore I. The Emperor approached Isidore for his opinion and edits for the content, and Manuel's own letters suggest that Isidore was chosen to deliver the eulogy at the ceremony. Such an honour gives weight to the speculation that he had imperial blood.

Bessarion was not so high born. He was probably the son of labourers who raised him in Trebizond, the capital city of a satellite Byzantine kingdom on the southeast coast of the Black Sea (in present-day northern Turkey). Situated at the natural crossroads between the best sea routes to the interior of Anatolia and to Iran, today Trebizond is part of northern Turkey. When Iohannes was born it was a heavily fortified city established on a steep hill overlooking a flourishing port and market.

The ruling family in Trebizond at the time of Bessarion's birth was the Comnenoi, the dynasty that had occupied the throne ever since the Crusader conquests of the Fourth Crusade in 1204 when Trebizond was founded. This diminutive empire was a mere strip of land with no physical links to Constantinople, yet it survived for another 250 years after Constantinople fell to the Turks in

The Champions of Byzantium: Isidore and Bessarion

1453. As Cardinal Bessarion, Iohannes would witness from afar the tragedy of Constantinople's demise, but he could take some consolation from the fact that his homeland represented one of the last bastions of the Byzantine Empire.

Nestled between the natural defences of the virtually impassible Pontic Mountains to the north and the manmade protection of the citadel around the city and its harbour, Trebizond was a secure home for the little boy. Over the centuries the Comnenoi rulers had further entrenched the little empire's strength through a series of strategic marriage alliances with the Ottomans and with vassalage treaties that they arranged with their larger neighbours. In fact, when Iohannes was born, Trebizond was a vassal state to the Mongols in return for their protection against Turkish aggression. The willingness of the Comnenoi to secure survival through these acts of realpolitik was a valuable lesson for Iohannes in his later life. He would advocate the unpopular union of the East and West churches as the most effective way to save the Byzantine Empire from the Ottomans. Much as Trebizond's ruling dynasty made arrangements with those who were distasteful to them, Iohannes would argue that having the protection of the western powers would ultimately preserve the existence of the Byzantine Empire.

Iohannes' parents may have been poor, but the environment in which he was born was not. The thriving trade and industry of this city port meant that the levels of disposable income were high. Residents and visitors spent this money on projects that made Trebizond one of the major Byzantine cultural and intellectual centres in the fifteenth century. Iohannes would have been accustomed to streets dominated by houses for rich merchants and to sprawling estates belonging to the landed gentry and to the Church. Trebizond boasted over ninety-five churches in its heyday, and there were several monasteries outside the city walls. These buildings were ostentatious in their architecture and art collections – the wealthy citizens were all too ready to donate and commission visible projects that would bring them kudos in the present, and eternal salvation in the afterlife.

Wherever Iohannes' residence was located in the city, his home would have been in the shadow of Trebizond's crowning glory: the citadel at the summit of the hill where the imperial palace, church and government offices were situated. The Comnenoi spared no expense on these buildings, and their generous patronage attracted many highly skilled artists and craftsman.

Iohannes was immensely proud of his Byzantine roots, even though he would ultimately uproot them and immigrate to Italy. Trebizond was perhaps the source of this pride. Despite his young years, the city and its imperial buildings made an impact on Iohannes that resonated loudly in his later life when he described the palace's vestibules and halls, 'which are quite beautiful and large and able to accommodate a great many people. [The] …floor is paved with white marble, and its ceiling gleams with gold, a variety of colours and masterpieces of painting. The entire vault shimmers with stars casting their light in imitation of the sky and displaying extraordinary refinement and luxury of the painting.'

It was not just a deep sense of patriotism that Trebizond gave to Iohannes. The energy and dynamism of this thriving city infused the boy and was reflected in the passion and energy that he brought to the causes he championed throughout his career. By the harbour and in the merchant quarters there must have been a riot of colours, smells and tastes, all competing to dominate the senses. Trebizond was located on the trade routes for spices, silks, basketry and dozens of other items. It was a dynamic trading hub but also a major centre of ship building where the craftsmen specialised in long ships and cargo vessels.

The Champions of Byzantium: Isidore and Bessarion

As a flourishing mercantile centre in the Byzantine Empire, the streets would have been bustling with people from many different nations. The city was relatively small, with only 4,000 inhabitants recorded in 1438. However, Iohannes would have rubbed shoulders with western Europeans (especially Genoese and Venetians), and Asians from Persia, from China and from other lands along the trading routes. In the local markets that teemed with foreigners from eastern Europe, he almost certainly encountered Byzantines from the Balkans and from further afield. It is clear from his writing about Trebizond that Iohannes relished this cosmopolitan environment: 'We intermingle with all foreign peoples, we interact with all races. There are no cities or minds of men about which we do not know.'

For this boy, foreigners were not threats, but repositories of potential to contribute and to enhance the Byzantine world, 'We become wiser and better than them because we collect what is best from everywhere, selecting what is useful and trading in every kind of knowledge.'

He sustained and developed this attitude into his manhood when he argued for the eastern Church to embrace union with the West, believing that the salvation of the Empire depended on the physical, spiritual and financial support of western powers.

Looking back on his childhood, Iohannes credited his training and education to his upbringing in Trebizond. These were very early years – by the time he reached his early teens he had already left for Constantinople, but clearly Trebizond inspired a deep loyalty in him: 'I shall adorn my fatherland with words, which God the Word challenged us to love above all else, not only because it reared us, but also because it was responsible for us acquiring this skill, as it provided us with more than an abundance of talent for speaking, and also made us capable of learning from others.'

The education of both Isidore and Bessarion, even though a decade apart, followed the same typical Byzantine model, which was unlike that on offer in the West. Schools and universities did not really exist, and students would seek out an individual teacher who would tutor them. Isidore was probably brought to Constantinople from the Morea in the retinue of Manuel II, when the Emperor stopped over on his return from a diplomatic trip to various regions of Europe. He may also have been tutored by the renowned Greek scholar Manuel Chrysoloras. Bessarion's first tutor was the bishop of Trebizond, a leading scholar called Dositheos. It seems that Dositheos became his mentor in 1415, when Iohannes would have been twelve or thirteen years old. His parents probably 'gave' him to the Church, a common practice in those days for unprosperous but aspirational families. The most likely scenario is that the child showed some academic aptitude and was noticed by Dositheos, who took him under his wing. When the bishop moved to Constantinople in 1416, the young Bessarion went with him.

In contrast, we are less certain where Isidore lived his earliest years, but if he was born in Constantinople, he would have endured the intermittent land blockade that Sultan Bayezid prosecuted over eight years. Conditions for the residents were intolerable during this period, as Constantinople experienced economic failure, cycles of plague and the inevitable breakdown of society. The intellectual and educational institutions also suffered, and by the end of the blockade the buildings were dilapidated and the teachers and students had fled. When Manuel II acceded to the throne at the end of this period, he invested in reviving the intellectual reputation of Constantinople. He had been travelling in the West, at the time of his father's death, campaigning for political and military support to oppose the Turks, and he stopped in the Morea on his way home.

The Champions of Byzantium: Isidore and Bessarion

The Emperor and his retinue spent several months there in the city of Monemvasia. It is possible that Isidore was living there when Manuel arrived and that he joined the imperial retinue when it left for Constantinople. Isidore would have been one of the first students to benefit from Manuel's revival of teaching in the imperial city.

Based on the writings that Isidore produced later in life, his curriculum most likely included the scriptures, the literature of the Church Fathers, ecclesiastical law, and ancient Greek (specifically the fashionable Attic dialect). The adult Isidore copied numerous manuscripts over the course of his career, and these display a high-quality calligraphy, suggesting that he had been trained from an early age in transcription and penmanship. The books that he borrowed as a Cardinal from the Vatican Library revealed an interest in the occult, ethnography, astronomy and antiquity – all topics that he had probably been schooled in as a child.

In the fifteenth century, humanists flocked to Constantinople to study, and both Bessarion and Isidore (though not in the city at the same time) were taught by many of these resident scholars. They were immersed in the classical Greek writers, schooling Isidore and Bessarion to write in the style of the late antique rhetoricians, a highly stylised and contrived manner. Isidore became a superb calligrapher and copyist of these manuscripts, and Bessarion's passion for preserving this ancient literary culture was seeded during these formative years. But it was not just classical Greek they encountered here. They had their first exposure to western literature in Constantinople, studying Latin writers with Italian humanist scholars, specifically Guarino dei Guarini of Verona, Francesco Filelfo, Giovanni Aurispa (a renowned book dealer), and the writer Cristoforo Garatone. The boys were unlikely to have had any proficiency in Latin during their years in Constantinople, and they would have only been able to read texts in Greek translation. But they must certainly have been aware (even if indirectly) of the Italian academic movement that we now call the Renaissance. The impact of these influences would be profound in their adult lives.

Constantinople would have presented Isidore and Bessarion with a medley of experiences whose contradictory nature inspired them to take the very unorthodox decisions to leave their homeland that they made at the end of the 1430s. On the one hand, Constantinople's mystique was still buoyant, but it was based on the reputation of a previous golden age rather than on the current reality. Its spiritual pedigree was rivalled only by Rome, and it is likely that this spirituality influenced Iohannes and Isidore in their choice of career. Constantinople was the home of an unsurpassed collection of relics. In 1200, it was estimated that the city held approximately 3,600 saintly body parts from 476 different saints. The Augousteion, a public space, was packed full of curiosities and dominated by the Great Palace of the Byzantine emperors and the magnificent cathedral of Hagia Sofia. The dome of this legendary church was so immense in scale that it was visible to sailors out at sea, who reported that it seemed to float mystically in the air. Inside the cathedral, the young men would have been dazzled by light from over 100 chandeliers and from shafts of sunlight piercing the interior at different angles throughout the day. The altar was made of solid gold and sat beneath a bejewelled and gilded canopy. Constantinople's Hagia Sofia would have been unlike anything Bessarion or Isidore had ever seen.

On the other hand, they only had to scratch the surface of this ancient glory, and they would have realised that Constantinople had fallen into a sad state. Continuous harassment by the Ottomans was increasingly effective in strangling the local economy. Pero

The Champions of Byzantium: Isidore and Bessarion

Tafur, a Spaniard from Cordoba, travelled extensively for several years in Europe and Asia. He wrote a detailed narrative of his experiences, and the manuscript survived in an eighteenth-century copy that was first printed in Madrid in 1874 under the title, *Andancas é Viajes de Pero Tafur por diversas partes del mundo avidos (1435–1439)*. Tafur's account of his visit to Constantinople captured a snapshot of the deplorable state of the city:

> The Emperor's Palace must have been very magnificent, but now it is in such a state that both it and the city show well the evils which the people have suffered and still endure. At the entrance to the Palace, beneath certain chambers, is an open loggia of marble with stone benches round it, and stones, like tables, raised on pillars in front of them, placed end to end. Here are many books and ancient writings and histories, and on one side are gaming boards so that the Emperor's house may always be well supplied. Inside, the house is badly kept, except certain parts where the Emperor, the Empress, and attendants can live, although cramped for space. The Emperor's state is as splendid as ever, for nothing is omitted from the ancient ceremonies, but, properly regarded, he is like a Bishop without a See... The city is sparsely populated. It is divided into districts, that by the seashore having the largest population. The inhabitants are not well clad, but sad and poor, showing the hardship of their lot which is, however, not so bad as they deserve, for they are a vicious people, steeped in sin. It is their custom when anyone dies not to open the door of the house for the whole of that year except in case of necessity. They go continually about the city howling as if in lamentation, and thus they long ago foreshadowed the evil which has befallen them.

Groomed from an early age for a career in the Church, Bessarion entered the monastery of St Basil in 1423, aged twenty. Three years later he was ordained as a deacon and became a priest shortly afterwards. Similarly, Isidore entered the private imperial monastery of Saint Demetrios and was appointed head of the institution three years later. There was an inevitability about becoming a monk. Taking the habit was probably planned for both men from their childhood. Monasticism commanded a very high profile in the Byzantine Empire, and it was common for men and women to take their vows. Although the records are sparse, it has been estimated that 1-2% of the imperial population was affiliated to a monastery at any given point during the empire's lifespan. The average age for a person to become a monk was twenty-four to twenty-five. At twenty, Bessarion was a little younger than most, while Isidore was a little older. Religious men could become politically powerful: they were regularly appointed as bishops and patriarchs of the Church. Many of the more prominent monks were consulted by emperors before major decisions were made. In the political arena, the monastic communities commanded a level of prestige that reflected their role as spiritual defenders of the Empire. For a young man like Bessarion who had no notable lineage or wealth, or for an illegitimate imperial child like Isidore, this was an obvious career path.

Despite their parallel educational experiences, it is not in Constantinople where Isidore and Bessarion finally met, but in the Morea where Isidore remained for a prolonged period after delivering Manuel's eulogy for Theodore I. Isidore had settled in Laconia, taking up residence in the monastery of Konstostephanos where he copied manuscripts and made regular visits to Mistra, the main city of the Peloponnese and the intellectual hub of Byzantium. Around 1411, a new metropolitan for Monemvasia was elected and Isidore became his assistant, accompanying him on his travels and composing texts for him to deliver to his flock. During this period, Isidore clearly had the ear of powerful rulers, including Despot Theodore II. He wrote to him to champion the cause of the residents of a town called Helikovounon, part of the diocese of the Metropolitan of Monemvasia. They were winemakers and their crops had been destroyed, leaving them unable to pay the high taxes demanded by the Despot. Isidore included a gift of Indian perfumes for Theodore in his letter, a reflection of the monk's love of luxuries.

Bessarion arrived a few years later, once again following his first mentor, Dositheos. He had been at the side of the bishop ever since he had left Trebizond to pursue a legal case with a higher authority in Constantinople. Dositheos continued to labour in this cause for a decade – in 1422 Bessarion even wrote the defence that the bishop presented to his judges. However, in 1430 the Synod in Constantinople finally threw out the case, and Dositheos was forced to resign his bishopric of Trebizond. He was then appointed as Archbishop of Monemvasia in the Morea and Bessarion once again followed him, this time settling in the Peloponnesian city of Mistra. To leave Constantinople at the beginning of his career was a surprising decision. Did he leave because he was outraged on behalf of his mentor at the lack of support from the synod? Perhaps his loyalty to Dositheos usurped his career aspirations.

Both Isidore and Bessarion complained of the Morea to their friends back in Constantinople. Isidore lamented to Guarino that the locals were backwards, that he missed his friends, the beautiful churches, the elegant houses and the superior food. He regularly chastised his friends for not writing to him more often and made eloquent efforts to fill them with guilt, on one occasion describing, in graphic detail, the suffering he experienced during a bout of the plague. Bessarion shared his misery with George Scholarios, complaining that he felt isolated and missed

Constantinople. He judged the local aristocratic families to be lazy and self-indulgent.

The men felt differently about Mistra, the city where the imperial court resided. Mistra was intellectually progressive and esoteric compared to the more conservative and religious Constantinople. For two decades the local ruling family had hosted a notorious philosopher, Gemistus Pletho, at the court. Pletho had been expelled from Constantinople for promoting what the religious authorities deemed to be paganism. He devoted himself to the study of Plato, and the ancient philosopher's texts inspired him to propose the revival of the Olympian gods, along with social and military reforms that he drew from the practices and theories of ancient Sparta. When Bessarion arrived in Mistra, Pletho had established a sort of commune, including men such as Isidore. Bessarion and Isidore were attracted to the refreshingly innovative thinking in the Peloponnesian community, and the time they spent with Pletho influenced the shape of their later careers. Pletho's advocacy of radicalism and unorthodox approaches to societal problems inspired in Bessarion and Isidore an outlook that would ultimately lead to their emigration to the West.

Both men faithfully followed the expected career trajectory, and both dramatically deviated from it at the same time in a bid to save Byzantium from the Turks. In 1433, Isidore left the Peloponnese and returned to Constantinople where he joined the monastery of Saint Demetrios. Back in the capital, he was ideally placed to launch a career in ecclesiastical politics, and the opportunity presented itself when he was chosen to be one of the Byzantine delegates for the Council of Basel, a gathering that had been convened for many years in an effort to limit papal power in the Church. Afterwards, Isidore was appointed bishop of Kiev and All Rus'. The Church of Kiev was not an

The Champions of Byzantium: Isidore and Bessarion

independent institution; it was a metropolitanate (bishopric) of the Church of Constantinople, where the Metropolitan was selected and appointed from almost exclusively Greek candidates. The Metropolitan of Kiev was expected to be a representative of the Byzantine church in the Rus' lands, and a conduit of Byzantine spiritual and cultural values. It was a position for the elite, and Isidore, with his learning, education and experience, had been groomed for such a role. Bessarion was also appointed as a Metropolitan, but for Nicaea. The Metropolitanate of Nicaea was in Bithynia (present-day Iznik in Turkey). It had a prestigious reputation; the city became the capital of the Byzantine Empire during the thirteenth-century occupation of Constantinople by the Crusaders, and the Patriarchate's seat in exile. In 1331 the Turks captured it, but the bishopric remained active. Its proximity to Constantinople and its historical prestige made it a useful appointment for bishops who needed a title but wanted to pursue a political career in the imperial court. The high-powered positions in the Church, held by Isidore and Bessarion, gave them authority in the eyes of the Emperor.

It is at this point that our story begins. More than two decades later, Isidore would pass away, having survived Russian prison, bubonic plague, combat on the walls of Constantinople in 1453, a head injury from the battle, and imprisonment by the Ottomans. Throughout these years he and Bessarion would demonstrate an unwavering commitment to defend Byzantium and to unify Christendom to defeat the Ottoman Turks. In addition, Bessarion would power a cultural and spiritual programme from his base in Italy to preserve the concept and cultural identity of the Empire. In pursuit of their goal, they sacrificed the goodwill of their fellow Greeks and their high-ranking positions in the imperial court and Orthodox Church. Bessarion would die in 1472, on his way back from yet another diplomatic mission to levy a crusade to take back Constantinople.

At no point during their youth, their manhood, or their old age would either Isidore or Bessarion have recognised Runciman's assessment of the Empire as dying and doomed. There were contemporaries who predicted that the end was nigh – such doomsayers exist in every society – and both men were almost certainly aware of their apocalyptic messages. However, it is only through the lens of hindsight could such predictions be seen as clear-sighted. To Isidore and Bessarion, and to many of their contemporaries, not only could they 'have reasonably predicted [in 1391] that Byzantium would last two generations more', but that it could and would continue to flourish without end. With the benefit of retrospect, we know that the Empire did ultimately collapse. This book, however, explores these years as those who lived at the time experienced them: without pre-judgement of the future or any prejudice that the end was inevitable.

2

EMPEROR JOHN VIII, SULTAN MURAD II AND THE BYZANTINE EMPIRE IN THE FIFTEENTH CENTURY

In the story that unfolds we follow the unorthodox efforts of Bessarion and Isidore to save Byzantium. But what did they believe that they were trying to save? The speech that Isidore delivered on a mission for the emperor to the Council of Basel in 1434 goes some way to answering this question.

> Do not think that the nation of the Greeks is small and unmoving. It has been under siege for many years during which it lost territories and came under stress. Yet it has not been totally worn out. The Lord protects it to a great extent. All of the Peloponnese is included in the empire of the Romans [Byzantium]; so are Lemnos, Imbros, and the greatest part of Thrace in the vicinity of the city of Constantine [Constantinople]. In addition to other areas under tribute, there is all of Corfu, Kephalonia, Zacynthos, Leukas, all of Epeiros, Illyria, Achaea, Phocis, Boeotia, Attica, Hellas, Macedonia, Thrace, Upper and Lower Mysia, Euboea, the

Cycladic islands, Crete, Rhodes, Cyprus, Chios, and Lesbos. All these areas are inhabited by Greeks. All territories in Asia under the barbarians [Turks] are mostly inhabited by Greeks. They are also [inhabited by] a great number of Syrians. There are many other kingdoms, which do not speak Greek, but are under the Greek Church. The great kingdom of Iberia [Georgia], the kingdom of the Lazians [Lazikans], the regions of Chechens, Alans, Circasians, and Goths, not to mention Moldowallachia, Great Wallachia, and the area of the Triballians [Serbs]. In addition, there is the land of the Albanians and to the extreme north the most extensive democracy of the Rus' (along the Ungrates) and the so-called king of Great Rus', along with other kings in the area, as well as lower Rus' with its upper and neighbouring kings. All these are subjects of the emperors of Constantinople. These neighbouring nations surpass in number your neighbours.

During the years Isidore and Bessarion were advancing in the hierarchy of the Orthodox Church, what did the Byzantine Empire look like? There is no dispute that its physical territory was much reduced since its heyday, and it was now a series of somewhat isolated autonomous kingdoms bound together by ties of religion and dynasty. These included regions as far flung as Trebizond in the east and Epirus in the west. The archipelago islands of the Aegean Sea changed hands between the Byzantines, Latins and Turks on a regular basis. The citizens frequently suffered the side effects of disputes over imperial succession as rival Palaeologan siblings periodically raised small armies and engaged in skirmishes for power. In reality, plague, civil wars, dynastic quarrels, uneasy peace treaties with enemies and scattered autonomous regions defined most of the political entities in the fifteenth century across Europe and Asia Minor, including the Ottomans and the western kingdoms and states.

Even the decay of the city of Constantinople was no different from that of Rome during the same period. If anything, Rome was in a worse state: cattle grazed in streets that had been left to crumble, church buildings were in a state of collapse, and local families battled for ascendency. Pero Tafur, who made such a negative assessment of Constantinople's state, was equally disparaging about Rome when he recorded his observations in the chronicle that he wrote about his travels through Europe to the Near East:

> The city of Rome is very sparsely populated considering its size. It is the opinion of many now that it is thrown down and depopulated, there issues from the ruins of the great buildings, and from the cellars and cisterns and houses, and from the deep vaults, now uninhabited, such poisonous air that it affects human bodies, and therefore it is said that Rome is unhealthy ... there are parts within the walls which look like thick woods, and wild beasts, hares, foxes, wolves, deer and even, so it is said, porcupines breed in the caves... Rome, which used to be the head of the world and is now the tail, has lost nothing of her ceremonies of what she was when she held the whole world in subjection, but such is now the miserable condition of the city that it is a shame to utter it.

Isidore and Bessarion came of age during the reign of the co-emperors Manuel II and his son, John VIII. Manuel had a stroke that physically incapacitated him in the early 1420s, and John increasingly assumed the role of autonomous ruler. As Isidore and Bessarion rose through the ecclesiastical and political ranks of the imperial court, John VIII and his political convictions would be a formative influence on the two young men. They became kindred spirits with this emperor – men who did not resign themselves and the Byzantine Empire to an inevitable demise.

Saving Byzantium: The Struggle to Salvage an Empire

John Palaeologus grew up in the genteel poverty of a royal city that was in decay. He was born in December 1392, the eldest of the six sons of Manuel II and Helen Dragaš. In 1414 while his father toured the courts of western leaders to generate financial aid and military support to defend Byzantium from the Turkish incursions, John ruled as regent. On the Emperor's return, he elevated John to co-emperor. In 1425, Manuel passed away, and his son became the sole ruler of Constantinople until his own death in 1448. During the 1420s, John became increasingly disillusioned with his father's approach to the Ottoman threat. Manuel had walked the tightrope of appeasement and realpolitik in his dealings with the sultans throughout his reign. He had attempted to manage the Ottomans through diplomacy, hoping that the Turks would restrain themselves out of fear that if they went too far, the West would muster a concerted military campaign against them. In reality, despite Manuel's frequent appeals to western leaders for support, including the prolonged embassy that he led in person, he saw that there was little appetite to support the Byzantines with soldiers. However, he made huge diplomatic efforts to give the Turks the impression that Byzantium had the backing of western princes. He created dynastic ties, negotiating the marriage between John and the Latin princess, Sophia of Montserrat. At the ceremony John was also officially elevated to co-emperor – a statement that the Byzantines were dynastically bound to the West at the highest level.

Similarly, he counselled John to pursue negotiations for the union of the Churches, dangling the promise and the threat of unification to Latins and the Ottomans. However, Manuel was a realist, not a pacifist. He identified the Morea in the Peloponnese as the area of his Empire with the potential to be a springboard for a Byzantine stand against the Turks, and this is where he focused a military campaign. He sent his sons

John and Theodore to consolidate the territory, leading an army that successfully took back large areas of the Ottoman-occupied south-western regions of the Peloponnese peninsula, Messenia and Elis in 1416.

Inspired by these successes, John had larger hawkish aspirations, rejecting the notion that the Byzantines could co-exist peacefully with the Ottomans by acquiescing to all their demands, and his divergent approach was reflected in a growing factionalism in the imperial court. Isidore and Bessarion, both relatively early in their careers, joined the court during this period, and were heavily influenced by those who demanded a more robust response to the Turks. Emperor Manuel, though paralysed by a stroke, was still sound in mind right up to his death, and his chronicler, George Sphrantzes recorded his concerns about his son John:

> My son, the Emperor, seems to himself a suitable emperor – but not for the present day. For he has large views and ideas such as the times demanded in the heyday of the prosperity of his ancestors. But nowadays, as things are going with us, our empire needs, not an emperor, but an administrator. I am afraid that the decline of this house may come from his poems and arguments, for I have noticed his propensities and what he thought to achieve with Mustafa, and I have also seen the results of his doctrines, to what danger they have brought us.

Like the Byzantine ruling dynasty, the Ottoman sultanate suffered from internal division that sometimes coalesced around a challenger to the throne. One of these potential usurpers emerged around the time that John began to be involved in governing with his father, and as the situation evolved over a period of many years, he saw it as an opportunity for his own Empire. At the end of John's regency in Constantinople, a man claiming to be Mustafa, the brother of Sultan Mehmed I, approached the Byzantines and Venetians for assistance to overthrow the Sultan. His attempt to usurp the throne was thwarted in the Turkish territory of Rumelia, and he fled to Thessalonica. Mehmed demanded that the Byzantines surrender Mustafa to him, but Emperor Manuel refused and promised to keep him imprisoned on the Sultan's behalf. Mehmed was required to fund the incarceration, and Mustafa was exiled to Lemnos. John became involved after being appointed to escort Mustafa from Thessalonica to his island prison in 1416.

Five years later, Sultan Mehmed I died, and John spotted a window of opportunity for the Byzantines to take advantage of the Ottomans during the period of relative weakness as a new sultan, Murad II, took power. Opposed by Manuel, who was too physically weak to impose his will, John released Mustafa and negotiated a deal to provide him with military support to take Rumelia on condition that he reward the Byzantines with Gallipoli, the peninsula that was part of the Rumelian province. This was a shrewd calculation to restore control of the Dardanelles passage to Byzantium, effectively cutting off the Ottoman navy's access from Asia to Europe. Unfortunately, John's meddling backfired. Mustafa initially made progress and seized Rumelia but refused to surrender Gallipoli, citing the Muslim tradition that forbade giving territory to non-believers. In the meantime, Murad II mustered his forces and drove Mustafa out of Rumelia. His supporters deserted him, and he fled to Europe. This time, though, the Sultan pursued him until he was captured and executed. Furious with the Byzantines for supporting the usurper, Murad turned his forces on Constantinople. In 1422 he besieged the city as punishment.

Murad commissioned the construction of an earth rampart from Sea of Marmara to the Golden Horn, and he ranged his army with their cannons and catapults along this wall so that the defenders had to spread themselves thinly to contend with a threat that stretched the length of their landside fortifications. A full assault began on 24 August 1422, but Constantinople also had artillery, and the battle was long. The Constantinopolitan soldiers were supported by residents and led by the co-emperor John VIII. A Greek chronicler, John Kananos, described the battle: 'Not only the soldiers and those skilled of the countryside and all of the common people, [but] the whole of the priests and monks and the braver of the archpriests and the holiest of spiritual holies all contributed to defence.'

John was not deterred from his policy of meddling in Turkish affairs to create instability. The Byzantines next approached Murad II's younger brother, also called Mustafa, a child of only thirteen. They proposed to support Mustafa to claim the Ottoman throne. Mustafa came to Constantinople and accepted the proposal. He got as far as Anatolia with John's help, but he was strangled by his own tutor before he could mount a significant threat to Murad II. Although the challenge failed, Murad was forced to divert his army to quell the rebellion. His attempt to take Constantinople had to be abandoned, and the attackers fled.

Once again, the Emperor's failed interference provoked repercussions, and Murad besieged Thessalonica in 1424. The Sultan targeted the city partly in retaliation for the Palaeologan support for the Pretender and partly because he was convinced that the city, which had been under Turkish control until 1403, was an inalienable territory of the Ottoman Empire. A year after the siege began, the Byzantine ruler of Thessalonica, John VIII's brother Andronikos Palaeologus, gave the city to Venice. He hoped that such a major naval power would have the resources that he did not to defeat the Sultan's army. Venice, however, had little interest in a military confrontation over Thessalonica, and they accepted the offer from Andronikos on the misapprehension that they could persuade Murad to accept their ownership of the city. This miscalculation failed to take into account the Sultan's emotional agenda to repossess Thessalonica. For a further seven years, the Ottomans maintained a naval blockade interspersed with occasional attacks on the city, which the Venetians, having allocated inadequate forces for the defence of the city, were unable to suppress.

The Republic continued to look for diplomatic solutions, appealing to allies to support them in ending the siege. In the meantime, the residents, increasingly worn down by the corruption and incompetence of the Venetian administration that treated the starving population with contempt, rallied around a pro-surrender movement. They believed defeat was inevitable and surrendering would spare them the brutal aftermath of an Ottoman victory by force. Venice suppressed this pressure group and formally declared war on the Sultan in 1429. The following year, Murad sent a large force to Thessalonica and took the city. A three-day orgy ensued in which the soldiers pillaged, raped and killed indiscriminately. Of those who survived, a fifth were enslaved and Thessalonica was left a shell of its former self.

Let down by the Venetians in Thessalonica, the Byzantines waged their own unsuccessful war and were forced to agree an annual tribute of 10,000 ducats to Murad in exchange for ending attacks on land in the Peloponnese and leaving Constantinople alone. The Greeks also forfeited land to the Ottomans on the coast of the Sea of Marmara and the Black Sea. Under this treaty, the Byzantines seemingly settled into a state of uneasy peace with Murad, and on the surface they honoured the terms that the Sultan had imposed.

During this decade of failure against the Ottomans, the Emperor turned again to the West for support. Appointing his brother Constantine as regent in Constantinople, John followed in the footsteps of his father and set off on a tour of the courts in western Europe. He hoped that his visit in person would bring sufficient pressure on the leaders to motivate them to contribute soldiers and money to reverse the recent military successes of the Turks. The Emperor started in Venice, then went to Milan, Mantua and Hungary. His efforts were futile, and he returned to Constantinople after a year with little to show for his efforts.

The loss of Thessalonica and the indifference of the West compelled the Emperor to revive another of his father's strategies: the consolidation of the Morea as a Byzantine stronghold from which a potential recovery could begin. The territory was flourishing, and John divided it into three regions, giving his brothers Theodore, Constantine and Thomas rule over each of the areas in the Despotate. Over the course of a decade, Constantine led successful military campaigns in the northern Peloponnese, and by the end of the 1430s he had expanded the Despotate of Morea to include most of the Greek territories. Constantine did not stop there; he continued his land grab, restoring Athens, Thebes and Boeotia to the Empire. These successes in the Morea demonstrated that the Ottoman advances could be reversed, but to achieve a similar set of victories throughout the Empire, the Emperor needed to muster support from the West.

A major obstacle to motivating the western nations was the mutual suspicion in which the Roman Catholic and Greek Orthodox Churches held each other. Just as the Roman Empire had cleaved in two, so, too, the practice and doctrine of Christianity split into two spheres along the same dividing line of East and West. However, it did not start out that way. Ecclesiastical councils in the fourth and fifth centuries had declared Constantinople to be the New Rome, a bishopric founded by no less a figurehead than the Apostle St Andrew. For several centuries Rome remained aligned with Constantinople in a Christian empire. These ties began to loosen in the early Middle Ages as Rome looked to the Carolingian rulers of the central and western European lands for protection from the chaos of the warring tribes that threatened the western churches. Maintaining a close relationship with the Byzantine Church became less of a priority for the popes, and the differences between the two institutions increased at the expense of collaboration and a sense of cohesion.

As ties with the West became strained, the Russian lands were converting to Christianity; they drew their liturgy from the East and were influenced far more by Constantinople than by Rome. Byzantine Christianity became more and more entrenched in its eastern identity, and with this the importance of the Church hierarchy of the Pentarchy grew (the five patriarchs of Rome, Jerusalem, Constantinople, Antioch and Alexandria). In this hierarchy there were five equal patriarchs; the pope as the patriarch of Rome held no greater authority than that of the others. The papacy's claim to supremacy became an increasingly sore point. By this time the churches of the East and West followed different rites and subscribed to differing doctrines. Frequent conflict and accusations of heresy provoked several schisms over the centuries, resulting in hostility and suspicion that belied their common roots as Christians. Catholic popes excommunicated Orthodox patriarchs on and off from the fourth century in an effort to assert their authority and that of the papacy over the Orthodox Church. In 1054, another edict of excommunication was passed by Pope Leo IX, and, as this one was technically never lifted, it is referred to as the Great Schism.

The Roman pontiff claimed papal supremacy over the whole Christian Church, insisting on an elevated authority inherited from the first disciple of Christ, St Peter himself. The patriarchs of Constantinople, Antioch, Alexandria and Jerusalem rejected this claim and maintained that a pope was the head of only the western churches and their peer in the hierarchy of church leadership. Set against the backdrop of diverging practices, along with disagreements over fundamental issues of doctrine, the stage was set for the Great Schism, a complete breakdown in relations. Almost 400 years later, those who tried to bridge the gulf between the East and West churches, as we shall see, were accused of heresy and immorality by both sides.

Two hundred years before Bessarion and Isidore were born, the tension between the Churches took another dramatic turn that would have repercussions in the negotiations for western support in the fifteenth century. The Seljuk Turks captured Jerusalem, provoking the Christians to launch the Fourth Crusade. Western armies gathered on the Dalmatian coast with the objective to wage holy war and recapture Jerusalem from the Turks. At the same time, the ruling Constantinopolitan emperor, Isaac, had been deposed by his brother, and Isaac's son thought it would be a good idea to see if he could make use of the nearby standing army to restore his father to the throne. Promising money to the crusaders in exchange for their support, he led them to Constantinople where he encountered fierce resistance from the residents. The crusaders ended up sacking the city and occupying it for the next fifty years, along with the kingdoms of Thessalonica, Achaia, Athens and Thebes. The resentment of the local populations was huge and long lasting – it continued to be a source of collective anguish for many generations of Byzantines.

The western soldiers pillaged the churches and shipped their treasures to Venice, where Bessarion, Isidore and their Greek companions would see them over 200 years later, still on display in Venice's Basilica of St Mark. The Pope imposed a Latin patriarch without consultation and attempts were made to force the local clergy to adopt the Latin rites. The Constantinopolitans ejected the occupiers in 1261, but the harm done to the relations and trust between the East and West was never repaired. In the next chapter we will see how, as late as the fifteenth century, the Greeks had not forgiven the Latins for the trauma of this subjugation.

Despite their misgivings, successive Byzantine emperors tried many strategies to motivate their Catholic Christian brothers to support them. Italian scholars and envoys were hosted for years in the Constantinople court, and when they returned to Italy they acted as campaigners for western aid to Byzantium against the Ottoman threat. Concerted efforts to build dynastic bridges between East and West motivated marriage between the Byzantine rulers and western leaders. The daughters of the Marquis of Montferrat and of the Count of Rimini married Emperor John Palaeologus and his brother Despot Theodore. The impact of these alliances was minimal, as the western families were very minor players.

After Emperor John returned empty handed from his diplomatic tour to Venice, Verona, Pavia and Hungary, he reluctantly agreed a treaty of vassalage with Murad II. Clearly, John viewed this treaty as playing for time. In spite of terms restricting him from activities that could be interpreted as hostile to the Ottomans, he started his programme of reinforcing the walls of Constantinople and expanding Byzantine territory in the Peloponnese.

As diplomatic mission after mission to the western powers had failed, John VIII realised that he needed more than minor marriage alliances and begging rounds to motivate the West to support the Byzantines. The Emperor and prominent members of the Orthodox Church, including the Patriarch, became increasingly convinced that the path to engendering this motivation lay in the unification of the West and East Churches. How much more effective would it be for the Orthodox Church to 'marry' the Roman Catholic Church? To form an alliance; a marriage of convenience to repel the Turks? In Bessarion and Isidore, the Emperor found supporters with a radical commitment to this idea that would shape the rest of their lives. Their involvement in the events of the next decade created the perfect conditions to cultivate these seeds.

3

SALVATION THROUGH SPIRITUAL UNION

'...[If] with our own hostilities resolved, united and harmonious as Christian princes should be, we would rise up to defend the Christian religion, [then] he [Mehmed II] would not only refrain from invading foreign lands, but would withdraw.'

Bessarion to Doge Francesco Forari

Emperor John VIII hoped that by uniting the churches it would be possible to position the Turkish threat to Byzantium as an existential threat to Christianity as a whole. He calculated that by shifting the perspective of the West, he was more likely to leverage military support in defence of Christianity. If the spread of Islam was deemed a menace to all Christendom, then its defence would be an obligation imposed by the pope on the wealthy nations of Europe. Negotiations for a council to discuss Church unification had been half-heartedly pursued since the 1420s, when John VIII had acceded to the throne. A decade later the Emperor intensified these discussions as he laid the groundwork to push the Ottomans back and reinvigorate the Byzantine Empire.

John's renewed interest in uniting the East and West Churches overlapped with the papacy of Eugenius IV (1383–1447), who had been the Venetian Cardinal Gabriele Condulmer before he was elected pope in 1431. Eugenius clung to an extremely perilous position in the first few years after his election. He found himself at the helm of a papacy that had only just emerged from a century of traumatic schism in which a series of popes and antipopes wrestled for dominance over the Church. It was only as recently as Eugenius's predecessor, Martin V, that the Church had been united again in Rome under a single pope. Pope Martin had established a fragile renaissance of power in the Eternal City, but Eugenius initially lacked the political acumen to sustain and nurture this.

In the 1430s, two rival Roman clans – the Orsini and Colonna – were once again struggling for dominance. Their dynastic feud had persisted for centuries, periodically erupting into outright war. Eugenius enraged Rome during the first three years of his papacy as he clumsily attempted to deal with the rising tensions. Amidst the backdrop of this escalating civil war, the Pope was forced to over-tax the resident Romans in a bid to raise money for defence. There were food shortages, poverty was acute, and crime was rife. On top of that, he closed Rome's gates, forbidding anyone from entering or leaving. The Colonna family (rightly) suspected that Pope Eugenius favoured their Orsini rivals. Acting on this suspicion, they incited a Roman rebellion to oust Eugenius.

The crisis peaked in the spring of 1434. Eugenius sought refuge in a small palazzo attached to the Church of San Callisto. Realising that he did not have the resources to suppress the uprising, the Pope forged a desperate plan. Dressed in a long black tunic and deep pointed hood, Eugenius snuck out of Rome disguised as a Benedictine monk during the traditional siesta hour on 4 June. It was a narrow escape: Eugenius was recognised, and a mob of angry Romans chased his getaway boat along the banks of the Tiber. He made it finally to a vessel that was waiting in the Ostia harbour to speed him away from the hostile Roman lands.

Eugenius was welcomed by the Florentines and invited to set up his papal court in their city. His position was shaky: he had lost his historic seat in Rome, and depleted the papal coffers waging multiple expensive wars, including against Naples. Many secular leaders in the papal states had mutinied against him and stopped paying papal taxes, preventing him from replenishing his treasury.

Not only was Eugenius practically insolvent, beleaguered by external secular adversaries and exiled from Rome, he was battling enemies within the Church. The proposed council to unite the East and West was not the only council to be held during Eugenius' papacy. From the beginning of the fifteenth century councils were convened to wrestle with the growing demand for reform of the church leadership and the papacy. As a Cardinal, Gabriele Condulmer had been fully committed to these reforms and even swore to uphold them if he were ever to become pope. However, by the time that he became Eugenius IV, the power base for these reforms was in Basel, and the Pope perceived the efforts to reduce papal power as a Germanic coup to dominate church politics and to sideline the Italians. Whilst Eugenius wanted spiritual reform, he was also deeply committed to upholding the Vatican's domination of the western Church. Faced with these secular and religious crises, Eugenius needed to consolidate his power base.

When Emperor John VIII appointed Isidore as his official ambassador to the council in Basel, signalling his renewed interest in a union of the churches, the Pope saw a political opportunity. Were he to orchestrate a union that led to a single, united Christendom, papal power over the Conciliarists would be strongly endorsed. How powerful would Eugenius be if he were to succeed in affirming his supremacy over not just the western Church leaders, but the entire Christian Church? This would put the Pope in an unassailable position and effectively quash those who were challenging his authority.

Isidore's mission was to represent the Byzantines at a meeting hosted by the Basel officials to sound out the possibility of holding a separate council dedicated to the unification of the Churches. His efforts were stymied from the outset. Setting out on the journey to Basel in the depths of winter in 1434, Isidore's ship was forced to land after being damaged by a violent storm. Determined to fulfil his commitment, he continued overland. After a gruelling and arduous trip that included an ambush by bandits, he and his retinue arrived in Basel in the summer. What motivated the priest to overcome such adversity in service of the Byzantine court and church? Isidore was a committed advocate for a union of the Churches that would unlock an arsenal of western military support for Byzantium in their struggle against the Ottomans. A speech he gave at the Council of Basel reflected the depth of his passion for the cause of Christians uniting against Islam:

> The rays of the sun illuminate your virtue. I respond and I beg that you zealously hasten, under the influence of the Holy Spirit, to reach our goal. Spare nothing that will bring about the union of the Church so it may recover its former status through harmony between the Church of the Greeks and the Church of the Latins. May the Greeks embrace with affection the Church of the Latins as if it were their own. Let both sides enjoy the pleasurable advantages, as it was in the past. Rewards, benefits, and advantages over the divine, and the most loveable to God union will come.

Isidore came away with an agreement that a separate synod would be held and that the Emperor and Patriarch would attend. A budget of 8,000 florins was allocated to the Greeks to fund a congregation of eastern prelates in preparation for attending. It was agreed that there would be no restrictions on the topics for discussion at the synod, and that all delegates would participate peacefully and honestly. They could not settle on a venue, and potential locations included Constantinople, Bologna, Milan, Calabria, Buda, Vienna and Savoy. From the beginning, everyone recognised the depth of emotion and mutual mistrust that these discussions would unleash. As a reward for their cooperation at Basel, the western Church leaders sent a small force of two large galleys, two light galleys and 300 crossbowmen to help the Byzantines defend Constantinople.

It took another three years before the preliminary discussions over the logistics were finally concluded. Ferrara had been chosen as the venue for the council, and the Byzantine delegation prepared for departure. By this time the Emperor and Patriarch had promoted Isidore to the position of Metropolitan of Kiev after he returned to Constantinople from Basel. This meant that he was in Russia by 1437, so it was only Bessarion who joined the 700 delegates assembling at the port of Constantinople in November that year. They boarded the merchant galleys sent by the Pope to carry them to Italy to attend the council that had finally been convened.

Ostensibly, the delegates came together in Italy to discuss a religious matter. However, you do not have to scratch too far below the surface to realise that there was a powerful ulterior motive: survival. Survival in the East for the Byzantine Empire and survival in the West for the autonomy of the papacy.

Saving the Byzantine Empire and eliminating political challenges to the papacy were powerful motives for the East and

West delegates respectively, and men like Bessarion were genuine in their bid to unite the Churches. Hopes were high on both sides, and one of the Byzantine delegates showered praise on his Roman Catholic counterpart, whom he deemed to have played a significant role in bringing about the Council:

> Don't you think it is something for the holy Emperor, the absolute ruler of the Romans, to set off and depart from the City [along with] the holy Patriarch, the bishops, the officials, the whole eastern Church, amongst whom are also old and infirm people, and for all of these to go to the Pope? This is something and you have accomplished a great feat indeed. And may the result be good!

It was a dull and wet day in February 1438 when Bessarion and the Byzantine delegates were formally greeted in Venice. In defiance of the gloomy weather, the doge put on a display of pomp to honour the guests. The Emperor's galley was escorted by a flotilla of Venetian ships, including the ceremonial ducal ship, the *Bucentaur*. As Emperor John VIII came ashore, a peal of bells from churches all over the city broke out to greet him, and the crowds sang and cheered. The city officials displayed the Patriarch's symbols throughout Venice, and the doge sent him gifts of sugar cakes, candles and wine.

With such a promising start, the mood of the Emperor, Patriarch and their delegates must have been positive, and the tribulations of their long journey seemed worthwhile. Unfortunately, their western hosts did not capitalise on this initial goodwill but proceeded to erode it with behaviour that served only to affirm pre-existing prejudices.

The doge led a ceremonial visit to San Marco where Bessarion and the other delegates saw the display of treasures that western crusaders had looted from Hagia Sofia in Constantinople when they sacked the city in 1204. What type of emotions must this have elicited from the Byzantines as they gazed on their captured relics? These items were not just valuable, they were endowed with holiness. For the Venetians these treasures were housed with reverence fitting to their holy status, but for the Byzantines they symbolised a shameful triumphant display of war booty. And now the Byzantines were in Italy to invite crusaders back into Constantinople. Could they trust them?

The Italians continued to commit insensitivity upon insensitivity. From the very first encounter between the Pope and the Greeks, issues of etiquette and seating arrangements overshadowed the Council. When the Pope received the Emperor and the Patriarch, he expected them to kiss his foot as all visiting dignitaries would do. For the Byzantines the act implied subordination, and Patriarch Joseph was offended. He expected, as head of the eastern Church, to be treated as a pope's equal. One of the most high-ranking ecclesiastical officials in the delegation, Sylvester Syropoulous, described the painful exchange between the imperial ambassador Theodor Karystinos with the Patriarch of Constantinople over the issue.

> ...he [Karystinos] said to the Patriarch, 'The Pope is expecting that your great Holiness, on arrival, will make your obeisance and kiss his foot. The Emperor, however, is opposed to this and has been striving for three days that this may not take place. He is making this known to your great Holiness that you may consider how you may approach [the Pope].' But the Patriarch said, 'I do not owe him such a greeting since we are brothers; we should instead embrace and kiss each other in a fraternal fashion. Therefore I shall not do otherwise.'

This issue of primacy would blight the entire proceedings. On three occasions talks broke down, and the Byzantines threatened more than once to walk away from the discussions. In these opening ceremonies the western Church leaders continued to demonstrate a level of intransigence that bode ill for the outcome. To conform to Latin practice, the Roman Catholics forced the Greeks to remove their monastic habits at the welcoming service that Eugenius held for them. Seating arrangements in the cathedral triggered another conflict over primacy. Once again, Syropoulos vividly captured the debate between the Greeks and the papal representative Cardinal Giuliano Cesarini.

> 'Since your Reverence has said that we are in two groups, the Pope should instead sit and be amongst his own group, just as the Emperor and the Patriarch [should] again be with their own [group].' But Julian [Cardinal Cesarini] said, 'But it is necessary for there to be some kind of link between the groups. The Pope will therefore be in the middle.' But we said, 'There is no need for this link. Nevertheless, if the Pope wishes to sit incontrovertibly in the middle, it necessarily follows that the Emperor and the Patriarch should also sit in the middle and be near him; for it is impossible for them to sit in any other manner.'

The Greeks failed to convince the Roman Catholic leaders with their argument. Pope Eugenius was seated on an elevated chair above the Patriarch, and the Byzantine deacons were given seating at the rear of the church nave. This seating plan was deeply insulting. One of the delegates, Bishop Dositheos of Trebizond, Bessarion's mentor and ex-tutor, foresaw the problems that would lie ahead:

> Even as I saw the throne and the rank in which the Pope placed you [the Patriarch], as well as the superiority which he assigned to himself, I was confused and said to myself, 'Can it be the Patriarch,

the Lord Joseph, who has accepted such treatment? And how does he endure such things?' And from then, I speculate that nothing healthy will occur for us as a result of this.

Pope Eugenius was motivated by his need to assert his primacy among the western churchmen. His statements and actions throughout the duration of the Council were intended to make an impression on these men, but they were not conducive to fostering a good relationship with the Orthodox leaders. Were these slights made out of ignorance or were they deliberate? To Bessarion and those who were driven in their determination to achieve this union, these acts were unfortunate but not malicious. Many delegates, however, interpreted their hosts' behaviour as intentional slights designed to demonstrate their sense of superiority.

Meanwhile, in Rus', Isidore was struggling to convince the Grand Prince Vassily Vasil'evich to let him leave for Italy to attend the Council. The Metropolitan prevailed, and twelve months after the first delegates had arrived in Italy, he was able to join them. By the time Isidore finally arrived, in August 1438, the mood of the Greeks had soured, and their list of woes was longer. Bessarion and his fellow delegates were dependent on a living stipend, which had been agreed by the Pope during the negotiations for holding a council. Five months after their arrival in Italy no money had been provided, and the Greeks were petitioning the Patriarch and Emperor to abandon the discussions so that they could return home. The pomp and splendour with which the Latins had greeted the Greeks contrasted starkly with the relative poverty of the Byzantine delegates. Syropoulos described their plight from the outset:

Then the Marquis [of Ferrara] gave lodgings to all of us, but beds only to those who were in the Patriarchal household. The others unwillingly slept on a pallet or on the bare ground, and if ever they were suffering from this, and said something to any one of the Pope's entourage, we heard nothing but, '*Habeas patientiam!*', which means, 'Have patience!', and they consoled our hardship with such words.

The Greeks were struggling to fund their upkeep without any sort of income. There was a growing consensus among them that the Catholics were withholding the money to put pressure on the Byzantines to abandon their religious and philosophical challenges in the council meetings, and to accept a union on the terms of the western Church.

These religious and philosophical challenges were immense and deep. Both sides were fanatical in their intransigence over the many areas of doctrinal disagreement. The Emperor had chosen many of his delegates based on their intellectual capabilities, and these men (Bessarion among them) led the Greek side in the many heated debates. Bessarion was elected by his peers to be one of six orators who would represent the eastern Church's point of view at the Council, and he grappled with a range of disputes. Some of these seemed petty: debates over the type of bread used in the Eucharist or the traditions of facial hair for the clergy. Other issues concerned fundamental tenets of doctrine such as disagreement over the nature of Purgatory. Isidore seems to have deferred to Bessarion on these dogmatic issues, keeping a lower profile in the intellectual debates. His primary contribution to the Council lay in his role as an imperial consultant and go-between, representing the Byzantine Emperor's position before the Pope. Over the course of the Council, Isidore and Eugenius formed a close relationship based on mutual respect.

The greatest conflict revolved around an amendment made centuries earlier to one of the foundational texts of

Christianity, the Nicene Creed. The amendment related to the hierarchy of the Trinity. In the original unadulterated Nicene Creed, God the Father and His Son were identified as a single and equal entity. The amendment to the creed professed that the Son proceeded from the Father and was therefore subordinate to Him. The Catholic Church subscribed to the amendment, but the Orthodox Church did not recognise this addition to the creed, insisting that the original document could never be altered. Cesarini, one of the Latin cardinals, offered proof that there was precedent to make changes and that these earlier changes had been accepted at the time by Orthodox church leaders. The Greeks divided between those who were convinced by his argument and those who believed that the westerners were simply bamboozling them with academic obfuscation. Eight heated sessions on this topic took place between 2 March and 24 March 1439, but no agreement could be reached. Again, the Greeks stormed out and, this time with the backing of the Patriarch, demanded that the Emperor abandon the negotiations so that they could go home. Finally, the impasse was broken by Bessarion, who had been persuaded by the Latin argument. He drafted a theological statement that dealt with the issue by a semantic sleight of hand. He explained his theory in his treatise, *De Processione Spiritus Sancti*:

> The words of the Fathers by themselves alone are enough to solve every doubt and to persuade every soul. It was not the syllogisms or probabilities of the force of arguments that led me to believe this, but the plain words of the doctors. For when I saw and heard them, I immediately put aside all contention and controversy and yielded to the authority of those whose words they were, even though until then I had not been moderate in my opinion.

Bessarion put forward the argument that the debate could be resolved firstly by establishing the correct versions of the Greek and Latin texts and secondly by understanding why the patristic authorities appeared to contradict each other. He gave a persuasive speech that won temporary Greek support by way of a linguistic manoeuvre which achieved a compromise, equating the Greek word for 'through' with the Latin word for 'from'. Thus, both parties could claim that the Son proceeded from the Father as well as through the Father. Isidore sided with Bessarion in the matter, and in a bid to win endorsement for the proposed accommodation he hosted a sumptuous dinner for a group of influential and high-ranking Orthodox churchmen. His skills as a negotiator and intermediary, coupled with fine dining, achieved the goal. The Byzantines grudgingly accepted Bessarion's compromise.

The Decree of Union of the Latin and Greek Churches was proclaimed on 6 July 1439, and Bessarion delivered the Greek version of the proclamation. Was the union going to save the Byzantine Empire and the Orthodox Church from collapse and eventual annihilation by the Turks? Bessarion clearly believed so. He introduced the statement of union with a quote from Psalm 96:11: 'Let the heavens rejoice and let the earth be glad.' Bessarion was apparently convinced that full spiritual union had been achieved, and he believed that this rapprochement with the pope would be the key to eliminating the Ottoman threat and to Byzantium's salvation. Almost all the delegates signed the decree, and the court at Constantinople upheld the union in the State Church of Byzantium. Buoyed by this success, Bessarion and the Greeks set out to deliver the results to the people of Constantinople, and Isidore departed for eastern Europe with the same agenda.

Sadly, the optimism of Bessarion, Isidore and the other Greek delegates was short-lived. In the late summer of 1439, Emperor

John VIII left Florence along with Bessarion and the other Byzantine delegates. It took them about six weeks, stopping briefly in Bologna, to reach Venice, from where they embarked for Constantinople. The convoy stopped off at a handful of destinations to deliver the union decree: Pola, Corfu, Modon, Coron, Negroponte, and the Dardanelles. Finally, in February 1440 they arrived in Constantinople – the Emperor and his delegates had been absent for over two years, and six months had already elapsed since the decree was signed in Florence.

These months were plenty for rumours to spread and entrench themselves among the local population. Anti-unionists seized on the reports that the Byzantines had been restricted to mere observation rather than participation at the Florentine church service to celebrate the union. They pointed to the inequality implied throughout the document that declared unification. Furthermore, according to the anti-unionists, the Roman contingent had insisted on signing the Tome of Union before the Byzantine officials. The precedence of the signatories seemed to imply an order of supremacy. These slights, combined with the words of the union document declaring that the popes 'possess the primacy over the whole world' as 'the successor to St Peter' and as 'first among the Apostles, true Vicar of Christ' outraged the anti-unionists. They delighted in telling the story of the Emperor's dog who, in a gesture of foreboding, howled beneath his master's chair in the church as the decree was signed.

The anti-unionists were organised around a formal group spearheaded by the monk and Metropolitan of Ephesus, Mark Eugenicus. The bishop had accompanied the Greek delegates to Italy but had not been convinced by the pro-union arguments of compatriots like Bessarion and Isidore. He refused to sign the Decree of Union, and he returned to Constantinople with an agenda to undermine it. As a monk, he had the support of the monastic institutions and lesser clergy who had the ear of the local Constantinopolitans. They believed that the political survival of Byzantium was secondary to the preservation of the Orthodox Church's doctrinal integrity. Accepting a compromise that encompassed elements of the Latin doctrine was positioned as morally corrupt, a sin that would lead to damnation. Eugenicus and his followers preached that suffering in the living world (i.e. occupation by the Turks) would be worth the rewards in the afterlife.

After Mark Eugenicus passed away, the leadership of the anti-unionists was assumed by George Scholarios, a scholar, layman and friend of Bessarion, who had not only accompanied the delegation to Florence but had even authored many of the pro-Union Greek scholarly arguments. Mysteriously, he left Florence before the Council ended, despite the pleas of the Emperor, Patriarch and Bessarion. Clearly something had shifted his view, and on his return to Constantinople his misgivings grew exponentially. Over the next ten years he became a monk, claimed he had been duped into using his scholarship to support the union, and eventually took over the anti-unionist movement that so undermined the imperial court in the final years before the fall of Constantinople.

From the perspective of the anti-unionists, the union was a spiritual failure that gave almost nothing to the Byzantines. The amended Nicene Creed was accepted to all intents and purposes, thanks to Bessarion's semantic solution to the impasse. The primacy of the pope was asserted. Many of the delegates began to feel that they had been complicit in the Latinization of their own religious and cultural practices. During the 1204 Latin occupation of Constantinople the local population had been forced to recite the Nicene Creed and to use unleavened bread for the Eucharist. Two centuries later, their Byzantine representatives were making these concessions of their own free will. Many of Bessarion's peers saw themselves as the architects of a union that would erode the Byzantine national identity.

It was crucial, in this febrile atmosphere, for the pro-unionists to take charge of the narrative, but unfortunately that did not happen. As Emperor John disembarked, he was greeted with the news that his wife had passed away in his absence. Prostrated by grief, he withdrew from active governing and failed to take steps to promulgate the decree officially. To put the seal on the political vacuum, Patriarch Joseph had died in Florence leaving the throne of the Byzantine Church empty. The anti-unionists, led by former delegates like Bishop Mark of Ephesus, seized this opportunity to wage a propaganda war fuelled by emotive arguments aimed at harnessing the natural suspicion and prejudice of the local secular population and its parochial church leaders.

From the moment the Emperor and his delegates disembarked in Constantinople, they found themselves under attack from those who were opposed to the union. The recrimination was so intense that prominent delegates publicly repudiated the union on their return to Constantinople, claiming they had signed under duress. Although Mark of Ephesus had been a notable participant in the Council, on his return home he actively campaigned against it, and soon took on the mantle of the leader of the anti-unionist movement. Having refused to sign the decree in Florence and returning to Constantinople before Bessarion, the Bishop was celebrated as a champion of Orthodox Christianity. Church officials refused to participate in services that were held or attended by anyone who had been a delegate at the Council.

Bessarion felt the furious rejection of the Council's results, but did not allow this reaction to sway his support for a unified Christianity. It must have been painful for him to witness the response of the Constantinopolitans to a union that he believed would be the salvation of Byzantium. He was subjected to a vitriolic personal campaign waged by the anti-unionists. Mark Eugenicus's brother, John, broke off his friendship with Bessarion in a public letter titled 'Before he became a unionist'. Later in life when Bessarion wrote a text outlining his reasons for joining the Roman Catholic Church, his former friend George Scholarios was provoked into publishing a treatise in which he laments the loss of their friendship following the Cardinal's change of fortune. This reference to Bessarion's wealth reflected Scholarios's opinion that pro-unionists were 'beguiled by ambition', and some held that their loyalty was purchased by the Pope. One of Bessarion's closest friends, the pro-unionist George of Trebizond, complained of hostility from fellow Greeks, including his own parents. Several of Bessarion's friends, and even his former tutor, Gemistus Pletho, turned their backs on him.

The unification of the Orthodox and Roman Catholic churches was a bid for survival: it was presented as the politically necessary price of papal support against the Turks. The aftermath of the Council generated emotional and political turmoil in Byzantium. Accusations of spiritual betrayal vied with expectations of salvation from the Muslim threat. Out of this maelstrom two men emerged, who not only understood how critical a united Christendom was to the survival of the Byzantine Empire but who also believed that God wanted the Churches to be as one. Driven by their deep convictions and passionate determination, Bessarion and Isidore took radical steps to do whatever had to be done to save their culture, homeland and their Church.

4

SAVING BYZANTIUM AS THE POPE'S MAN

In his role as intermediary at the Ferrara-Florence Council, Isidore had established a working relationship with Pope Eugenius. At the conclusion of the Council, it was the Pope and not the Emperor who harnessed Isidore's commitment to the union and sent him on a mission to deliver the decree to the eastern Slavic Churches. In the meantime, as Constantinople rejected the union, it became clear to Bessarion that Byzantium would have to be saved despite the Constantinopolitans and not by them. So when Pope Eugenius offered the position of cardinal in the Curia to both men, they accepted the appointment. They were driven to take such radical action by their belief that this would be the only way to sustain pressure on the Pope and other significant Church leaders to pursue the union and guarantee the survival of Byzantium.

These men identified ways to wield their own political power within the hierarchy of the Roman Catholic Church. Isidore used his role as a papal official to act as a missionary, taking the message of union to the Orthodox Churches. He was determined to persuade them that the salvation of Christianity could only be guaranteed through unity – acting as one strong body of Christians against the Ottoman threat. Wielding the same power as Isidore – that of a high-ranking official position in the western Church – Bessarion had a different approach. From his inside position, he sought to influence the western church leaders to take action. He also led a campaign, explored in a later chapter, to preserve the cultural and spiritual empire through the curation of a prolific Greek library and other acts of patronage. This more subtle approach led to questions about the sincerity of his motivation, a debate that continues today. How did these two men, who were highly placed officials in the Byzantine court and Church, justify what seemed to many of their fellow Greeks as unforgivable disloyalty?

Byzantines like Bessarion and Isidore feared that the Decree of Union, secured only on paper, would not be enough to ensure the survival of Byzantium. When Bessarion made the decision to return to Italy, he claimed that his reason for accepting the cardinalate was his belief that he was more likely to achieve his goals with a power base in Italy than in Constantinople. In Pope Eugenius, Bessarion and Isidore saw a man committed to a united Christendom; to preserving Byzantium; and to upholding universal Christian values in his leadership. In their minds, Eugenius's actions contrasted starkly with the self-serving agenda of the religious and political elites in Constantinople. These churchmen and secular leaders, whom they believed were presiding over the decay of Byzantium, seemingly preferred subjugation to the Ottoman Turks to union with the western Church.

Cardinal Isidore and the Papal Mission

When he appointed Isidore to deliver the Decree of Union to the Slavic regions, Eugenius assumed that his new missionary, in his role as Metropolitan of Kiev, had some authority over the Church leaders there. However, Isidore had spent no more than a few months in this position before he left to attend the Council in Italy, and his experience of the region and its politics, along with his authority, was limited. Coupled with this inexperience, the new Cardinal's relationship with the Grand Prince was strained after the Russian ruler had opposed Isidore's attendance at the Council. Under these circumstances, the bravado with which Isidore assured Eugenius of his success seems grossly misplaced.

> Not one of them dares argue with me; the Grand Prince is young and under my will ... their bishops are ignorant and they, too, fear me... I shall always intone your name in the Mass, and will bring over to you from the Greek faith all the princes and all the Eastern Christian folk... No longer will they go to the Imperial City [Constantinople] but I will bring them to Rome and it will be to you that they bring their gifts.

Did he make this rash promise to Eugenius out of gratitude for such a papal vote of confidence? Isidore was genuinely passionate about his belief that a united Christianity was the spiritual and physical salvation of the Orthodox Church, but he cannot have been completely oblivious to the monumental challenge he faced to convince the Slavic Church leaders and secular rulers. In his mind, the new Cardinal was positioning himself to the Pope and to the Slavic rulers as a bridge between the East and West Churches.

With equally oblivious optimism, Eugenius prepared a letter for Isidore to deliver to the Grand Prince, which was intended to give authority to the Cardinal's mission. In his statement the Pope stressed the hard work of 'our esteemed brother Sidor [Isidore], your Metropolitan of All Rus' in contributing to the union. He called for the Grand Prince and any relevant officials to 'assist him in all deeds' especially those that furthered the promotion of a single Church and its ceremonies. The Pope then invoked his authority in God – 'And in our Lord we beseech your Excellency, and with the greatest desire and with much zealousness' – to consult with Isidore on the nature of the new ecclesiastical customs. Finally, he outlined the rewards for following his instructions. 'Thus you will fervently be the helpmate to him with all your assistance that will gain popular commendation and glory, and from us you will have the blessing and from God an eternal gift.'

Furnished with his papal endorsement, Isidore set out on a journey to Moscow by way of Poland, Lithuania and Kiev. With several key stops along the way, including Zagreb, Lepsény, Belgorod, Buda, Krakow and Vilnius, it took him a full year to disseminate the Decree of Union. Buda in Hungary was a key destination. Like Constantinople and all of Byzantium, the kingdom of Hungary faced the threat of Ottoman annihilation. The Hungarians' anxiety made them pro-union as they, too, hoped for western military and financial support in their struggle. Buda had even been briefly considered as a venue for the Council that ended up in Ferrara and Florence, so it was not surprising that Isidore used Buda as the base for his mission to the Slavs.

Here he wrote and published a papal encyclical addressed to the Hungarian king, circulated to all the Slavic lands. The contents offer an insight into how the Cardinal envisaged the union in the Orthodox context. He declares that there is only one Christian Church to which everyone who has been baptised belongs. According to Isidore, the acts of baptism, holy communion and confession are equally valid whether they are performed following eastern or western rites. With the Turks on their doorstep, the Hungarians and Poles were ready to accept Isidore's vision. However, the story was very different in Kiev and Moscow.

Wearing a red hat, the symbol of a Roman Catholic cardinal, the Metropolitan of Kiev and Rus' processed to the main gates of Moscow preceded by three Roman bishops' croziers and a cross of Latin design. (A traditional Orthodox Cross has four equal sides, unlike a Roman Catholic cross whose vertical bar is longer than the horizontal.) Equally provocative was Isidore's decision to parade the highly popular native churchman, Simeon of Suzdal, in chains for spreading anti-unionist propaganda in Novgorod. Isidore held a service at the gate, replacing the name of the Patriarch with that of the Pope in each of his prayers. The incendiary parade proceeded through the streets to Uspensky Cathedral, where Grand Prince Vassily and high-ranking dignitaries awaited the Metropolitan. Although the Grand Prince must have been aware in advance that Isidore was coming to Moscow with a plan to implement the Decree of Union, the Metropolitan's ostentatious display of Roman Catholic conformity was undoubtedly shocking.

Vassily had been persuaded to allow Isidore to attend the Council of Ferrara-Florence only after he had extracted a solemn promise from the Metropolitan that he would defend their Church's practices and reject any changes to them. The Prince's disbelief initially paralysed him, as Isidore celebrated the service according to Latin rites, invoked the name of the Pope and got a protodeacon to recite the contents of the Decree of Union from the pulpit. This stunned astonishment quickly turned to horror and anger: Vassily refused to accept Isidore's benediction at the end of the service, and he swiftly ordered him to be deposed as Metropolitan and imprisoned in the Chudov monastery to await trial for heresy.

The intensity of the Grand Prince's fury rings through in a letter to the Byzantine emperor that he composed soon after Isidore's return to Moscow:

Saving Byzantium as the Pope's Man

> Oh great sovereign Emperor; why did you go to them [the Pope and western Church]? What were you thinking of? What have you done? You have exchanged light for darkness; instead of the Divine Law you have received the Latin faith; instead of truth and righteousness you have loved flattery and falsity. Formerly you were the agent of piety, now you are the sower of evil seeds; formerly you were haloed by the light of the Heavenly spirit, now you are clothed in the darkness of unbelief.

How did Isidore, an astute diplomat by all accounts, make such an enormous miscalculation? Had he been lulled into a false complacency by the muted reaction to the decree that he encountered on his long journey from Florence to Moscow? The Hungarians had enthusiastically accepted the union, and the Poles had demonstrated no objection to it. Even in Kiev, where Isidore had spent six months before proceeding to Moscow, there had been very little reaction to his papal message.

The consensus among historians is that this extreme rejection was politically, not spiritually motivated. With his repudiation of the Decree of Union with the Roman Church, the Grand Prince was actually engineering an excuse to break away from the Byzantine Orthodox Church. By ousting Isidore, the Patriarch of Constantinople's appointee and emissary of the union, the Russians were carving a path to make the Russian Church independent. The papal encyclical and its heavy-handed delivery further splintered the very notion of a united Christendom that Isidore was so passionately promoting.

Isidore managed to escape from prison and fled Muscovite Rus'. Despite losing his position in Moscow, he set out again on a tour of the areas over which he still held authority as metropolitan. He continued to preach union as he made his way back to Italy, arriving in Venice in the summer of 1443 before joining the Pope in Siena.

Much has been made by later commentators of Isidore's failure to sell the union to the Russian Church. In addition, the literature produced by Russian writers at the time criticised the Metropolitan's disregard for the Grand Prince's instructions to oppose any change to the Byzantine rites at the Council of Ferrara-Florence, and it condemned his presumptuous actions on his journey to Rus' to implement the Decree of Union. However, it should be remembered that Moscow was still a small princedom among several in Rus', and the Grand Prince had not yet established the city as the unchallenged centre of the Russian Church. In time, Moscow would expand, but its power was still very much in its infancy, and there was no concept of a Russian nation. While the imprisonment of Isidore was dramatic, the immediate impact of the rejection of the union with the Latin Church by Moscow should not be overestimated. Isidore and his message of union had been welcomed and accepted in many of the Slavic states that he toured on his way to Rus'. He retained his title of Metropolitan of Kiev until he resigned the office as late as 1458.

Certainly, Isidore was outraged by his treatment in Moscow, and he complained bitterly to the Pope about his imprisonment. However, he did not return to Italy because he thought he had failed in his mission. After fleeing Rus', he ended up in Buda in Hungary where negotiations for a crusade against the Turks were in their final stages. Isidore returned to Italy to continue pushing for military intervention and relief for Constantinople. This was his true passion, and he intended to be at the heart of the action. When Isidore arrived back in Italy, it was not as a failed missionary. On the contrary, the Pope celebrated his return by holding the ceremony to invest him as a cardinal.

Shortly after his return to Rome, Isidore turned his attention to the Morea, writing to Eugenius to suggest that he send a legate with Patriarch Gregory III to the despots of the Peloponnesian lands, Constantine and Thomas who were reluctant to accept the Union. In 1445, Isidore himself was posted there as the papal representative, but the visit was short and unproductive. It is clear, as we will see in the work that Isidore would perform over the subsequent years, that the Cardinal had lost none of his appetite to save his homeland and its Church.

Cardinal Bessarion: A Career in the Curia

Traumatised by the intense hostility directed at him back in Constantinople, Bessarion did not take long to accept the cardinalate and move to the papal Curia. Eugenius offered him a cardinal's hat along with a pension of 300 florins, and he promised to double the pension if Bessarion agreed to reside in Italy and attend the papal court. Taking the greatest gamble of his life, Bessarion accepted the appointment and moved to Italy permanently in 1440.

This was undoubtedly the most significant moment in Bessarion's career. At the Council he had witnessed first-hand the prejudice and suspicion of the Italians towards the Greeks. He had to convince his new peers that his conversion was sincere, and he had to convince himself that his ambitions could be realised under the Pope. This first sally into Italian politics would make or break his reputation for years to come. Would being a leader in the Roman Catholic Church put him in a stronger position to save the Byzantine Church? Would he be accepted as loyal to the Pope?

If Bessarion had had any doubts about the finality of his break with the Greek Church, the words spoken by the Pope in the ceremony to appoint him as cardinal left no room for ambiguity.

To the praise of the Almighty God, and the honour of the Holy See, receive the red hat, the distinctive sign of the Cardinal's dignity, by which is meant that even unto death and the shedding of blood you will show yourself courageous for the exaltation of our Holy Father [the Pope], for the peace and outlet of the Christian people and for the augmentation of the Holy Roman Church.

By participating in this ceremony, Bessarion declared his commitment to upholding both papal supremacy (the honour of the Holy See) and the supremacy of the Holy Roman Church, a declaration that was abominable to his Greek friends and former supporters.

Bessarion's inauguration would have been protracted over several days, if not weeks. He was becoming a prince of the Church, and the length and elaborate ceremonial etiquette all served to enhance the mystique and regal pomp of this status. Initially, Bessarion's name would have been added to a formally published list of men whom the Pope intended to appoint as cardinals. After this public declaration, Bessarion was required to set in motion a prescribed set of bewilderingly complicated preparations. In his residence he would have designated one of the rooms to be a reception hall, to be sealed until the Cardinal Secretary of State arrived to present the *biglietto* personally to Bessarion announcing the Pope's intentions.

Within the designated room the backdrop was created for the initial ceremony. A gilded throne facing the wall to symbolise the cardinal designate's lack of power would have been set up on a raised platform. A baldacchino was raised, the ceremonial canopy above the 'throne', and a portrait of Eugenius IV attached to the folds of the drapery. Opposite this installation, a second baldacchino would have been erected, also draped in scarlet velvet or silk, with Bessarion's own coat of arms attached. This, however, was to remain covered until the hat and ring (symbols of the position of cardinal) were received.

When the Cardinal Secretary of State arrived at Bessarion's sealed room, he would have brought with him the parchment on which the papal appointment was written. Following the strict etiquette, he would have passed the parchment to Bessarion who, after reading it silently, then passed it to the highest-ranking member of his retinue who was tasked to read it aloud. Bessarion would have approached his throne but not sat on it while the Papal Master of Ceremonies announced the date and hour for bestowing the cardinal's hat.

Then the cardinal designate would have processed to the cathedral, dressed in the formal attire of the position: red Moroccan leather shoes with buckles, a scarlet *zucchetto* (robe) and a hat with gold threaded cords. Bessarion would have then advanced to the papal apartments where the enthroned Eugenius presented him with the silk scarlet *mozzetta* and the symbolic hat, the *biretta*, a wide brimmed red hat with thirty hanging tassels.

The following day Bessarion and his retinue would have returned once again, this time for the Second (secret) Consistory. The ceremony that took place in this meeting was heavily infused with a symbolism that made it irrefutably clear to Bessarion that the position of cardinal was granted to him with the expectation of loyalty to the Pope above all else. There were two complementary elements to this process: the ceremonial 'opening of the mouth' (*aperitio oris*) and 'closing of the mouth' (*clausura oris*).

As Bessarion submitted to the *aperitio oris*, he would have heard these words spoken, 'I open your mouth that in Consistories, Congregations and in other ecclesiastical functions you may be heard in the name of the Father, Son and the Holy Ghost.' This episode in the ceremony conjures the image of a cardinal acting as a puppet through which the Pope speaks. And the *clausura oris* was intended to represent the closed mouth that would enable Cardinal Bessarion 'to keep the secrets of their office and to give wise counsel to the Pope'.

The climax of this ceremony was the spiritual marriage of Bessarion to his titular church in Rome, the Basilica of Santissimi XII Apostoli, chosen for him by the Pope. However, it would not be until three years later, in 1443, that this union was 'consummated' when Eugenius returned to Rome and Bessarion took possession of SS Apostoli. Up to this point, the titular church was as symbolic to Bessarion as the gem-encrusted ring engraved with the name of Eugenius and his coat of arms that he had received from the Pope during the inauguration.

Bessarion justified his conversion to Roman Catholicism as a politically strategic move. He argued that by exercising power within the papal court he would be in a position from which he could campaign more effectively for military relief of Byzantium from the advance of the Ottomans. During the opening years of Bessarion's new life as a Roman Catholic cardinal, he worked tirelessly with the Pope to overcome the reluctance of the western secular princes and leaders to support a crusade.

Many contemporaries and historians have questioned the sincerity of Bessarion's conversion, with both Greeks and Italians suggesting that he was motivated by money and power. However, one of his earliest cultural projects demonstrated a genuine conviction for that united, Catholic Church that he had advocated in the Council of Ferrara-Florence.

Between 1451 and 1460 Cardinal Bessarion commissioned around eighteen large-format, heavily illustrated choir books for the Franciscan Monastery of St Anthony of 'Chypriss' or Padua in Constantinople. The Franciscans were established in Constantinople by 1220, and were influential at the Latin court in the city. They were known for their cultural pursuits and proficiency in the Greek language, even owning a library in Constantinople with Greek books. Although the Order was exiled from the Byzantine capital in 1261, they returned before 1296 and retained a monastery in the city until 1307, when they were forced once again to leave. In 1449, Pope Eugenius IV sent a special commission to found another Franciscan institution to be located within the Constantinopolitan walls. The monastery was known as St Anthony of 'Chypriss' and was dedicated to St Anthony of Padua or to St Anthony the Hermit. Construction was complete by 1451. The choir books never made it to Constantinople as they were still unfinished when the city fell to the Turks two years later. It took ten years for the commission to be completed, and Bessarion changed the beneficiary from the monastery in Constantinople to the Rimini noble family, the Malatesta. Today, the choir books are kept in the Biblioteca Malatestiana, a local library in Cesena.

Why was Bessarion commissioning a set of Latin choir books for a Franciscan establishment in Constantinople? What does this say about his relationship with Greece? If the books had been delivered to the Constantinopolitan monastery, it would have been a rare instance of the Cardinal's patronage acting as a conduit of western culture to the East. Bessarion's commission reflected his involvement and endorsement in a papal project to promote a missionary Catholic Order in the Byzantine Empire. The Franciscan Order proselytised globally with vigour, and its role in Constantinople served to maintain a strong Catholic presence in Byzantium and to convert Orthodox Christians to Roman Catholicism. Bessarion's motivation to bring about the Roman Catholic supremacy and union of the Churches to save Christendom from the Turks was so strong that he was not deterred by the image he might project among Greeks as a 'former' national now prepared to command a major Latin cultural project in Constantinople. The Cardinal made a potent declaration of his sympathies with these elaborately and expensively decorated choir books.

Bessarion was not the only one to perceive the increasingly critical situation in the East; the magnitude of the crisis facing the Church was described by Bartolomeo de Giano, a Franciscan monk living in Constantinople. In this letter he listed the large groups of Christians that populated the East to convey a sense of how many 'souls' were under threat from the Ottoman advance. The monk succinctly summarised the speed at which the Muslim forces were progressing through these Christian lands and demonstrated that the Europeans should not be complacent under the assumption that this problem did not concern them. Finally, Bartolomeo ranted against the secular princes who took no action and preferred to isolate themselves in their own domestic lives.

> For although Greece has been lost as has all of Turkey (which is elsewhere called Asia where the seven churches mentioned in the Apocalypse are and where Teucer, the enemy of Christ, reigns), at the present time innumerable Christian peoples still remain beyond the Black Sea, governing themselves under the Greek rite to this very day. First, there is to the East of Trebizond the not insignificant kingdom of the Georgians, i.e. of Georgia, where King Alexander rules today. And who can traverse under the open sky the homeland of the Russians and the Ruthenians to the marshes of Meotis (which is called the Sea of Habbakuk when interpreted)? I leave out Circasia, Vogaria, Mingrillia, Wallachia, Patras on the sea, though at present these are under the Greek rite. I'll say nothing about the Armenians, whom, I hope, you will soon see coming to Italy along with our father Jacob so as to be led back to the Catholic faith. They are far more eager than other nations for ready conversion and for receiving the truth and most favourably inclined to the Latins. Furthermore, you know from experience

that innumerable Christians are scattered in the Caesian mountains and here and there in Persia and Scythia, where the houses of our brethren stand devoid of friars, and that some are still living even among the Tartars. I therefore think that your personality and others like yours would be not without benefit—indeed, they would be most appropriate in those regions—once the sacred union is celebrated, if God should permit it... It was only eighty years ago or so that not a single Turk was found in Greece. They even crossed over carried by the Christians themselves and have filled that entire country. Indeed, unless it is provided with some swift remedy, Greece shall soon become like Arabia or Egypt. I am speaking of a broad and populous country adorned by the most glorious cities which have all been, for the time being at least, reduced to nothingness, so to speak, since they have been emptied of their inhabitants. It is the land where Alexander the Great ruled, and where there are the cities of Athens, Corinth, Sparta, Thessalonika, and Philippi ... cities that now it is painful to see. What I have described is nothing in comparison with the following deeds that have or will occur there unless someone pays attention and offers help. Where, I ask you, are the countries now of Dalmatia, Croatia, Bosnia, Rascia, Bulgaria, Albania, and Wallachia—not insignificant kingdoms that were despoiled of their inhabitants in just a few years? I come now to Hungary from which, it is said, three hundred thousand (though I would say more truly six hundred thousand) souls have been carried off in just a few days [by the Turkish armies]. Don't you believe that what I fear could happen, namely that by the just judgement of God this fire shall advance so far that it could occupy the border of [European] Christians? What then are those wretched Christians doing now? What are their princes doing? What about the pastors of the Church? Do they not sleep or do they suffer instead from lethargy so that they simply await Christendom to be consumed bit by bit? They play around—or rather hurt themselves—with lances and dances! And in the meantime, the Turk snuffs out the name of Christ and has already sworn, has already vowed himself to his own God, not to remain at peace under any agreement, unless he hears the praises of Muhammad sung in all of Hungary as soon as possible.

A month after the union was decreed, Eugenius and Bessarion called on the western rulers to contribute to the raising of a crusade force. It was not good timing. England and France were preoccupied with fighting each other in yet another stage of the Hundred Years' War, an Anglo-French conflict that also included a civil war on French territory. Technically, it began in 1337 when the King of England, Edward III, made a claim to the French throne. It was an intermittent conflict, marked by truces and lulls in hostility, eventually ending in 1453 in favour of the French. By the 1430s, the conflict had flickered back to life with major events like the English siege of Orleans and the rise of Joan of Arc. Both England and France were stretched militarily and financially; they were unable to divert much attention or resources to the plight of Byzantium.

At the same time, the leaders of the German states were still reluctant to recognise Eugenius as the legitimate pope after his efforts to sideline the Conciliarists at the Council of Basel. Resentful and truculent, they were disinclined to support any papal initiatives, especially those that would incur costs. Turning eastwards was equally unrewarding. Poland and Hungary, whose Baltic borders were physically threatened by the Turks, were too distracted by their own domestic territorial disputes to allocate military and financial assets to a crusade. Shortly after the King of Hungary, Albert, died in 1439, his wife Elizabeth gave birth to their son Ladislaus and claimed the throne for the infant. She had him crowned even though the Estates of the Hungarian realm had already offered the throne to Vladislaus, King of Poland. Vladislaus accepted the offer and was crowned a few months after Ladislaus. When a civil war erupted, the leading statesman and military general, John Hunyadi, also known as the White Knight, took the side of Vladislaus. He brought an end to the civil war after winning victory at Bátaszék, a pivotal location of conflict. Nonetheless, peace was elusive: Ladislaus's partisans were entrenched in the Transylvanian lands, and Hunyadi was unable to invest time or resources in a campaign against the Turks until he had established stability in those outlying territories of Hungary.

The only secular prince who responded positively to the call for a crusade was Philip III, Duke of Burgundy. Like Emperor John VIII, Isidore and Bessarion, Philip the Good was convinced that the Ottomans could be defeated and the Byzantine Empire saved. One of the few western princes to respond consistently to Byzantine pleas for military assistance, he commissioned courtiers to travel to the Near East to gather intelligence on the strength of the Ottoman's army. He actively pursued allies who would support him with troops, and committed oaths, financial support and men to papal entreaties for a crusade.

Despite the poor response, the Pope managed to secure funding (in principle) from the main banks in Venice, Florence and Genoa, and he chased the doge and senate for the fleet that they had promised the Byzantines. In the autumn of 1442, Eugenius outlined his plan to offer the Constantinopolitan emperor a number of armed galleys for twelve months, and 300 funded archers to join the soldiers in Constantinople.

In the same year, a contingent of Greeks from the Constantinople court arrived at the Vatican to remind the Pope of his obligations to them according to the terms of the Decree of Union. Eugenius issued an encyclical (a papal order to the entire

Roman Catholic Church) announcing the launch of a crusade on 1 January 1443. A year before Eugenius announced his crusade, with Hungary more or less settled under John Hunyadi and King Vladislaus, the Polish ruler and several of his barons launched the 'Long Campaign' against the Turks. The King sent men, and reinforcements arrived from Moldavia and Poland. Hunyadi hired over 10,000 mercenary soldiers whom he paid with money from his own treasury. He was deeply committed to the defence of Christendom, and he used his own income from his vast lands (nearly four million acres) to fund his military efforts. Although Vladislaus was the leader in name, it was Hunyadi who led the troops to victory against four Ottoman forces and captured the Serbian cities of Kruševac and Niš, as well as Sofia in Bulgaria. His successful military campaigns against the Ottomans earned him the nickname, the 'Turk-buster'.

Buoyed by these successes, Eugenius and the Hungarians believed that the Ottomans were fatally weakened and that the time had come to expel them from Christendom with a crusade. The Venetians were also sufficiently enthused by Vladislaus's victories to overcome the economic self-interest that usually motivated them to avoid conflict in order to protect their trade treaties forged with the Turks. The senate held a procession of thanksgiving culminating in a ceremony outside St Mark's attended by the doge, aristocracy and clergy. Senators wrote to the Pope to explain that the long-promised ships were ready but that they required additional funding to arm them. In response, Eugenius conducted several fundraisers, including the sale of indulgences to those who visited designated churches as far afield as the Church of St Mary of Eton near Windsor and to those who donated to the preparations of the military campaign. The Pope sent envoys to preach about the crusade in Moldavia, Lithuania and Wallachia, and he set aside one-fifth of the revenue of the apostolic camera to fund it. He also levied a tithe of one-tenth of all revenue on the archbishops, bishops and abbots of the western Christian nations. Three years after his conversion, Bessarion was finally able to hope his gamble had paid off and that he would be instrumental in rescuing the beleaguered Byzantine Empire from the Ottomans.

Together, King Vladislaus of Hungary, John Hunyadi, the Venetians and the Poles conceived an ambitious plan. Vladislaus and Hunyadi set out with an army to march through Ottoman-occupied Bulgaria. They expected the Bulgarians would rise up against their Turkish overlords, and initially the crusaders met little resistance. The Venetians planned to re-supply them with soldiers and weapons at a rendezvous on the coast of the Black Sea. In the meantime, a blockade, also led by Venice, was established to prevent Sultan Murad from leaving Anatolia and joining his troops in Europe. This is where their luck ran out. Hunyadi's troops were increasingly rowdy, pillaging and looting as they advanced, turning the local Bulgarians against them. The Genoese traitorously accepted money from the Sultan to transport him and his army through the blockade. The Ottoman army in Europe swelled to 60,000 men versus the West's 20,000 soldiers. To compound the crusaders' woes, a violent storm prevented the Venetians from reaching Hunyadi's army at the agreed meeting point.

The soldiers had no choice but to fight despite the odds. They set up camp at Varna, the large Bulgarian city on the coast of the Black Sea. On a chilly November night in 1444, a final Mass was held for the army and at sunrise they awoke to find themselves surrounded by the Turks. The fighting was desperate, and the crusaders were not easily overcome. During a lull, King Vladislaus led a foolhardy charge. He was killed, and his death was the beginning of the end for the crusade. This was the most damaging defeat for the Christians prior to the Fall of Constantinople. It brought about the end of the Hungarian-Polish alliance, and the Ottomans now believed nothing stood in the way of a complete defeat of the Byzantine Empire.

The defeat at Varna was a major setback for Isidore's and Bessarion's cause. It gave the impression that the West was weak, even when it united in defence of Christian territories, and it gave the Ottomans a sense of confidence in their own military capabilities. They were re-energised to expand further west. In November of 1446, Murad led a large army of around 50,000-60,000 men, seizing the territories in Greece that Despot Constantine had conquered only the previous year. The Byzantines retreated behind the Hexamilion wall: a supposedly impregnable defence system constructed around the Peloponnesian lands of the Morea. Constantine tried to sue for peace, sending the writer Laonikos Chalkokondyles as ambassador to Murad, who rejected the Despot's proposition and imprisoned the unfortunate envoy.

Constantine and his brother Thomas mustered around 20,000 men to defend the walls, although a substantial number of the soldiers were Albanian mercenaries, not known for their reliability. Although vastly outnumbered and forced to spread themselves too thinly, the Byzantines held out for two weeks before Murad successfully breached the Hexamilion, which could not withstand the modern cannon fire of the Turks. The despots of this key imperial territory lost their autonomy – from now on they would depend on the good will of Murad to maintain their position. Saddled with a hefty annual tribute and forbidden from repairing the damage to the Hexamilion, Constantine and Thomas focused on rebuilding the homes and farmsteads ravaged by the Turks. The victors had pillaged mercilessly and taken more than 60,000 inhabitants prisoner, depleting the local population.

Saving Byzantium as the Pope's Man

At this crucial moment, when a swift and decisive response to the invasion of Morea from the western princes might have stopped the Ottomans, Pope Eugenius died. Bessarion and Isidore feared that time was running out for Byzantium. The prospect of using their position in the Roman Catholic Church to bring about the union of the East and West and to save the empire from collapse looked very bleak. Apart from the Hungarians, the eastern European regions were even more resistant to the Decree of Union's terms than the Constantinopolitans. The first attempt at a crusade had ended in defeat. Bessarion and Isidore had lost their sponsor, who had promoted their Roman careers and believed as passionately as they did in a crusade and a unified Christian Church. No one yet knew who would succeed Eugenius and whether he would be equally concerned with the plight of Byzantium. The two men had taken a huge gamble in 1440 when they accepted their cardinalates; in 1447 the uncertainty had grown as the cardinals waited to find out whether they would have a friend or foe in the new pope.

5

GREEK HAWKS IN THE SACRED COLLEGE

After Eugenius IV passed away, the electoral college chose a recently appointed Cardinal, Tommaso Parentucelli, to be the new pope. He took the name Pope Nicholas V. At the time of his succession, the Byzantines and Ottomans were maintaining an uneasy peace, and the new Pope had little reason to focus on this issue. Nicholas V faced seemingly more serious challenges elsewhere. The western continent was in turmoil; England and France were at war, the authority of the Holy Roman Emperor Frederick III was under threat, Bohemia had cut ties with the papacy, and the Italian leaders were engaged in multiple struggles for power. The Vatican's treasury was empty, and little income came from the papal states ravaged by decades of warfare. Law and order had broken down, villages had been pillaged and destroyed, leaving the papal states' subjects vulnerable to famine and enslavement.

In such dire circumstances, the Pope's noble vassals were plotting to sever themselves from Roman control. Faced with such a range of crises, Nicholas positioned himself as a bringer of peace. Domestically, he set about settling the papal states and restoring the revenue stream. He sent Bessarion as papal legate to Bologna – an important state that needed a firm hand to quell its increasing resistance to papal authority. At this stage, Bessarion took a backseat in the diplomatic efforts to raise a crusade. Despite the diversion of his appointment in Bologna, he did not give up his defence of Byzantium. As we will see in a later chapter, Bessarion's energy was still sharply focused on saving the cultural and spiritual empire during these years.

Internationally, the Pope used his own substantial skills in diplomacy, supported by equally talented appointees, to orchestrate a series of new alliances and agreements. He made the first overtures to the hostile King Alfonso of Naples by offering him a prominent place in the papal coronation ceremony, and it was shortly afterwards that Alfonso instructed his ambassadors to pledge Naples' allegiance to the Pope.

The German princes were more challenging for Nicholas, but he won them over by enlisting the support of Emperor Frederick. Some leaders of the German states had hoped to use the transition period from Eugenius IV to Nicholas V as an opportunity to revive the claim of the antipope, Felix V, to the Vatican. Frederick summoned all the electors, nobles and clerics to a council convened in Aschaffenburg, where the papal ambassador and the Emperor persuaded them to proclaim Nicholas V as pope. In the end, they all signed the Concordat of Vienna, essentially closing the rift that had been at the heart of the Council of Basel.

Pope Nicholas was fully absorbed by these issues during the first few years of his papacy, and he effectively de-prioritised the Byzantine crisis. He was not oblivious to the Turkish advances, but the immediate threat posed by the Ottomans at the end of the 1440s seemed to focus more on Hungary and Albania than on Constantinople. By nature, Nicholas was not a warmongering pope, and his preference for diplomacy and political manoeuvring over direct military action was reflected in his dealings with the Ottoman threat to Europe. He invested time in resolving internal conflicts in Hungary and Albania so that they could cooperate and unite against the exterior enemy. When Rhodes and Cyprus became a target, Nicholas diverted funds raised from indulgences to fund their defence, but he did not try to muster an army.

The death of Murad II and the accession of his son Mehmed II in 1451 shattered the relative calm. Passionate and religious to the point of messianism, Mehmed believed himself to be the great warrior leader that the Prophet Mohammad had foretold. He cultivated the persona of imperial sanctity and needed a target for his holy war; that target was Constantinople. A poem he composed under the pseudonym, Avni, evoked the sincerity of his conviction. Such rhetoric confirmed the warnings of Isidore and Bessarion that the Ottoman threat was more than a danger to the Orthodox Church: it was a threat to all Christianity.

> To obey and fight hard for Allah is my aim and my desire;
> 'Tis but zeal for Faith, for Islam, that my ardour doth inspire.
> Through the grace of Allah, and the assistance of the Band Unseen,
> Is my earnest hope the Infidels to crush with ruin dire.
> On the Saints and on the Prophets surely doth my trust repose;
> Through the love of God, to triumph and to conquest I aspire.
> What if I with soul and gold strive here to wage the Holy War?
> Praise is God's! Ten thousand sighs for battle in my breast suspire.
> O Muhammed! through the chosen Ahmed Mukhtar's glorious aid,
> Hope I that my might may trump over Islam's foes acquire!

Despite his youth, he had keenly observed the victory at Varna and the absence of a western response to his father's attack on the Morea. Over the next couple of years, he pursued a dual strategy of military aggression and treaties. In one of his first and most overtly aggressive challenges, Mehmed ordered the construction of a fortress, Rumeli Hisarı on the European shore of the Bosporus straits separating the Asian and European Ottoman territories. Mehmed summoned a thousand masons, lime slakers and workmen to construct the castle, named Boghazkesen (cut throat), that he had designed on the site that he had selected at the channel's narrowest point where the current was swiftest. The chronicler Michael Doukas captured the anxiety of the Byzantines as they watched the fortress's construction:

> ...he [Mehmed II] undertook another against the Romans which inflicted deadly injury. At the onset of winter, mandates and proclamations were sent to every province in the East and West to furnish one thousand skilled masons as well as an equal number of labourers and limestokers. Provisions were also to be made for the transportation of building materials required for the construction, in the spring, of a fortress at the Sacred Mouth above the City. When the Romans heard the bitter news, the Christians of Constantinople, Asia, Thrace, and the islands trembled in their deep distress. Their only comment was, 'Now the end of the City is at hand. Behold the omens of our nation's ruin. Now are the days of Antichrist. What will become of us and what will we do? Let our lives be taken from us, O Lord. Let not the eyes of Thy servants see the destruction of the City. Let not Thine enemies say "O Emperor, where are the guardian saints of this City?"' It was not only the Christians in the City who lamented aloud in such a manner but all the Christians dispersed throughout the East and West and those dwelling in the islands also wept loudly.

Mehmed's fortress gave him full maritime control over Constantinople's Black Sea trade: 'in order to deny passage to all vessels, big and small, sailing from the Black Sea toward our [i.e. the Byzantine] harbour and to provide easy passage from Asia Minor to Thrace for his [Mehmed] troops'. The Sultan took responsibility for the construction of the walls between the towers, each of which he assigned to his viziers, who were also required to fund their allocated projects. During the construction, which took only four months, tensions ran high between the local Byzantine residents and the Turkish workmen. There were attempts by individuals to obstruct the building work, and several incidents of injury and even murder. The fortress was immense; the towers rose to around 60 metres above sea level and the entire structure was 245 metres in length. The Byzantines sent their objections to the Sultan's court at Edirne but were ignored. Mehmed garrisoned four hundred men in the fortress with the remit to stop all ships, and his instructions were reported by Doukas:

> Do not allow ships sailing from the Hellespont to the Black Sea or from the Black Sea to the Hellespont, no matter under whose flag they may be sailing – Genoese, Venetian, Constantinopolitan, Kaffatinian, Trapezundian, Amisinian, Sinopean, or even under my own flag, and no matter what class they are, triremes, biremes, barques, or skiffs – to sail through without first lowering their sails and paying customs duties; only after they have done so will you permit them to proceed on their way. Use the cannon to sink the ship that does not comply and submit.

A range of cannons, some capable of firing balls of around 270 kilos, targeted any ships that did not obey Mehmed's directive. It was not a bluff. When a Venetian merchant ship failed to stop at the end of 1452, the guards launched an attack, sinking the vessel and arresting the captain and his crew. Brought before Mehmed, the sailors were beheaded, the captain was impaled, and their bodies were left on display in the street. Not only did the fortress put pressure on the trading activities of Constantinople and other western maritime powers, it also made them increasingly isolated in the event of a Turkish attack.

Hand-in-hand with this display of force, the Sultan forged a series of strategic relationships with those whom he feared might challenge his actions. Bessarion and Isidore looked on in horror as former allies in the Balkans, including George Brankovic, despot of Serbia, and even John Hunyadi, were courted by Mehmed and persuaded to sign treaties. Other important Christian players in the area – the Knights Hospitaller of Rhodes, the Genoese based at Chios and Lesbos, and the Wallachians in the north – also came to an agreement with the new Sultan.

Constantinople had a new ruler, the Emperor Constantine Dragaš Palaeologus, who took the title of Constantine XI. A year after Pope Eugenius died, Emperor John VIII also passed away. He had been close to his younger brother Constantine and had designated him as his successor. At the time of his death, the heir apparent was quite far away ruling his Peloponnesian territories from the throne in Mistra, and it looked like there might be an imperial challenge from his brothers Thomas and Demetrius. A known anti-unionist, Demetrius, in particular, had significant popular support. However, the siblings' mother, Helena, was still living and she favoured Constantine. Taking control of the situation, she filled the dangerous vacuum by assuming the regency of Constantinople while Constantine was invested as emperor in a civil ceremony in Mistra. Demetrius and Thomas backed down and resentfully accepted Constantine's position. However, the new Emperor could not be crowned without a patriarch, and the serving cleric at the time was the pro-unionist Patriarch Gregory III. His authority had been rejected by the majority of the Constantinopolitan clergy and monks, who refused to accept a pro-union leader for their church. To hold a crowning ceremony led by Gregory III was to risk inciting a rebellion.

This omission would haunt Constantine's government in the run up to the fall of Constantinople when the legitimacy of his rule would be challenged by his opponents. While Constantine recognised the practical necessity of accepting the Decree of Union, he was not philosophically committed to it. His attempts to impose the decree on Constantinople were half-hearted, partly from lack of conviction and partly through fear that his subjects would revolt.

Mehmed's acts of aggression drove Constantine to send an embassy to Rome to beseech the Pope to come to the Byzantines' aid. A contemporary, writing after the fall of the city, described the heightened alarm at the imperial court: 'Dragaš the Emperor of the Greeks was under the impression that the enemy [Turks] would come back once more, and he sent numerous noble emissaries to the highest priest [Pope Nicholas V], to the Roman Emperor [Frederick III], to King Alfonso, and to the Venetians to announce that, unless he received help, he would find himself unable to resist the Turks.'

In response to the Emperor's pleas, Pope Nicholas turned to Cardinal Isidore to lead a papal delegation to Constantinople. Like Bessarion, Isidore held the title of official papal Consiliarius for Eastern Affairs. As Consiliarius, he advised the Pope on the eastern Church, facilitated communication with the Byzantine secular and religious leaders, and monitored the Ottoman incursions. Bessarion was proving to be indispensable to the Pope in Bologna and this left Isidore as the obvious candidate.

Despite the urgency of the imminent threat to Constantinople, Nicholas briefed Isidore to convey the Pope's uncompromising stance over the acceptance and implementation of the Decree of Union. Byzantine pro-unionists understood the peril that Constantinople faced at this moment and renewed their efforts to achieve the alliance with the West that would have been crucial to Byzantium's survival. A decade earlier, Pope Eugenius IV had committed to mustering western support in exchange for the signatures of the Greeks on the Decree of Union. This was not enough for Pope Nicholas. He demanded evidence that the decree was being implemented before he would provide any military assistance. The papal message that Isidore delivered to Constantine was brutal and demonstrated little of the diplomacy that the Pope had employed in other situations:

> Some other sin must have provoked Divine Justice, and this sin is the schism which was begun under Photius and has since lasted for five hundred years. Full of sorrow and with a heavy heart do we make this complaint, and we would willingly have buried it in everlasting silence, but if a remedy is to be applied the wound must be laid bare. For almost five hundred years Satan, the author of all evil, and especially of division, has seduced the Church of Constantinople into disobedience to the Roman Bishop, the successor of St Peter and representative of our Lord Jesus Christ. Innumerable negotiations have meanwhile been undertaken, a great many Councils have been held, countless embassies have been sent to and fro, until at last Emperor John and Patriarch Joseph of Constantinople, accompanied by numerous prelates and great men, met Pope Eugenius IV, the Cardinals of the Roman Church, and a considerable body of Western Prelates at Florence in order, with the blessing of God, to put an end to the schism and establish unity... These negotiations were carried on before

the eyes of the whole world, and the Decree of Union drawn up in Greek and Latin and signed by all present has been made known to the whole world... And now many years have already passed during which the decree of the Union has been disregarded by the Greeks, and there appears no hope of any readiness to accept it... We will wait until this letter of ours has received your consideration, and if you, with your great men and your people ... accept the decree of the Union, you will find us, the Cardinals and the whole Western Church always ready for you and well disposed towards you.

Up to this point there had been little effort to impose the decree in the Byzantine lands. Faced with the highly emotional and well organised opposition, the pro-unionist patriarch, Gregory III Mammas, fled Constantinople and the anti-unionists, taking refuge in the Vatican. Imperial authority was at a low ebb, and there was virtually no functioning ecclesiastical administration. Neither the Emperor nor the church leaders were in a position to suppress the anti-unionist movement. Like the earlier mission to impose the Decree of Union on the Slavic churches, Isidore found himself once again charged with a daunting task: to persuade the Constantinopolitans to accept the Decree of Union so that the Pope would agree to send military help to oppose the Ottoman Turks. This time, though, the stakes were higher: the survival of Byzantium's main city, Constantinople.

The Cardinal set out on a journey from Rome to Constantinople that lasted six gruelling months. As a representative of the Vatican to Constantinople, he was expected to deliver the intransigent papal message to the Byzantines. As a fellow Greek, Isidore understood that he must also provide tangible proof of the West's good faith, evidence to be used as leverage in his discussions with the anti-unionists. He planned, therefore, to arrive in Constantinople with soldiers who would join the defenders of the city walls. As he travelled, he stopped at several ports to recruit mercenaries for this purpose. He faced significant recruitment challenges, which may account for the many months it took him to reach Constantinople. Mercenaries had no particular loyalty to the Cardinal's cause; they were equally comfortable fighting for the Sultan who was offering far better terms and the prospect of loot.

Constantinople was in a state of internal chaos. The imperial treasury was empty, and the Emperor's attempts to levy a tax on the Venetian merchants to raise defence funds met with such fierce resistance that he had to abandon his plans. The majority of the wealthy Constantinopolitans preferred to invest their money in Italy rather than in the protection of their homeland, reducing Constantine to raiding church treasuries for the means to defend the city. The polarisation of the unionists and anti-unionists was at fever pitch – the anti-unionists would rather die at the hands of the Ottomans than to make any concessions to the West in exchange for military aid.

Upon hearing the conditions imposed by the Pope in exchange for aid against the Turks, the fanatical scholar monk George Scholarios posted a statement addressed to the pro-union Constantinopolitans declaring, 'Ah benighted souls, not only have you lost everything, but now you turn your backs on that which is most holy. Instead of finding solace in God during these iniquitous times, it is rather separation from God that you seek... Now I bear witness before God that the Union of yours is evil...'

In a letter to Bessarion, Isidore complained about his arduous experience: 'Around the month of May of last year [1452] I left Rome, bringing no help or garrison ... and everything seemed to be against me. I met with no luck. I omit each instance. Finally

I spent six months in transit and only managed to reach the most unfortunate city of Constantinople on the twenty-sixth of October. It was already under threat of arms and surrounded on every side.'

When he arrived in the autumn, he found a city that had been terrorised by Sultan Mehmed over the preceding months. The Constantinopolitans were feeling the effects of having their access from the Black Sea to the Sea of Marmara essentially severed by the menacing fortress of Rumeli Hisar. Supplies were low, and the citizens felt trapped. Mehmed had also besieged several of the city's satellite towns and castles. The Cardinal described the ruthless slaughter of the Christians in these places and mentions the hatred for them that seemed to motivate the sultan: 'He [Mehmed] considers it an abomination to look upon a Christian and he subsequently washes and cleanses his eyes to rid himself of the pollution.'

By the time, however, that Isidore reached Constantinople, Mehmed had withdrawn his troops to regroup over the autumn and winter of 1452. The city remained in a state of high alert, and there was a realistic fear that the Ottomans would be back and would go further in their next campaign. The local population warmly welcomed Isidore and his motley force. The gunners and crossbowmen that the Cardinal managed to muster were a welcome addition to a threadbare army. These were the first combatants to arrive from the West; Isidore had called at Naples and several of the Aegean islands en route to Constantinople, recruiting men at each port.

The chronicler Doukas mentioned Isidore's efforts in his account: 'The Cardinal came to the island of Chios on board a very large Genoese vessel, where he remained a number of days ... he had with him up to fifty Italian recruits and many other Latins from Chios.'

Initially, the signs were positive for Isidore and his mission. The Ottoman threat, visible on the doorstep of all Constantinopolitans, along with the promise of military aid, put pressure on the anti-unionists and gave Emperor Constantine hope that a deal could be made. Pope Nicholas's demands included the appointment of a pro-union patriarch: either by reinstating the current patriarch, Gregory Mammas, or by replacing him with Isidore. His second demand was that the leaders of the anti-unionist movement convene for discussions with Isidore to achieve an agreement to implement and follow the terms of the decree.

Unfortunately for Isidore, George Scholarios, sensing that there was potential for the Decree of Union to be successfully implemented, focused his rabid invective on the Cardinal. He spread rumours that the soldiers who had accompanied Isidore were not there to defend Constantinople from the Turks, but to impose the Latin rites on the Orthodox Church by force. According to Scholarios, subjugation to the Ottomans was better than to the Roman Catholics. He declaimed prophecies of the end of Byzantium as divine punishment for accepting a union with the western Church. To Emperor Constantine he inveighed that: '…what they [the Latin Church] wish to accomplish will invite every evil from God, from men, from friends and from external enemies. Consequently, neither union nor non-union will result. The Church of Constantinople will no longer exist for the Orthodox from this point on, if you [Constantine] enact your wishes [to accept the Decree of Union in return for military support].'

Scholarios and his followers refused to participate in the discussions held by Isidore with Constantine and the pro-unionists in Constantinople. They insisted that the Council of Ferrara-Florence must be reconvened and that new terms, more favourable to the Orthodox Church, be drawn up. In the meantime, Scholarios called for the supply of military support from the West to be divorced from the issue of union. Both sides were aware that these demands were unrealistic, and Isidore proceeded to convince the Emperor to revive the existing Decree of Union, as Pope Nicholas demanded. Constantine duly ordered that a mass be held in Hagia Sofia to celebrate the union in December of 1452.

Scholarios was predictably outraged and persuaded the local clerics to boycott Hagia Sofia. Emperor Constantine was not prepared to force the union on his people, and he made it clear that he held Isidore entirely responsible for convincing the locals to accept the decree. Ubertino Pusculo, a student in Constantinople at the time, and later bishop of Brescia, recorded details of Isidore's exchange with the Emperor in his epic poem *Constantinopolis*, written between 1455 and 1460:

> The Emperor appeared concerned and kept his eyes fixed on the ground. Then he said a few words: 'It is not solely up to me to join the Pope and there is no dignity to compel my people. They must do so willingly. It is up to you to use all your cunning to convert the monks and the high clerics. I would be delighted to find any way to avenge myself upon the Turks and to wipe them out. Try to convert my people, who have been numbed by the impending danger.'

This demonstration of imperial weakness served to perpetuate the chaos and increase the polarisation of the two sides. A growing anti-court movement intensified the internal strife, resurrecting the controversy over Constantine's right to the throne since he had not been formally crowned by a patriarch after the death of Emperor John VIII. His opponents seized on this to raise doubts about the legitimacy of Constantine's decisions regarding the union. The Emperor's dilemma was unenviable: to have a chance to save Constantinople from the Ottomans he had to declare and enforce the decree. To do so would risk his position as the anti-unionists mustered more and more support against him.

In this context, his decision to order the celebration of the decree but not to enforce it could be interpreted as an effort to appease both camps. It backfired: he did not meet the conditions required by the Pope, but he still managed to alienate his subjects. Isidore doggedly continued to pursue his agenda and did his best to use his influence to persuade the inhabitants and the clerics to support the union. Ubertino Pusculo described these efforts in detail.

> He [Isidore] urged them and tried to persuade them to unite with the highest lord of the Christians [the Pope] and not perish willingly left by themselves. In addition, he employed similar arguments in his talks with the foremost citizens in various gatherings. He pressed his admonitions on those who were wavering. He performed labours with all of his strength day and night, but in vain.

Isidore was angry, and his raw emotion came through in his speech to the Constantinopolitans: 'I would never have faced the dangers of the sea. I am an old man and should not have taken upon my shoulders such hard work. I would not have come to your city, but our common threat to our homeland forced me to retrace my steps to my sacred fatherland.' Time had run out for Isidore and Bessarion. The West failed to acknowledge the enormity of the threat looming over the Byzantine Empire.

Nicholas was very clear that he would withhold support until the Decree of Union was implemented. A crisis was about to unfold for Constantinople, and had the Pope mustered forces sooner, the city might have withstood the siege. And yet, in the end, this calamity would be harnessed by the two cardinals and their peers to wake up western Christians. This event did not signal the end of the entire empire for those who were living through these events. However, it took the magnitude of this grievous blow to make the West understand the existential threat they faced if they did not save Byzantium.

6

THE BATTLE FOR CONSTANTINOPLE

Isidore's actions in the run up to and during the siege of Constantinople are testament to his conviction that the Empire could be salvaged. There had been many crisis points for the Byzantines over the years preceding 1453, and as the greatest of these calamities unfolded, Isidore found himself in Constantinople. He seized the opportunity to take a military role as a defender of the city and of his fellow countrymen. In the weeks following the siege, the Cardinal wrote a series of letters vividly describing what had happened and what he believed it would mean for the future. These letters were addressed to prominent leaders in the west and played a key role in Isidore's campaign to save the Empire. His words alongside those of eyewitness accounts compiled by a contemporary papal official, Henry of Soemmern, reveal Isidore's role and actions during the siege.

The winter of 1452 was a frenzy of activity for Isidore and the Constantinopolitans. Not only was the Cardinal embroiled in the difficult negotiations over the Decree of Union with the Emperor, he committed his personal energy and resources to preparations for the struggle the city was about to face. Constantinople depended on its harbour and its land and sea walls for its defence. As Isidore and the citizens prepared for war, the poor condition of the walls became a focus for them. Emperor Constantine was struggling to find the money to finance the work. Obstructed by an uncooperative upper class, he had to raid the Church's coffers to pay the labourers, who refused to work unless they received hard currency. To make the situation even worse, corrupt contractors were skimming the scant funds, leaving a shortfall in pay for the workers. An eyewitness, Nicolo Barbaro, alleged that the aristocracy had claimed penury when Constantine asked them to contribute to the costs of repairing the city's fortifications. After the city fell, he claimed that their homes were found to be filled with treasure and money. He described how some nobles took gold to the Sultan to purchase his clemency. It is rumoured that Isidore sold his own vestments to raise money for the repairs, and various contemporary sources mentioned his personal contribution to the work on the towers of the Xyloporta and Anemades gates.

Constantine appealed to individuals and to states in Europe for assistance, offering imperial concessions in exchange. No support came from Trebizond, Wallachia or Iberia-Georgia. Despite offering the island of Lemnos to Alfonso of Aragon, the only support he gave was a single ship provisioned with food. Similarly, Constantine promised Mesembria and Selymbria to John Hunyadi, but to no avail: Hungary did not provide any help. The best that Emperor Frederick could muster was a threatening letter that he wrote to the Sultan; and Constantine's brothers, Thomas and Demetrius, were tied down by raids in the Peloponnese that Mehmed had ordered to keep them from coming to Constantinople's aid.

Isidore also contributed to the harbour defences, and in the letter that he would later send to Bessarion after he escaped the Turkish occupation, he boasted that he had managed to assemble a defensive fleet over the winter months. His contribution was crucial in convincing the Venetian merchants and local population to stay and defend Constantinople alongside the Greeks. A year earlier, as the Ottoman threat intensified, Emperor Constantine had begun to detain the Venetian merchant vessels that called at the port of Constantinople en route between Caffa (now in Ukraine) and Trebizond, commandeering them for military service. He had come dangerously close to losing the support of this community when he attempted to raise cash by imposing additional levies on foreigners in the city.

Grasping the importance of the Venetians and their ships to Constantinople's defence, Isidore and the head of the Venetian community (the *bailo*) called a meeting in the city's church of San Marco. Isidore had cultivated close ties with the Venetians back in Italy – as early as 1443 he had been granted citizenship of Venice by the Grand Council. As a citizen and a papal envoy, the Cardinal held substantial influence among the Venetian community in Constantinople. At the San Marco meeting he convinced them to vote almost unanimously to stay and defend the city. The merchant captains were also persuaded to swear an oath to stay until the end of the siege and adapt their ships for use as defensive vessels.

By December, the Cardinal had achieved an immense amount: an official proclamation of the Decree of Union in Hagia Sofia and the mustering of a naval campaign to oppose the Turks. In his letter to Pope Nicholas, written in the aftermath of the city's fall, Isidore described these efforts: 'Care had been exercised to guard and bar the harbour of Constantinople with a chain, as that port resembles a bay and it is enclosed, like a strait, across by the city of Pera. This was done. In addition, five Venetian triremes and twelve, in number, large ships under contract undertook to guard and secure the chain itself.'

Six months had passed since the Emperor and Isidore celebrated the Decree of Union in Hagia Sofia, as requested by Pope Nicholas. Constantine and his subjects were waiting anxiously for the papal armies that had been promised in return. They never came. By the time the Pope and the Venetians finally grasped the severity of the threat to Constantinople, it was too late. Nicholas sent three Genoese ships and sourced five more that were to be equipped by Venice. These were delayed by disputes over the funding of the equipment and the crews' wages.

In the spring of 1453, Mehmed was back. Isidore and the residents of Constantinople woke on 5 April to find the Ottoman forces camped outside the city walls. The Sultan issued his terms of surrender, which were rejected by Emperor Constantine, and the siege began. Isidore described a vast Turkish army in his letter to Pope Nicholas, numbering: 'beyond three hundred thousand individuals, two hundred and twenty large and small triremes, bombards [a type of cannon] and other effective war engines, as well as other weapons of war, which would be too difficult to enumerate.'

While this was an inflated estimation, there is no doubt that the Sultan's forces considerably outnumbered the defenders (in reality there were around 80,000 Turkish soldiers and only 6,000-7,000 Greeks). It is clear from the Cardinal's account that not only was the Ottoman army larger, but it was also much better equipped than the Byzantine soldiers. A few days after the siege began, Mehmed's enormous cannon arrived on a vehicle that required sixty oxen to pull it. Capable of firing a ball weighing 1,200 lb over a distance of more than a mile, the weapon was a significant threat to the walls of Constantinople. Isidore noted that, out of the entire Ottoman arsenal of weapons, only the three largest cannons were a true challenge to the defences of the city.

> He cast very many bombards, as many as one thousand. Among them, three were the largest. The first ejected a stone that measured eleven palms in circumference and weighed fourteen cantars; the second ejected a stone of ten palms that weighed twelve cantars; and the third ejected a stone of nine palms in circumference that weighed ten cantars. There were other smaller pieces ... and there were countless firearms. All the other cannons did no harm, but those three bombards that fired almost seventy large stones caused a great deal of damage.

Despite the Turkish advantage, victory was anything but a foregone conclusion. The efforts of the Emperor and men like Isidore to prepare the city for the siege had not been in vain. Isidore's efforts to persuade the Venetian residents of Constantinople to support the Byzantines were rewarded. Only a month earlier, in April, the Italo-Byzantine fleet guarding the Golden Horn defeated an Ottoman naval attack. The Constantinopolitans and the resident foreigners put up a strong defence, and there were reports of many dead Turks. Damage to the walls was speedily repaired overnight, and the siege seemed to be stalling. In response to the pleas of the Emperor, and to acknowledge the progress Isidore had made in implementing the Decree of Union, the Pope sent a flotilla full of supplies to relieve the city. The ships succeeded in evading the blockade and delivering the desperately needed commodities. In a further setback for the Sultan, his navy failed to win an engagement with the Italo-Byzantine fleet that Isidore, Emperor

Constantine and the Venetian *bailo* had managed to assemble to guard the Golden Horn. This defeat forced the Ottomans to withdraw and reconsider their plans.

In his letter to Pope Nicholas, Isidore described the ingenuity of Mehmed, who faced the formidable resistance of the Byzantines. Realising that he was not going to be able to get past the chain and the boats protecting the port, the Sultan devised what the Cardinal referred to as 'unprecedented and even miraculous, evils'. He commanded his soldiers to construct a three-mile track of wooden beams across the hills behind Galata, so that the Ottomans' seventy-two triremes could be dragged across the greased logs to bypass the chain. Isidore wrote how it seemed as though the vessels 'were sailing over the sea, propelled by the wind, with oars extended over the sides, and with their standards and tents, resembling their normal way of travelling'. The Turks could now enter the harbour.

By crossing Galata (Pera), they could circumvent the Venetian fleet and defensive boom that blocked access to the harbour of Constantinople. Against the odds, the Ottomans managed to keep their engineers' plans secret and to transport, undetected, the supplies they would need in the construction of this bridge. When the construction had been finished, the vessels were transferred across land under the cover of night, and the Constantinopolitans woke up the next morning to the unwelcome surprise that their harbour was filled with enemy ships. Isidore described the event twice, to Pope Nicholas and to Bessarion:

> To begin with, the harbour had been contained and secured, from the side of Galatas mountain to the Beautiful Gate and access was admirably blocked to the Turks by fifteen Venetian triremes and

another twelve round ships and especially by those immense chains. When the Turks concluded that they could not force their way, they moved their anchorage at Diplokionion, where they had amassed their ships. A few days later the Turk ordered that a three-mile (or even longer road) be constructed over the mountain to transport ninety-two biremes and uniremes from one side of the mountain at Galatas to the other; and so it was done and the Turk assumed total control of the harbour.

Mehmed's ingenuity was not limited to this feat, according to Isidore. In his letter to Bessarion, he compared the Sultan to the Xerxes the Great, with his legendary bridge over the Hellespont to invade Greece. According to the Cardinal, the Sultan outdid the Persian ruler by constructing a portable bridge that, at 370m, was twice the length and wide enough for five men and their horses to pass. This bridge enabled the Turks to access the stretch of city wall along the Golden Horn. Isidore and many other eyewitnesses were deeply impressed by the Sultan's ingenuity. The Cardinal wrote to Bessarion:

> Then he [Mehmed] thought of something more admirable, something that Xerxes had also done in antiquity: he devised and constructed a very large bridge stretching from the shore by Hagia Galatina as far as our walls at Kynegion, double the distance bridged by Xerxes long ago. Over it many horsemen could cross at the same time.

The psychological impact of these actions should not be underestimated, but it is unlikely that Mehmed had any real intention to assault the sea walls of Constantinople. By giving his troops access via the water to these walls in the harbour and over the water by the bridge, he forced the defenders to move troops that they could not spare from the land walls to the sea fortifications.

To both Bessarion and the Pope, Isidore detailed the overwhelming weaponry available to the Turks, and the assaults that came from above and below ground. He described over 300 towers that could be moved and positioned against the walls like ladders. These towers had hooks that secured them so that they could not be dislodged by the Constantinopolitan soldiers. Mehmed had ordered the construction of shelters for the men climbing the ladders to protect them from the defenders who were firing down on them. At the same time, he deployed sappers to dig tunnels leading up to the walls near the Kaligaria Gate so that mines could be laid to destroy the foundations. Isidore and the Greeks resisted by digging tunnels to meet the Turks and laying counter-mines that repelled the advancing sappers.

The siege dragged on. Supplies and morale drained away at an equal rate. The western religious and secular leaders, consumed by their own domestic issues, continued to underestimate the severity of the threat to Constantinople. Venice equipped and launched a galley to come to the aid of the besieged city, but this contribution was too little too late, and it never made it there in time.

Still, it was not a clearcut situation for the Sultan. The resistance of the city had been fierce, costing many Ottoman lives over the fifty-three days. Rumours were spreading about a Christian force that would imminently arrive from the west, and several of Mehmed's advisors recommended withdrawing. Clearly, the aggressor did not assume a successful outcome. If victory was not a foregone conclusion in the minds of the Sultan and his generals, then there is no reason to believe that the fall of Constantinople was inevitable in the minds of

The Battle for Constantinople

the Greeks and the wider Christian world. Mehmed nearly abandoned the siege, fearing an alliance between the East and West existed and that their combined forces would overwhelm him. Had that alliance existed in reality, Constantinople's story, and even that of the entire empire, might have been very different. Overruling his more cautious generals, the Sultan decided, nonetheless, to attempt a full assault. After firing on the walls throughout the night, the Turks stormed in the early hours of 29 May 1453. Despite the extensive damage from the night's bombardment and the exhaustion of the defenders, the first and second waves failed. Mehmed himself rallied his soldiers to lead a third attempt, and finally the Turks breached the walls. Isidore described the attack in detail in one of his letters to Bessarion.

> Therefore, on the twenty-ninth day of the recently concluded month of May, as dawn was breaking and the sun's rays were even assaulting us, the Turks, attacking by sea and land, assaulted the part of the city that had been most half-ruined near Saint Romanus. Many brave Latin and Greek men were there, though they were without their king and emperor, who had already been wounded and slain by the enemy, and his head had later been given as a gift to the Turk, who rejoiced greatly at its sight and mocked him with insolent taunts and immediately sent it to Andrianople for a triumphant procession. ... The ascent to the walls in that area was indeed easy because, as previously mentioned, it had been almost entirely bombarded and severely shaken, hence the invaders entered the city with ease, as no one was found there to repel the attack of the enemy or defend that part.

Isidore was not merely an eyewitness to the events in Constantinople that May. As a tireless champion of the

Byzantines, he threw himself wholeheartedly into the defence of the symbolic city. He attended the meetings held by the commanders throughout the siege, and he was assigned to lead the defenders in the area around the Monastery of St Demetrios. Before his appointment as Metropolitan of Kiev, he had been the abbot of this institution and knew the area well. After the city walls were breached, the Cardinal left his sector and headed to the more vulnerable area of the Augustaion, where Hagia Sofia was under attack.

It is not known whether Isidore actually bore arms during the fight, but he was wounded and recounted the injury in his letter to Bessarion: 'And by the immortal God, before whose eyes all things are open and manifest, I have cursed and cursed that cruel Turk who struck me with an arrow and wounded me on the left side of the head in front of the door of a certain monastery, time and time again.' He continued his description to Bessarion, covering the aftermath of the breach:

> ...it was like seeing the entire city itself fighting, besieged both within and without the walls. Indeed, all the streets and alleys were covered with blood and gore, flowing with the bodies of the slain and the dead. Nobles and freeborn women were dragged out of their homes, their necks bound with ropes, slave and mistress together, and many were barefoot. Their sons and sisters were seized, torn away from their fathers and divided from their mothers, abducted from here and there.

The invaders executed noble families and sold the young boys and girls into slavery. Soldiers brought three severed heads on poles to Mehmed: one was that of the Emperor Constantine, one had belonged to Orhan (a relative of the Sultan who had fought on the side of the Christians) and the third was a monk of the Order of St Basil, whose head was mistaken for that of Cardinal Isidore.

Isidore was very much alive, and he lamented the treatment of the churches and their caretakers, noting that nuns and laywomen were captured and driven out of the city. The Ottomans rampaged through Hagia Sofia, smashing statues and icons of Christ, the saints and other holy figures. Isidore described the Turkish soldiers leaping onto the furniture and altars where they sang hymns to Allah. They broke down the doors and looted sacred objects and relics, stealing those with financial value and trashing those with only religious value. The miraculously preserved body of St Theodosia was dismembered and fed to the dogs, while horses were saddled with holy vestments that were seized from the churches, and driven to trample on books from the church libraries, including any copies of the gospels that the soldiers could find.

At the end of June, Mehmed took Pera, a Genoese suburb of Constantinople. He conscripted recently enslaved Christians to fight against their brethren, and he imposed a draconian prohibition on the practice of Christianity. Contemporary accounts talk of a ban on the ringing of church bells. Now that Mehmed dominated Constantinople and the surrounding territories in the Aegean Sea, he was able to levy huge taxes from the subjugated Christian population, money that many feared would fund campaigns against Christian nations further west.

The narrative of Isidore's escape from Constantinople was taken up by Henry of Soemmern, writing a few months after the defeat. Not much is known of this writer, but he was likely to have been an official in the papal palace or chancery where he had access to a range of sources. Henry claimed that his account was drawn from letters written by the Venetian naval Captain

General Jacopo Loredano, by Doge Francesco Foscai, by the head of the Franciscans in Candia (where Isidore took refuge) and by Isidore himself.

After the Ottomans entered the city and the Cardinal managed to reach Hagia Sofia, he expected to find Christian soldiers in battle. Allegedly incensed that no one would resist and all were fleeing, he declared that he would engage the enemy, despite his injuries. His servants managed to restrain him and persuade him to hide in the church. Here, he was captured but not recognized. The Turks unknowingly held Isidore in a camp for three days – the rumour that he had already been killed probably saved his life during this period of captivity:

> Finally the Cardinal was ransomed for one hundred ducats and was conveyed to Pera; he remained hidden for eight days, as he secretly fled from house to house. But after he heard that Pera would surrender to the Turks, he concluded that it would not be safe for him to stay any longer and, as he could not flee through Christian territory, he boarded a Turkish galley and stayed on board three days; he was not recognized, as his head was covered with bandages because he had been wounded by an arrow on the face.

Isidore disembarked in Bithynia (Bursa in modern Turkey), where he pretended to be an impoverished man who was seeking to raise the funds to ransom his captured sons in Constantinople. He continued to make his way out of the occupied region but was inadvertently identified by fellow Genoese travellers. The Cardinal boarded a small boat to Chios and eventually ended up in Candia (Crete), one of the first ports of call for the ships fleeing the city. Here, he was finally able to take refuge at the beginning of July.

The Battle for Constantinople

It took time for news of the city's fall to reach the West. Rumours began to circulate from the middle of June, carried by the boats that sought refuge in Candia. An annotation, dated '29 June 1453, Candia' in a Greek manuscript that is now in the British Library (British Museum Add. 34060 f.1v) reads:

> In the year 1453, on June 29, a Friday, there came from Constantinople three Cretan caravels – those of Sgouros, Hyalina, and Philomatos. They said that on the 29th of May, the third day of Saint Theodosia, at the third hour of the morning [9 am], the Hagarenes, that is the troops of Mehmet Celebi [Sultan Mehmed II], entered the city of Constantinople. They also said that they killed the emperor, the Lord Constantine Dragas and Palaiologos. Then there was great sorrow and much weeping on Crete because of the sad news that had arrived. Indeed nothing worse than this has ever happened or ever will happen. May the Lord God be merciful to us and free us from His fearful threats.

These reports were confirmed by the end of the month, as the Venetian and Genoese ships that had participated in defending the Golden Horn limped to the safety of Candia and disgorged their cargo of refugees. Exiles continued to pour into the island aboard vessels of all sizes.

Was this the end of the Byzantine Empire? With hindsight, historians identify it as the nail in the coffin. For Isidore and his contemporaries, who had fought for a decade on the political front and in person on the front line of the siege, the Empire was not lost. They harnessed this catastrophe to galvanise the wider Christian world to take action. Isidore was one of the refugees who disembarked from a Genoese ship, and he was given accommodation from where he began his propaganda campaign for a crusade in a series of letters to Italian religious and secular leaders. He wrote eloquent and emotional missives to the Florentines, to the city of Bologna, to Cardinal Domenica Capricana, to Cardinal Bessarion and an official report to Pope Nicholas V.

His propaganda machine was wide-ranging in terms of themes, drawing on biblical and classical precedents. He combined these historical comparisons with highly charged emotion to inspire and motivate the recipients of these letters. In his letter to Pope Nicholas, Isidore skilfully set the fall of Constantinople in the context of the destruction of Jerusalem by King Nebuchadnezzar in the sixth century. In his account, however, he described Constantinople's demise as far worse:

> Its fate cannot be compared to the fate of other cities. It goes beyond comparison. When King Nebuchadnezzar took Jerusalem, it was not as rich and was small, with less extensive territory. To be sure, it was pillaged of its treasures, but its inhabitants' hands and feet were not bound. They were gathered and taken to Babylon. Their sacred vessels were not snatched or trampled, but the king of Assyria kept them in his temples with respect. Similarly, the fate of no other city can provide a comparison. Nothing equals this sack.

In his most overtly polemic letter, he addressed all those of Christian faith (*universis et singulis Christi fidelibus*), framing his message in terms of a threat to Latin Christendom's existence from the Muslim Ottoman Empire. Recovering Constantinople was positioned in terms of survival. The true heirs to the Roman Empire had been defeated and their enduring existence was at risk. Western Christendom suddenly felt very vulnerable, and the Italian states began to panic that a conflict with the Ottomans was inevitable. Isidore set out the evidence of Mehmed's military preparations to give substance to his predictions:

These, therefore, are the things that have thus far been exacted by the Turks against the Christians; but who can describe what they are plotting against them in the future? First, he prepared a hundred and seventy triremes, both small and large, and sent them to the Aegean Sea to the Cycladic islands in order to subjugate them under his rule. Then he prepares himself with an infinite army to march across to three strong and powerful cities located near the Danube, to conquer and devastate them: one which we call Peristerii, another Fendorabium, and yet another Bellestadium. And so, he intends to cross all of Hungary and to destroy and obliterate it, in order to have no hindrance behind him, since in the coming year he has decided to migrate to Italy, where he is already introducing and proposing all of these actions in the present year.

Isidore harnessed religious indignation in his descriptions of the desecration of the churches by the Turks and of Mehmed's personal hatred of Christianity. He catalogued the plight of the nuns and monks along with the destruction of holy relics. Continuing the theme of righteous Christianity, he claimed his escape from the Turks to be a miracle. Through his portrayal of Sultan Mehmed as the Antichrist on a mission to world dominion, Isidore prophesied the westwards advance of the Ottoman terror. The Cardinal had a transparent agenda: to rouse an emotional response that would inspire a crusading fervour in which liberating Constantinople replaced the historical goal of Jerusalem: 'Let it be known to all, my lords and most faithful Christians, that now the precursor of the Antichrist is near, the leader and ruler of the Turks, whose name is Muhammad.'

After establishing the extent of the threat and provoking wild fear, Isidore explained what needed to be done. Reverting to his agenda in the years between the Council of Ferrara-Florence and before the siege, he called on the Christian nations to put aside their differences and unite against the Turks as a common enemy:

> Therefore, I implore, beseech, and exhort all of you Christians, to embrace zeal and love for the Christian faith and for your freedom. I earnestly entreat you to firstly have peace and unity among yourselves, and to cast out all misery and pusillanimity that seem to exist among you. Cultivate within yourselves the love of God, peace, and unity, and prepare yourselves to be courageous, steadfast, and magnanimous. Arm yourselves to valiantly charge against the enemies and unbelievers.

In the Cardinal's report to Pope Nicholas, he reminded him that he had fulfilled the papal mandate and that the Decree of Union had been announced publicly in a service at Hagia Sofia in the winter before the Ottomans attacked.

> It [promulgation of the union] was accomplished on the twelfth day of December of the last year. It was perfectly concluded and the entire city of Constantinople was united with the Catholic Church. Everywhere Your name was first commemorated and was followed by [the commemoration of the name of] the most reverend Patriarch Gregory (which had not ever been done in any church in Constantinople, including his own monastery) but, with the conclusion of the union, he was commemorated by the entire city, as it was said. All, to the last citizen, were united with the emperor and Catholics, thanks be to God!

His approach in this official report on the loss of Constantinople to the Muslims had a clear motive. Isidore was insinuating that the Curia did not uphold its promise to supply military aid to the Byzantines, even though they had fulfilled Nicholas's precondition that they accept the union. Cardinal Isidore drew also on his classical education and scholarship to extend his propaganda campaign to the humanists who held influence in both secular and religious courts. He was the first to compare Mehmed to Xerxes of Persia and to Alexander the Great.

In the aftermath of the city's fall, Italian humanists adopted and enlarged on the theme of comparing Mehmed to Xerxes, who invaded Greece. Isidore was its earliest proponent in his letters to Bessarion and Pope Nicholas. The King of Persia had sacked Athens, just as the Sultan had seized Constantinople, but the Persian invasion was ultimately stopped when they lost the maritime battle of Salamis. Isidore and fellow humanists interpreted the Sultan's aggression as a replay of the Persian campaign, predicting that it would end in a similar catastrophic defeat for the Ottomans. The western crusaders would recover Constantinople as the Athenians had taken Athens back from Xerxes.

As to the comparison with Alexander the Great, to the Florentines he wrote, '…daily he [Mehmed II] hears the life of Alexander in Arabic, Greek, and Latin.' In a bid to raise the levels of anxiety of the Italians, the Cardinal implied that the Ottoman leader saw himself as a latter-day Alexander, with aspirations to conquer vast territories in the Mediterranean and to establish his own empire.

Whether he embodied the Antichrist, Xerxes or Alexander the Great, Sultan Mehmed II's conquest of Constantinople served as a wakeup call for the West. Complacency and disbelief had thwarted the efforts of Bessarion and Isidore to galvanise the leaders of the Roman Catholic Church to take action. Losing Constantinople drove home the reality of the Ottoman threat to all of Christendom. Would Mehmed stop at the threshold of the West, or could even Rome be at risk? The stakes had been raised from that of assisting their Byzantine brothers to that of ensuring the survival of Christianity. Cardinals Isidore and

Bessarion were acutely sensitive to this shift and exploited it to promote their agenda to save the Byzantine Empire. With the fall of Constantinople, their challenge had become greater, but their motivation (and that of the westerners) had been boosted. A defensive crusade would no longer be sufficient: Bessarion and Isidore started to work on the Christian and secular leaders to raise an offensive campaign to take back Constantinople, and to eliminate the Ottoman presence in the Byzantine Christian territories and its threat to the West.

7

A CRUSADE FOR CONSTANTINOPLE

In the aftermath of the fall of Constantinople, the Byzantines and all Christendom faced an age-old dilemma that institutional powers continue to grapple with today. How should they respond to the aggressor? What would be his next move? What action should be taken in the face of such a great territorial and symbolic loss? Who would assume the responsibility for any such action?

And just as the questions were perennial, so were the answers. The Catholic Church and the secular leaders of Christendom's territories had spent the preceding hundred years hoping that the Ottoman problem would go away. This stance became untenable after Mehmed II took Constantinople. Arguments for military action vied with those for appeasement and containment; for peaceful coexistence; and for interfaith discussions between Christian and Muslim leaders. Bessarion and Isidore favoured a military response to recover Constantinople and to eject the Ottomans from the other Byzantine territories that they occupied. Over the next two decades there would be five different popes, and each one would tackle the Ottoman question. Bessarion would be one of the loudest voices calling for a military campaign (by now, Isidore was ageing and would soon pass away), and he would also be one of the most proactive papal agents in the efforts to muster a unified military response.

Bessarion and Isidore maintained a consistent conviction that the only way to halt the progress of the Ottomans and to save Byzantium's integrity was to unite the western and eastern Christians in these common goals. They held this position in their roles at the Council of Ferrara-Florence and in their political manoeuvring as papal legates. In the aftermath of the Council, an acceptable level of unity could have been achieved had the anti-unionists not hijacked the narrative by returning to Constantinople ahead of the pro-union delegates. In addition, the implementation of the union was deeply undermined by Emperor John VIII's grief-driven withdrawal from proactive government after he arrived home to find that his wife had died. In the short term, this did not impact on the papal motivation to help the Greeks – Eugenius IV organised the crusade that failed in 1444 at Varna, despite the equivocal behaviour of the Byzantines regarding the union. For Pope Nicholas, however, it was a dealbreaker. It took the seismic shock of losing Constantinople to shift the Pope's attitude.

By the autumn of 1453, Pope Nicholas V declared a papal campaign to raise a crusade in the Bull that he published, *Etsi Ecclesia Christi*. To this end he appointed a commission of cardinals, including Isidore, Bessarion and Francesco della Rovere (the future Pope Sixtus IV). Alongside this group, he established the Italic League, envisaged as a unified cohort of the leaders of the Italian territories that would form the core of any crusading campaign. The league was a long time in the making, and the Pope was less motivated by the defence of Christianity than by fear that the rising powers of Milan, Venice, Florence and Naples were a threat to the papacy and the autonomy of the papal states. Nicholas wanted to assert his authority by creating a league over which the Church presided. The rivalry between these powers had erupted regularly into open warfare, and the Pope convened a diplomatic conference in Rome as early as 1451 and again in 1453 with the ostensible aim of bringing about an agreement that would establish peace and security through a balance of power.

In the duke of Milan, Francesco Sforza, Nicholas found a supporter for his league. Together they made the first step in April 1454 when the Treaty of Lodi was signed, ending two years of war between Milan and the Republic of Venice. This treaty gave the league momentum, and a year later it was expanded to include Florence. After the fall of Constantinople, Nicholas announced a crusade, and Naples joined the league which was positioned as the vehicle for the military campaign. With all five major powers signed up – Venice, Naples, Florence, Milan and Rome – another 120 Italian states became members, and the Italic League was officially formed in March 1455. In essence it was a pact of non-aggression and a commitment to intervene militarily on behalf of any member who was attacked. The arrangement was decreed to last twenty-five years, and it sealed the supreme authority of the Church over the Italian secular leaders.

The Treaty of Lodi and its metamorphosis into a more general league went some way to dealing with the conditions that had prevented Pope Eugenius IV from successfully mustering support from other Italian states for a crusade. Under Nicholas V, the conditions were ripe for a unified Italian campaign. The Pope also commissioned a little-known humanist, Lampo Birago, to write a military handbook for the crusade, and Bessarion was appointed to supervise this project. Birago called the treatise, *Strategicon adversus Turcos* (A Strategy against the Turks). Scribes copied the manuscript, and Birago and Bessarion presented versions to the Pope and to the other cardinals in the commission. The author appeared to have very detailed information about the military capacity and structures of the enemy, suggesting that he had an informer. He harvested the techniques and strategies of ancient warfare from classical texts to compose a manual on how to prosecute a successful war against the Ottomans.

Birago took up Bessarion and Isidore's theme of solidarity between the Roman nations of east and west; a revival of classical Roman virtues in Italy would enable the 'First Rome' to come to the rescue of the 'Second Rome' (Constantinople). His text reflected Bessarion's agenda, forged in the fear that all Europe lived at risk of spiritual and cultural annihilation, to revive the Greco-Roman empire to repel the Ottoman threat. But he also insisted that, if necessary, the Italian states had sufficient military prowess to single-handedly eject the Turks from Constantinople without the support of other powers. Throughout, Birago reiterated that the Italians, newly bonded in a cooperative league presided over by the fairness and generosity of a unifying pope, had the power to achieve their military goals.

In the treatise, Birago envisaged an army of 27,000 to 32,000 soldiers armed with the most up-to-date weaponry. The force would be divided between 12,000 calvary, 15,000 infantry soldiers and 5,000 auxiliaries. He discussed ways to increase the mobility of the army, modelled on the speed and discipline of the classical Roman legions. The text included ideas for dealing with the sultan's specialist soldiers, the janissaries and spahis. He recommended that the new type of crossbow should be issued to the infantry to give their arrows greater range and to facilitate faster reloading. However, Birago advised against the use of firearms, citing the logistical problems of using gunpowder in open battle. He even drew up a budget for the campaign that he predicted would last between one and three years.

A maximum of 1.5 to 1.7 million ducats would be needed to cover the cost of the troops, auxiliary cavalry, and equipment. This did not include the cost of the navy, which would be met by Naples, Genoa and Venice. The treatise directed the armies to gather in Bologna, where Bessarion was currently serving Pope Nicholas, under the direction of an unnamed commander and the Cardinal. Birago wrote that the forces would advance to the south by land through Friuli or by sea, crossing from Brinidisi or Otranto through the Adriatic Sea to Albania, where Venetians and Albanians could help with landing. From there they would march to Adrianopolis or Constantinople, liberating the provinces from Turkish occupation as they passed through.

Pope Nicholas's efforts remained firmly theoretical, and not everyone was impressed, criticising him for investing far more money in his elaborate renovations to buildings in Rome than in preparations for a crusade. When Nicholas succumbed to a growing list of ailments and died in 1455, there was little for the pro-crusaders to mourn. His successor, Calixtus III, committed his papacy to recovering Constantinople and confirmed Nicholas's crusading bull, *Etsi Ecclesia Christi*, giving men like Bessarion and Isidore a reason to feel more hopeful.

> I, Pope Callixtus, vow to Almighty God and the Holy Trinity that by war, maledictions, interdicts, excommunications, and all other means in my power, even sacrifice my life if need be, I will pursue the Turks, the most cruel foes of the Christian name, to conquer again Constantinople, which has been captured and destroyed by

Mehmet II in punishment for our sins, for the release of Christians who lie in slavery to strengthen the true faith.

The new Pope's actions confirmed their optimism. Calixtus stripped the gold and silver embellishments from manuscripts commissioned by Nicholas and, along with other papal treasures, turned them into coins to fund the construction of a crusading fleet in the Tiber. He also launched an active campaign of preaching and taxation throughout the Catholic lands to raise revenue for the crusade. In these early years after the Ottoman occupation of Constantinople, Bessarion and Isidore rode a wave of momentum, emanating from the papal court and even beyond, to fight back. Alfonso of Aragon and his nephew Alfonso of Portugal committed (admittedly only on paper) 50,000 men and 400 ships to the cause. Emperor Frederick the Great took up the Cross in 1455.

By 1456, the Pope had armed sixteen galleys at a cost of 150,000 ducats. He assigned Bessarion to a council of cardinals appointed to supervise the provision of the papal fleet. This was timely, as Mehmed laid siege to Belgrade in the same year. Isidore and Bessarion's warning seemed to be coming true: Constantinople's fall had spurred the Ottomans to expand their reach westwards. John Hunyadi, supported by an independently organised crusading force, met the Turkish soldiers and managed to defeat them. The Christian world interpreted the victory at Belgrade as divine support for the crusading cause, and more successes followed. A few months later, Calixtus's fleet captured more than twenty-five enemy ships at Mytilene, the main port of the island of Lesbos, and they pushed the Turks back from the Aegean island of Lemnos. Hunyadi died shortly after the success at Belgrade and a couple of years later Calixtus also passed away.

A Crusade for Constantinople

Despite increasing infirmity, Isidore had sufficient strength to play a part in the conclave that gathered to elect Calixtus's successor, a contest fraught with corruption and drama. The Frenchman, Cardinal Guillaume d'Estouteville, vied with the Italian Cardinal, Aeneas Silvius Piccolomini. D'Estouteville allegedly bought the votes of Isidore and Bessarion, but Piccolomini prevailed and took the title Pope Pius II. Bessarion claimed that his opposition to Pius was merely related to the new Pope's age, not to his suitability for the role. The two Greek cardinals had more confidence in the relative youth and virility of the French candidate to prosecute a war against the Ottomans than they had in the veteran Piccolomini, who was also in poor health.

Bessarion and Isidore's opposition to Piccolomini was a miscalculation. The new Pope turned out to be even more aligned with their objectives than any others they had served. Fortunately, he did not hold a grudge, and the three men forged a productive relationship based on their common interests. An opportunity for collaboration between Isidore, Bessarion and Pope Pius II arose when Mehmed II invaded the Morea in 1458. After Constantinople fell, the fraternal despots in the Peloponnese, Thomas and Demetrius, negotiated a treaty to pay an annual tribute of 10,000 ducats to the Ottomans in exchange for their continued independence. Thomas and Demetrius shared the rule of the Morea: Demetrius governed the southern and eastern parts with a capital city at Mistra, while Thomas ruled the north-west and Corinthia. Shortly after making their agreement with Mehmed, they faced another threat from an Albanian insurgency. Too weak to repel the insurgents alone, the brothers appealed to the Sultan to help them quell the uprising. In exchange for Turkish assistance, the tribute rose to 12,000 ducats per year.

Saving Byzantium: The Struggle to Salvage an Empire

The despots were unable to raise such a hefty sum, and they secretly banked on the West to come to the rescue of Byzantium. For three years, Thomas and Demetrius failed to pay the Sultan, and eventually he lost patience. It was in Mehmed's interests to take the Morea as he feared that the many exiles from Constantinople who had gathered in these strategically positioned territories provided a rallying point for a military campaign against the Turks in the Balkans. Facing relatively little resistance, Mehmed seized most of the northern parts of the Morea. He left the southern territories for the Palaeologus brothers on condition that they honour their tribute. The pressure of the external threat, combined with the brothers' antipathy towards each other, was an explosive mix that erupted into civil war when Thomas led an army against Demetrius. The conflict grew out of quarrelling between the landowners of the Peloponnese, as described in the *History of Mehmed* by Kritovoulos.

> That same winter the Despots of the Peleponnesus quarrelled, to their own damage, and made war with each other for the following reason: the grandees who were under them, men who had domains and large revenues and were over cities and fortresses, were not content with these but, grasping in thought and malicious in act, were always aspiring for more. They sought revolution and were rebellious against each other, made war, and filled all those parts with disorder and uproar. They even drew Despots into the confusion, by attacking and disturbing each other, for first they would come secretly and accuse the opposite party, as if they were revealing some unspeakable mystery, and so by lies and slanders against each other they tried to stir them up one against another and to arm them Then later, unashamed, they deserted the one side and went to the other, enticing them with their towns and fortresses.

The brothers were also divided by their opposing attitudes towards the Ottomans and the West. Demetrius believed that Byzantium should rely on the Sultan for its survival, a lesser evil (in his mind) than cooperation with the heretical western Catholics. In reaction to this, Thomas positioned his military campaign against his brother as a holy war against the Muslims. He sent an envoy to Rome along with sixteen Turkish prisoners to appeal to Pius II for support. The Pope was convinced, sending 300 soldiers in the first instance, and initiating plans for a crusade.

Guided by Bessarion's advice, Pius II approached the challenge of raising a crusade in a different way to his predecessors. Rather than issuing the traditional papal bull, favoured by the previous popes, to be delivered by appointed delegates at the courts throughout Europe, Pius called a congress in which he invited attendees to contribute ideas and discuss the best way to raise a campaign. The Pope chose Mantua to host the congress, and accompanied by several officials, including Bessarion and Isidore, he spent the next six months making his way there from Rome.

Pope Pius officially opened the congress on 1 June 1459, but few of the delegates had arrived. In a growing fury, Pius wrote to the absentees and waited a further four months for them to turn up. By September, enough delegates had finally assembled; they included significant Italian leaders like Duke Francesco Sforza of Milan, as well as other important European rulers such as Philip, Duke of Burgundy.

Pius and Bessarion opened the proceedings with lengthy orations delivered in Mantua's cathedral. The Pope's speech, *Cum bellum hodie*, inspired the audience at the time and continues to elicit admiration from historians today. Pius drew heavily from the content in Isidore's letters written in the immediate aftermath of Constantinople's fall and described again, in detail, the atrocities of the Turks and the threat of Islam to all of Christendom.

> Every victory of his will be a step towards the next one until he [Mehmed II] has defeated all the Western kings, destroyed the Christian gospel, and imposed the law of Muhammad on the whole world. And do not think it will take long before he comes against you... Unless we go against them, they will come, the Turks, they will come, and take our country and people.

Pius warmed up his audience with this emotive approach and then built on it by addressing the objections that he anticipated from the delegates. He insisted that defeating the Turks was realistic, backing up his conviction by arguing that Mehmed's military strength had been exaggerated by the West, and that collectively the Europeans could easily overcome his forces. As Bessarion and Isidore had maintained in speeches and writings throughout their careers, the unity of Christendom was crucial to mounting a successful resistance to the Ottomans. Ejecting Mehmed II from Constantinople and the other Byzantine territories would be an entirely achievable military objective by an army of united Christian states.

In January 1460, the Congress concluded with the publication, finally, of a papal bull that declared a three-year crusade, with full indulgences granted to all serving soldiers and financial contributors. To raise revenue to support the campaign, the Pope imposed a tithe on all monasteries, convents and citizens of the papal states. Lay communities and the Jews were also subject to a crusade tax. The Congress appeared to have been a success, with the Holy Roman Emperor and the heads of several German principalities agreeing to commit 32,000 infantry soldiers and

10,000 calvary to a crusade. Other delegates promised arms, ships and additional funding.

Just a few months after the Congress disbanded, the Sultan invaded the Morea peninsula for the second time. He directed his forces against Demetrius in the initial campaign, and Corinth and Mistra fell. The Despot fled to Monemvasia with his family, a fortified island that commanded an important position on the route through the western Aegean Sea. The fortress was seemingly impregnable, perched on a rock promontory off Minoa and linked to the mainland by a single bridge. Monemvasia had managed to resist the Frankish attempts to seize it during the thirteenth century, holding out until it was finally taken in 1248. The Byzantines recovered the fortress in 1262 when the Palaeologus family took back Constantinople from the Latins. From then it was used as a base for recovering more territory in Morea, and it became a prestigious Metropolitan see for the religious elite at the Byzantine court.

Despite Monemvasia's reputation as virtually unassailable, Demetrius readily surrendered to Mehmed, agreeing to hand over his family and the town to the Ottomans in exchange for the promise of a generous income and a safe haven in Constantinople. The citizens and their governor, Manuel Palaeologus, refused to agree to the deal that Demetrius had accepted on their behalf. They declared 'We have no authority to hold and dispose of what has been built by God.' Apparently, this objection satisfied the Sultan, and he withdrew.

However, the Monemvasians were realistic about the unlikely prospect that they could deter the Ottomans in perpetuity. They turned to Despot Thomas for help, but he was also in the process of fleeing. As a last resort, they organised a delegation to approach Pope Pius II and to request that he extend papal protection to Monemvasia. Pius II recorded their meeting in his Commentaries.

> The ambassadors were given public audience and spoke as follows: 'Have regard to us Pope Pius. Unless you stretch out your hand, we are the prey of the Turks. Demetrius Palaeologus was our lord. He went over to the Turks and strove to bring us under their power. We detected and thwarted his schemes. We broke into the citadel, sent his wife to her husband, and closed the entrance against the Turks. We approached Thomas, Demetrius's brother, and begged him to receive and defend the city which was his now that his brother had deserted to the enemy. Thomas answered that he was not strong enough to protect us and urged us to adopt either you or someone else as our lord. In a council called to discuss these matters, we voted unanimously to throw ourselves on your mercy and to hand over the people and state to you. Receive then the suppliant, succour the wretched, and do not despise our city, which is the most convenient base for operations in Greece. If you decide to send a fleet to the East, it will find us with a harbour and the safest of refuges. If you abandon us we are forced to submit to the Turkish yoke, an event which will assuredly be a disgrace to you and a calamity to Christendom.'

Of all the Peloponnesian territories, Monemvasia held out the longest, eventually accepting rule from the Venetians in 1464 in return for their protection against the Turks. Despot Thomas, on the other hand, was not so resilient. After Mehmed had dealt with Demetrius and the despotate of Mistra, he turned his attention and military might against Thomas. Territory after territory fell: Bordonia, Kastritsa, Karitania, Androusa, and Ithomi. In Kiparissia the Sultan enslaved 10,000 residents and, in Leondarion he tortured 6,000 citizens to death, including women and children. Faced with such barbarity and apparent invincibility, Thomas did not fight back. He fled with his family, first to the Venetian port of Pilos and then on to Corfu in 1460 after the Venetians, fearing the Sultan's attention, asked him to leave.

The Byzantine rulers of the Morea begged for military support. Isidore managed to muster weapons from Brescia and Verona, and he organised a small fleet after travelling to Ancona. Bessarion petitioned Bianca, the Duchess of Milan to call up 300 mercenaries whom she sent to defend the beleaguered Morea. In the background, Pius was struggling to galvanise the Italians to honour the promises they had made at Mantua. Once again, conflict had broken out between them, and the rulers were too involved in their domestic battles to spare men or money for the battles in Byzantium. Undeterred, the Pope looked to the other European delegates who had attended the Congress. He appointed Bessarion to act as papal legate and sent him to Germany in the autumn of 1460. The Cardinal addressed the German princes fervently: 'We need arms, arms I tell you, and strong men, not words; an army well supplied, not neat and polished oratory; we need the enduring strength of soldiers, not the bombast of fine speeches.'

Mehmed remained in the Morea to complete his conquest of the Peloponnese. The fortresses submitted with little resistance, apart from that in Achaea where a minor member of the Palaeologan dynasty, Graitzas Palaeologus, held out at Salmenikon. For a year he refused to surrender despite the odds, and his bravery impressed the Turks. When he finally capitulated, he was allowed to leave unharmed, having earned respect for his unwavering resolution.

On Thomas's way to Corfu, he stopped over at Patras to rescue an important relic, the head of St Andrew, which he feared would fall into the hands of the advancing Turks. In Thomas, Bessarion saw an opportunity to champion a potential emperor of a New Byzantium and a pro-Latin leader, who could be installed following a successful crusade to liberate the Peloponnesian Morea. Such a plan might unlock the crucial support of the Venetians, who had an economic interest in seeing Constantinople sidelined as the heart of Byzantium. The Morea was a critically important strategic area whose conquest gave the Turks an immense advantage. Recapturing it would provide the surrounding Christian powers of Crete, Asia, Illyricum and Macedonia with a military base from which they could launch defensive forces against any Ottoman campaigns.

For Bessarion to realise his grand scheme he needed Despot Thomas to be beholden to Rome and the Morea to be seized back from the Turks. Pius II invited Thomas and his family to seek refuge for themselves and the relic in Rome. St Andrew's head became the rallying point for his and Bessarion's next push for a crusade. This time, however, the more modest objective would be to fight for the Morea, not for Constantinople.

Together, the Cardinal and Pope established a nexus of symbols embodied in the head of St Andrew, and they orchestrated an elaborate series of events around the relic to communicate all levels of the symbolism to an audience of spiritual and secular leaders. After Thomas had secured the relic, many Christian states approached him with offers of money and sanctuary for his family and their precious treasure. Pius made his position clear on the matter: 'Thomas must not trust so sacred an object to anyone without the Pope's orders, unless he wished to incur the anger of the Apostles. He need not plead poverty as an excuse, for if he came to live in Rome, he should be maintained in the style befitting a prince.'

The Pope was keen for St Andrew to be 'reunited' with his apostolic brother St Peter in Rome, and he offered Thomas and his relic temporary accommodation until they could be restored to their rightful places in Patras and the Morea. Coupled with this promise was Bessarion's agenda to make Thomas the new emperor of Byzantium. Unsurprisingly, the Despot agreed to the proposal, and the plans for the translation of St Andrew's head were set in motion.

This fraternal reunification of the apostles was a thinly veiled symbol of the unification of the East and West Churches that Bessarion and Isidore had campaigned for so tirelessly throughout their careers. Pius used the same motif to demonstrate the stability and superiority of the Roman Church, by providing the 'eastern' apostle with a strong place of safety and refuge while his own land was a place of weakness and threat.

In part of his speech at the ceremony of translation, Pius made this clear, '…you [Andrew] will be returned to your own seat, God willing, and one day you will say, "Oh happy exile, where such aid was found!" In the meantime, you will remain with your brother for some time, and you will have equal honour with him. For this is nourishing Rome, dedicated with your brother's precious blood.'

An elaborate and drawn-out procession to bring the relic to St Peter's was carefully choreographed to deliver a host of messages that promoted Church unity, Roman Catholic supremacy and the imperative for the West to launch a crusade. Cardinal Bessarion was chosen, along with two other cardinals, to go to Narni in Umbria, where Thomas was waiting with the holy head. With pomp and ceremony, they proceeded to accompany the head from Narni to the Milvian Bridge in Rome. This was where the Emperor Constantine had entered Rome in 312 AD to defeat Maxentius and bring Christianity to the heart of the Roman Empire. By choosing this venue and holding the ceremony on Palm Sunday, Bessarion and the Pope declared their imperial aspirations for Despot Thomas and reminded the world of Rome's historical role as the primary seat of a Christianised Roman Empire. After completing the traditional Palm Sunday celebrations to remember Jesus's triumphal entry into Jerusalem, Pope Pius met Bessarion to receive the relic and to process through the Flaminian Gate. They provided palm fronds to the crowds, ensuring that no one missed the implied connection between Jesus entering Jerusalem and the head of St Andrew entering Rome.

To attract an international audience, Pope Pius promised indulgences to all who attended the ceremony. He intended for the relic to generate renewed enthusiasm for a crusade, and the Pope exploited the emotive and visual potential of the event to the full. Weeping, Pius received the reliquary containing the holy head from an equally distraught Bessarion. The Pope composed a prayer, whose words highlighted St Andrew's plight as a symbol of the threat that the Turks posed to all Christians: 'Omnipotent and everlasting God, Who dost rule heaven and earth, Who hast today deigned to solace us with the coming of the precious head of St Andrew, thy Apostle, grant we pray that through his merits and intercession the insolence of the faithless Turk may be crushed, all infidels may cease from troubling us, and Christians serve Thee in freedom and safety.'

With all the cardinals following the Pope on foot, the parade wound its way through decorated streets ringing with celebratory music. It reached its climax at St Peter's where a staircase had been specially constructed for the ceremony. The Pope, bearing the reliquary, mounted the steps to the altar where a scripted play took place. Playing the role of St Andrew, Bessarion recognised the Apostle Peter as the ultimate head of the Church, and he begged the Pope not to abandon the campaign to raise a crusade.

Pius (playing himself) replied: 'Nothing is closer to our heart than the defence of the Christian religion and the orthodox faith which your enemies and ours, the Turks, are trying to trample under foot. But if the Christian princes and people will hear our voice and will follow their shepherd, all the Church will see and be glad that we have not neglected the duties of our office and that you will not come in vain to get your brother's [Peter's] help.'

Pius II timed the celebrations to welcome the relic of St Andrew to Rome with an unprecedented announcement. The infirm and ailing Pope had decided that he needed to lead by example and declared his intention to head up a crusader force in person. He hoped that by demonstrating that he was willing to sacrifice his own life for the sake of a crusade, he would motivate his flock to join the fight: 'We are determined to go at once into the war against the Turks and by deed as well as words to summon Christian princes to follow us. Perhaps when they see their master and father, the Pope of Rome, the vicar of Jesus Christ, going into the war old and ill they will be ashamed to stay at home.'

Defending Christianity with a sword was a personal mission for Pius, and his rhetoric stressed the threat of spiritual destruction on the doorstep of Christendom. His actions were an effort to appeal to the secular princes' sense of honour and chivalry. Philip of Burgundy was a named target – in 1453 he had vowed publicly at a feast he hosted that he would personally fight the Turks if any other Christian prince would accompany him. By leading an army, Pius II was taking on the role of the Christian prince and hoping to force Duke Philip's hand.

Isidore, though elderly and unwell, managed to attend the celebrations for the translation of St Andrew's head, but passed away shortly afterwards. Bessarion was still in good health and energised by his involvement in the preparations for a crusade. He took charge of allocating preachers to take the message of crusade to Venice and its territories. These men were empowered to recruit other clerics to support their efforts, and they were given permission to grant a remittance of penance owed by any sinner for up to 100 days to anyone who attended their sermons on the theme of the crusade. Bessarion prescribed a very precise set of instructions for his preachers. They were told to focus on the themes of the justice and sanctity of opposing the Turks, and on the atrocities perpetrated by the Ottomans against their fellow Christians. He expected his preachers to solicit direct volunteers, substitutes or money for the cause from the audiences who came to the sermons. Promises of eternal salvation and full forgiveness of sins were to be made to anyone who contributed to the crusade.

Bessarion dictated the words of the prayers that were to be said as the badge of the cross was pinned to the breast of any who volunteered to fight. The formula included words to use in instances where substitutes were sponsored by the faithful, and where religious groups sent soldiers in their name. Bessarion supplied the words of the letter of plenary indulgence that the preachers were to bestow on each volunteer. Alongside the incentives, the Cardinal instructed the preachers to threaten with excommunication anyone who obstructed them, stole funds or assisted the Turks.

The sickly Pope made his way to the port of Ancona, where he waited for the promised armies to assemble. Finally, in the summer of 1464 the Venetians arrived with their long-promised fleet to join 3,000 men from Burgundy, a band of individual crusaders from northern Europe and a small force mustered by the Duke of Milan, Francesco Sforza. An outbreak of plague wreaked havoc on the resolve of the assembled soldiers and many drifted away during the long period of waiting. Then tragedy struck: Pope Pius II died just three days after the Venetians arrived. In the absence of the papal presence, the ships turned around and returned to Venice to be disarmed. The crusade was not going to happen.

This was the last occasion in the lifetimes of Isidore and Bessarion that there would be a realistic chance for a crusade against the Turks. Before his death, Pope Pius II succinctly summarised the dilemma that he and men such as Isidore and Bessarion faced.

> Over and over again we have pondered as to whether we could muster the strength of Christians against the Turks in one way or another and take measures to prevent the Christian peoples finally falling prey to them. We have spent many sleepless nights in meditation, tossing from side to side and deploring the unhappy calamities of our time. Our heart swelled and our old blood boiled with rage. We longed to declare war against the Turks and to put forth every effort in defence of religion, but when we measure our strength against that of the enemy, it is clear that the Church of Rome cannot defeat the Turks with its own resources...If we send envoys to ask aid of sovereigns, they are laughed at. If we impose tithes on the clergy, they appeal for a future council. If we issue indulgences and encourage the contribution of money by spiritual gifts, we are accused of avarice. People think our sole object is to amass gold. No one believes what we say.

No pope ever managed to convince a western prince to champion the cause with empty rhetoric. What had happened to the surge of enthusiasm for a crusade in the aftermath of Constantinople's fall? A growing hostility to the Greeks, particularly in the years after the influx of refugees in 1453, motivated many to blame the Byzantines for their own fate. In their eyes, they had been divinely punished for rejecting the true Catholic faith. In the east, the victims were also blamed but for the opposite reason: divine punishment meted out for signing the Decree of Union.

An anonymous Russian writer held Isidore personally to account for the fate of Constantinople as late as 1460:

> But you, O Isidore, deceiver and apostate, how long shall you hate and persecute the Holy Church that shines with piety in the land of Rus'? How long shall you prove an obstacle to the grace of the Holy Spirit by introducing into the Holy Church of Russian Orthodoxy the unleavened bread that is offered by the Latins? You have done things hated and abhorred by God, you have loved gold, you have destroyed your faith, you have deceived the emperor, you have provoked the patriarch, you have filled the imperial city with ruin, and after having ruined the souls of some of the Orthodox, you have gone far from God. Therefore, O accursed Isidore, see now how because of your deception and violation of divine law—which had brought the Greek people the piety of the true faith—even the imperial city falls to ruin because of the union with the Latin heresy, and thanks to punishment towards you, which God has permitted through the invasion of the pagans, a tremendous number of Agarenes [Turks], men without God, has attacked and killed the orthodox people.

Blame lay more convincingly with the West which was too preoccupied with domestic challenges and short-sighted self-interest to provide the support that Byzantium required to overcome the Turks. Motivated by economic concerns above any spiritual obligations, Venice made treaties with the Sultan in 1430, 1446 and 1451. Byzantium had been an economic competitor to the Republic and its demise allowed the Venetians and Genoese to dominate the area's maritime trade. The participation of Venice in any crusade was a precondition for its success, but their involvement was arguably a conflict of interest. Florence and Naples were also blinded by the potential gain that cooperation with the Sultan could bring them. Mehmed gave Florence unprecedented access to the Levantine trade, a market from which it had been excluded when the Byzantines and Venetians controlled the seas. Further west, Burgundy and France were engaged in an interminable conflict that drained their manpower and finances. France and England continued to clash sporadically over the course of the Hundred Years' War. There was little appetite for focusing on a threat that was not yet on their own doorstep.

Bessarion must have been devastated by the death of Pius II, who had been so close to launching a crusade. To date, four popes had come and gone over the course of the Greek cardinals' careers; Isidore had passed away; and Despot Thomas died alone in Rome's Santo Spirito hospital in 1465. Thomas had been the last realistic chance for the Palaeologus dynasty to rescue Byzantium. Once again, misfortune had thwarted efforts to reverse the progress of the Turks. The Empire had reached yet another critical moment, and, at the age of sixty-one, the Cardinal found himself starting all over again under a new papal administration led by Pietro Barbo, who was elected as Pope Paul II. Other forces and characters would come into play as the struggle to salvage Byzantium continued.

8

BYZANTIUM AT THE CROSSROADS

The last hope of the Palaeologus dynasty was not the last hope of Byzantium. If salvation could not come from Thomas and the West, there was a chance it could come from the East. The Empire of Trebizond, where Bessarion had been born, was ruled by Emperor John IV Comnenus, and he began to assert himself as the head of an Oriental League, established to reverse the Ottoman conquests in Byzantium.

Trebizond, like Nicaea, was one of the 'rump' states of Byzantium that was independent of Constantinople and, in times of trouble, positioned itself as an alternative centre for the Empire. Ruled by an off-shoot of the Comnenus dynasty that had held the throne in Constantinople throughout the eleventh century, the Trebizond emperors had the pedigree and resources to take the lead. Geographically, their territory was seemingly impregnable. Situated along the southern coast of the Black Sea and the western half of the Pontic Mountains, Trebizond occupied much of what is now southern Crimea. The Turks raided their lands repeatedly over several centuries but failed to make any permanent inroads. In the late thirteenth century the Spanish king, Henry III of Castille and Leon, sent an envoy, Ruy Gonzalez de Clavijo, to meet with Tamerlane. The ambassador's journey took him through Trebizond, and his surviving description of the territory's natural defences and prosperity demonstrate why this Empire survived for so long.

> We were four days journeying through their country and then came to the sea-shore, at a place on the coast [of the Black Sea] that lies six days' journey east of Trebizond, and here journeying along a wretched road soon reached the little port of Susurmena [or Surmeneh]. The land is of the district of Trebizond, it lies along the sea coast and is very mountainous, the hillsides everywhere being covered by forests. The trees as they stand support many creepers, most of which are grapevines, and of the wild grapes a wine is made, but no vineyards are tended by these people. The population live in hamlets each of which bears the name of Curio, the same consisting of well masoned cottages, a few together standing in one place and elsewhere others. The paths we had to follow going through this country were so abominable, that it cost us the lives of near all the beasts of burden we had with us for our baggage.

Mehmed II was always going to feel threatened by Trebizond, whose emperor was now the figurehead for the Greeks and Anatolians who yearned to resurrect the glory days of the Byzantine Empire. As early as 1456, the Sultan mounted an assault on John IV's realm. The Turks were initially successful, but they held back from total occupation, preferring to raise an annual tribute from the Emperor in exchange for the cessation of hostilities. With such a costly and precarious arrangement, and with little sign of help from the West, John began to forge an alliance with eastern enemies of the Sultan.

He approached Uzun Hassan, grandson of the founder of the Persian Timurid Empire, Timur. Hassan ruled half the now-partitioned realm as the 'White Sheep' Turcoman. He wanted to reunite Persia under a single rule. John IV Comnenus took steps to forge an alliance with Uzun Hassan to give Trebizond greater leverage in his negotiations with Mehmed II. The Emperor married his daughter to Uzun Hassan, creating a dynastic link between the Comnenoi and Turcoman. When John IV died inopportunely, his work was left in the hands of his four-year-old son, whose guardian was John's much weaker brother, David.

David continued his brother's policy to build an Oriental League, but he failed to manipulate the relationship between Uzun Hassan and Mehmed to Trebizond's advantage. The Trebizond Emperor used Hassan to intercede with the Sultan to cancel the annual tribute, which his citizens were struggling to afford. When Hassan came before Mehmed, he made demands above and beyond David's brief. He demanded that the Sultan restore Cappadocia to the Comnenoi since that land had been promised to him by the late John IV as part of his wife's dowry. He also insisted that Mehmed resume a long-suspended tribute that the Seljuks had paid at one time to the Persians consisting of 1,000 horse blankets, turban cloths and carpets. Mehmed was deeply offended; his response to Hassan and Emperor David was so threatening that Hassan shortly afterwards agreed a treaty with Mehmed, precluding any assistance to Trebizond in the event of an Ottoman assault.

David attempted to use the nascent Oriental League as an incentive in the West. In this, too, he overshot the mark. Writing to Philip, Duke of Burgundy in 1459, he exaggerated the support he could muster in the east, claiming that Hassan would add 50,000 men to Trebizond's 20,000 soldiers and thirty galleys. He stated that the King of Georgia and one of his dukes had committed 60,000 men and 20,000 calvary to oppose the Turkish armies. Allegedly, the Goths and Alani tribes had promised to fight; and he claimed that the Prince in Armenia and his barons were sending 30,000 soldiers. David wanted Duke Philip to lead a diversionary expedition in Hungary so that his League could advance against the Ottomans in the east. In exchange, the Emperor promised that they would go as far as Jerusalem and make Philip its king after they had taken the Holy City.

In the meantime, at the papal court, a little-known Franciscan monk, Fra Ludovico da Bologna, adopted the eastern cause and convinced Popes Calixtus, Nicholas and Pius to appoint him as papal plenipotentiary, and later papal nuncio, charged with expanding Emperor David's Oriental League by recruiting the support of the Indian princes and the king of Ethiopia. Fra Ludovico was a con artist with aspirations to become the Patriarch of Constantinople. He fooled three popes and the Emperor of Trebizond. The monk brought David and a group of eastern rulers to Pope Pius's court with claims that they represented the Oriental League and had mustered 150,000 soldiers. All they needed now was a western commitment under papal leadership to join their forces in a campaign against Mehmed. Many of the members they listed in their League had not actually joined, and the numbers of men that they promised were far beyond anything these rulers could realistically raise. Guileless, Pius II allowed himself to be convinced but realised that he would need the agreement of the King of France and Duke of Burgundy. Louis XI of France and Philip were not so easily duped by the monk and his motley band of exotic eastern leaders. The discussions broke down, and the delegates retreated to Rome under a cloud of suspicion.

In the aftermath of both the abortive attempt to raise western support and the fiasco with Uzun Hassan, the Sultan realised that Trebizond, with its eastern and western relations, would always represent a potential threat to the Ottomans. Having cowed Hassan into withdrawing his support from David for now, Mehmed decided the moment was opportune to deal with Trebizond. Leading an army of reportedly 60,000 calvary and 80,000 infantry, the Ottomans took a circuitous route to Trebizond, passing close to Hassan's territories to reinforce the sense of threat to the Turcoman's position.

On arrival, the Sultan sent a message to Emperor David offering terms of surrender.

> To the Emperor of Trebizond of the imperial family of the Hellenes, Mehmed the Great King declares: You see how great a distance I have travelled after deciding to invade your territory. If you now surrender your capital without delay, I shall make land to you, as I did to Demetrius, the Greek prince of Morea on whom I bestowed riches, islands and the beautiful city of Aenos. He is now living at peace and is happy. But if you do not give ear to these proposals, know that annihilation awaits your city. For I will not leave this spot until I have levelled the walls and ignominiously killed all the inhabitants.

Emperor David accepted Mehmed's offer. He was allowed to keep his moveable treasures and servants; the imperial family was relocated to Adrianople where they lived for a short period supported by a grant from the Sultan. It was not a sustainable arrangement – Mehmed recognised that as long as descendants of the Comnenoi lived, they represented a potential rallying point for a Byzantine-inspired uprising against him. In 1463 he ordered David's execution, placed the women of the family in his harem, and forced the children to convert to Islam. A Comnenus revival of Byzantium was no longer a possibility.

Above: 1. Cristoforo Buondelmonti, A Chart of Constantinople, *Liber Insularum Archipelagi*, circa 1420. (National Maritime Museum, F1592. © National Maritime Museum, Greenwich, London)

Overleaf: 2. Frans Hogenberg, *Byzantium Nunc Constantinopolis*, from *Civitates Orbis Terrarum*, 1572. (University Library Heidelberg. Fine Art Images/Alinari Archives, Firenze)

3. Artist unknown, *Portrait of Cardinal Isidore*, eighteenth century. (Borys Voznytskyi Lviv National Art Gallery. Courtesy of the Ministry of Culture and Information Policy of Ukraine)

4. Artist unknown, *Isidore, Metropolitan of Kiev and Rus, Cardinal, Patriarch of Constantinople, Archbishop of Cyprus*. (The Picture Collection, Alamy)

5. Gentile Bellini, *Cardinal Bessarion and Two Members of the Scuola della Carità in Prayer with the Bessarion Reliquary*, circa 1472–3. (© The National Gallery, London)

6. Artist unknown, *Portrait of Cardinal Johannes Bessarion*, sixteenth century. (Gallerie dell'Accademia, Venice, Italy. Photo: Cameraphoto Arte, Venice / Art Resource, NY)

7. Bernardino Pinturicchio, *Pope Eugenius IV* (detail) from the fresco cycle of the Piccolomini Library, north east wall: 'Aeneas Sylvius makes an act of submission to Pope Eugenius IV, February 7, 1447'. (Libreria Piccolomini, Duomo, Siena, Italy. Photo: © Ghigo G. Roli / Art Resource, NY)

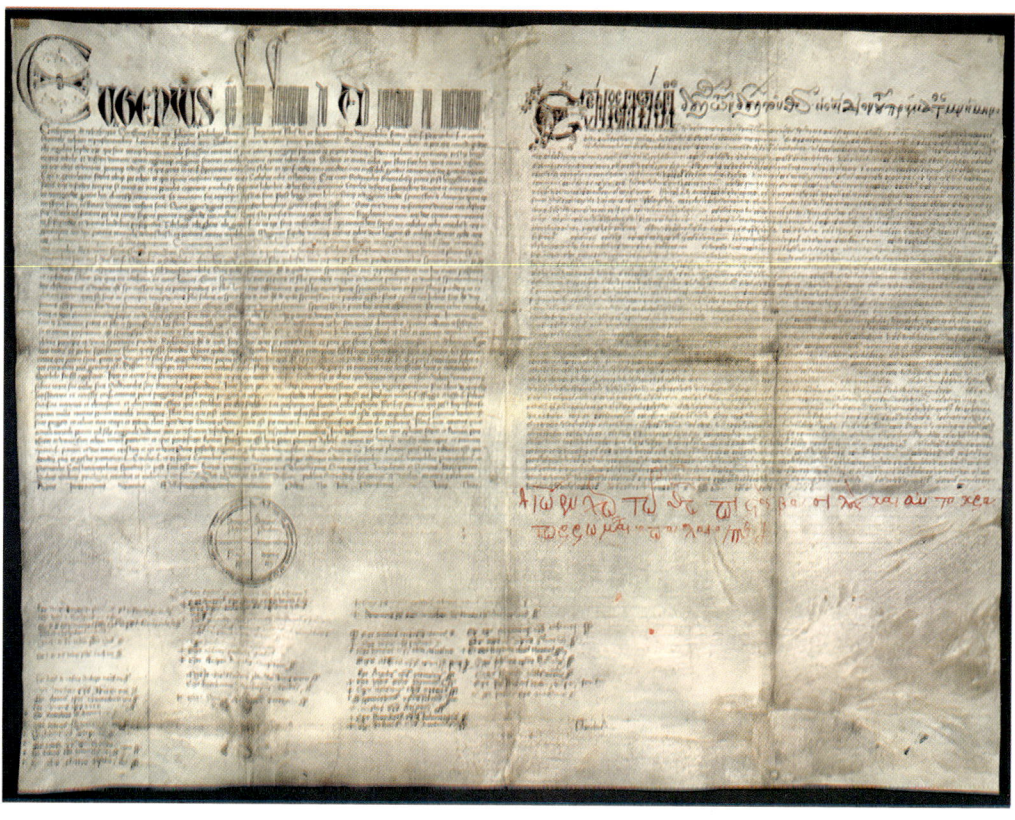

8. Bull of the Union of the Greek and Latin Churches, 1439. (Cotton MS Cleopatra E III, The British Library, London)

9. Peter Paul Rubens, *Portrait of Pope Nicholas V*, 1612–16. (MPM.V.IV.066, Stad Antwerpen, Museum Plantin-Moretus. Photo: Michel Wuyts)

10. Giovanni Paladino, *Medallion of Pope Pius II*, late sixteenth century. (Metropolitan Museum of Art, New York. Bequest of Rupert L. Joseph, 1959)

11. Artist unknown, *Portrait of Emperor John VIII*. (Library of the Holy Monastery of St Catherine, Sinai, Egypt, Cod.2123, fol. 30v. © 2024 St Catherine's Monastery at Mt Sinai)

Right: 12. Artist unknown, *Statue of Constantine XI Palaeologus* (1405–53). (National Historical Museum of Athens. Photo courtesy of NH Museum Athens)

Left: 13. Benozzo Gozzoli, *Joseph, Patriarch of Constantinople* (detail) from The Adoration of the Magi, 1459. (Palazzo Medici-Riccardi, Florence, Italy. akg-images / Erich Lessing)

Left: 14. Islamic-Ottoman, *The Fatih Sultan Mehmed II*, fifteenth century. (The Topkapi Palace Museum, Istanbul, Turkey. Alinari Archives, Florence)

Below: 15. Artist unknown, Siege of Constantinople, sixteenth century. (Moldovita Monastery, Suceava County, Romania. Photo courtesy of Diana Condrea)

Opposite: 16. Turkish School, *Miniature of the Siege of Constantinople*, 1453, watercolour. (Topkapi Palace Library, Istanbul, Turkey. © Album / Oronoz)

Above: 17. Paolo Romano, *Tomb of Pope Pius II* (detail of the relief showing the translation of St Andrew's Head), 1465–70. (Church of S. Andrea della Valle, Rome, Italy. Alinari Archives, Florence)

Left: 18. Shrine with the statue of St Andrew commemorating the arrival of the relic in Rome. (Milvian Bridge, Rome, Italy. Photo courtesy of Maya Maskarinec)

19. Byzantine School, *Icon of Saint Demetrios*, fourteenth century. (Museo Civico, Sassoferrato, Italy. Photo courtesy of Robert S. Nelson)

20. Antoniazzo Romano, *Madonna and Child*. (Basilica dei Santi XII Apostoli, Rome, Italy. Photo 52982180 © Jozef Sedmak | Dreamstime.com)

21. Artist unknown, *Reliquary of Cardinal Bessarion*, fourteenth century. (Gallerie dell'Accademia, Venice, Italy. Photo: Cameraphoto Arte, Venice / Art Resource, NY)

Surprisingly, Bessarion does not seem to have had much involvement in the efforts of Trebizond to raise an eastern-led opposition to Mehmed II. Perhaps this was because the alliances were with other Islamic powers, and Bessarion's political, religious and cultural motivation was centred exclusively in the Christian western sphere. However, in the final years of his life, the Ottomans made a conquest that roused a reaction in the West that resembled the depth of anguish evoked by the fall of Constantinople. The response briefly raised the hopes of Bessarion and Greeks like him, that a crusade might be successfully mustered. The provocation was the Sultan's capture of Negroponte (also known as Chalkis), a Venetian-held state on the Island of Euboea.

Up to this point Pope Paul II had shown little enthusiasm for dealing with the plight of eastern Christendom. Between the death of Pius II and Paul's election, Bessarion had been the dean of the College of Cardinals, and he had presided over a pre-election meeting of its members to draw up an agreement (called the Capitulation) to bind the new Pope to a set of obligations. One of these was a commitment to go to war against the Turks. All the potential candidates signed the Capitulation, including Pietro Barbo, who was then elected as Pope Paul II. For six years, the Pope took no action to honour the Capitulation, until the catastrophe in Negroponte.

The Venetians had seized Euboea in the Fourth Crusade, and Emperor Michael VIII had briefly restored it to the Byzantine Empire when he came to the throne. In the fourteenth and fifteenth centuries, Venice gradually resumed its control and gave Negroponte the status of a Venetian protectorate – its loss was, however, perceived to be a Greek tragedy with massive implications for the West. A friend of Bessarion, the bishop of Zamor, Rodrigo Sánchez de Arévalo, wrote to the Cardinal in consolation at the news of Negroponte's loss, comparing the plight of the Greeks to the Israelites under Pharaoh.

Since the fall of Constantinople, Venice had performed an uneasy balancing act between maintaining peace with the Ottomans to protect its trade routes and supporting the papacy in its various initiatives to launch a crusade. Ottoman aggression against Venetian-held territories in the Aegean and the renewed efforts of Pius II to muster military support combined to push Venice into what would be known as the first Ottoman-Venetian war. Of the hostilities that lasted from 1463 to 1479, Negroponte's demise was the most traumatic episode.

It was no secret that Mehmed II had Negroponte in his sights. Greek spies reported activity in the shipyards of the Sea of Marmara, where a large fleet was being built. They also observed the casting of large guns in Thessalonica. Piero Dolfin, a Venetian merchant, sent a letter to the Republic's Senate on 14 February 1470, recording that: 'On the first of December we heard from Pera that the Turk is preparing a fleet … he has come in person to Constantinople … to look after his affairs. This report leaves no doubt that he intends to move against Negroponte.' The Venetians were not complacent; they added another thirty-five triremes to their squadron anchored in Negroponte. It was an inadequate response. Islanders in the Aegean coastal settlements reported that there were at least 100 Ottoman triremes off the island of Tenedos and that the Turkish ships blanketed a stretch of sea for six miles. In preliminary skirmishes through the winter and spring of 1470, Mehmed's naval commander, Grand Admiral Mahmud Pasha, attempted to take Lemnos and Skiros. These efforts failed, but he and his navy sailed unopposed into the Euboean Sea. In the meantime, the Sultan set out at the head of the land army, crossing through Thessaly on the way to Boeotia, the mainland across from the island of Euboea.

The Sultan's forces arrived in Boeotia in the middle of June in the summer of 1470. Across the water, they faced Negroponte, a heavily fortified city where the officials had had time to repair any weaknesses in the walls and to collect supplies to withstand a siege for enough time to allow for the Venetian navy to relieve them. Mehmed's first task was to construct a pontoon bridge across the Euripus Strait that separated the island from the mainland. His men, weapons and forty-two giant bronze guns were then transferred to positions around the main city walls. The battle for Negroponte was almost as dramatic as that for Constantinople, and certainly its aftermath created equal shockwaves in the West. Rumours circulated that there were 70,000 men aboard the Ottoman ships and that the Sultan was leading 120,000 soldiers by land. These figures were exaggerated, but the Turks did massively outnumber the islander defence forces and the Venetian soldiers. Despite their numerical disadvantage, the defence of the city was vigorous. Mehmed sent waves of Janissaries to assault the walls, and each time they were repulsed. Thousands of Ottomans were killed, and the dead piled up in the moats around the city.

Negroponte clung on by its fingernails awaiting rescue by the Venetian fleet that had been assembled to defend the island. In July they spotted the first few ships, a small fleet commanded by Captain-General Niccolo da Canale had outpaced the bulk of the squadron and anchored off the coast of Negroponte. What happened next, or rather, did not happen, cost the Venetians the island. Da Canale made the decision to wait until the rest of the navy vessels arrived. He and his forces watched the battle unfold but did not intervene. The defenders were exhausted and frantically tried to signal to the Venetian ships that they needed immediate help. A monk inside the city walls, Fra Jacopo dalla Castellana, left an eyewitness account that captured the frustration of the situation.

> Our fleet from Venice entered from the part of the channel by the Bridge of Santa Clara [Chiara] to the east and was in good position to help our territory... His Magnificence, the Captain General Nicolo da Canale, made an error, as His Magnificence would not allow some of the ships of the Genoese that had been enlisted in Candia to attack and besiege the bridge or the two galleys from Cyprus and the two galleys from Rhodes that volunteered to sail to the aid of the city. His Magnificence would not issue permission to attack. The cause of this is not known but, consequently, our territory received no assistance. We within the territory realised that we were not going to receive any help; yet we fought on bravely until the second hour of the day. By the second hour of the day the Turks assumed command of all the walls of Negroponte; at noon the fighting went on in the main square. From the Gate that bore the image of San Marco to the Gate of the Church, the streets had been barricaded with beams and barrels. The women put to death a large number of Turks by pouring boiling water and lime on them from windows. On that day Negroponte was plundered, i.e. the entire territory, with the exception of the bridge that fell the following Saturday.

Unbeknownst to Niccolo da Canale, Mehmed was on the verge of aborting his assault when he saw the fleet arrive. He overestimated the number of ships, and he calculated that he would be unable to breach the walls while under attack from the Venetian navy. One of his admirals, however, persuaded him to make one last attempt. They were aided by a traitor within Negroponte; a garrison captain, Fiorio di Nardone, led the

Ottomans to the weakest point in the walls. The exhaustion of the islanders, combined with the galling inaction of Niccolo da Canale and the treason of one of their own, overwhelmed the defenders, and the Sultan's army breached the walls. The civilian population put up a fierce resistance as the soldiers advanced through the streets in a battle that lasted five hours. The Janissaries, facing armed women and children, had to fight their way from corner to corner. No mercy was afforded to the Greek residents or the Italian defenders. The Sultan ordered all prisoners with beards to be brought before him to be executed. Eight hundred captives were beheaded; women and children were enslaved and deported.

Giacomo Rizzardo, a Flemish naval commander, wrote an account of the fall of Negroponte in which he described the aftermath. He was not an eyewitness but probably learned the details when he was secretary to Captain Lorenzo Contarini whose ship had been one of the fleet led by Niccolo da Canale.

> The slaughter that ensued within the city was so great that no human being can adequately convey the bloodshed and the savagery committed by the Turks. This great slaughter took place because the Turks had been enraged by the insults that the townspeople had been hurling at them, when they had asked them to surrender. In truth, both the Lord Turk and his army had been humiliated and when they reported to him the insults offered by the besieged he had been extremely upset and had taken an oath from the bottom of his heart that, when he took the city, they would regret it. And so, after the fall of the city, the Lord Turk, mounted his horse and escorted by his sons, by the pasha and by a crowd of Turkish officials, patrolled the main square... All those whom he encountered were ordered to be sawn asunder in front of the Church of the Holy Apostles.

Saving Byzantium: The Struggle to Salvage an Empire

Losing Negroponte sparked an outpouring of collective mourning and fear. The Venetians held processions and offered prayers; they revelled in self-recrimination. There was a sense that the Republic and the West now faced an existential threat from Mehmed. Doge Cristoforo Moro wrote to Galeazzo Maria Sforza, Duke of Milan that, 'All Italy and all Christendom are in the same boat, we all face the same peril; no coastline, no province, no part of Italy, no matter how remote and hidden it may seem, can be considered safer than the rest.'

As he and Isidore had done in 1453, Bessarion harnessed the trauma to campaign again for action against the Ottomans. Writing to his namesake, Abbot Bessarion of San Severino, the Cardinal painted the alarming picture that he would refine into a propagandistic diatribe to all the princes of European states: 'The Turkish navy will soon be at Brindisi, then Naples, then Rome. With the Venetians defeated, the Turks will rule the seas as they do the land.'

Bessarion wrote *The Orationes*, two speeches addressed to the princes of Italy. In the text he analysed the Sultan's techniques and goals; assessed the political and economic pressures on his empire; and discussed whether Europe had any intention of withstanding the Muslims. Bessarion adopted a tone that conveyed the impression of a close relationship with the Italian leaders and the Pope, founded on mutual preoccupation with Latin interests.

Appended to the *Orationes* was Bessarion's translation into Latin of Demosthenes' *First Olynthiac to the Athenians*. Bessarion was using his Greek heritage to achieve a western goal: the promotion of a Crusade to save Christendom. In the course of presenting an acute political parallel between fourth-century BC Athens and western Christendom, Bessarion also contributed another previously inaccessible Greek text to the Latin repertoire. Between 350 and 347 BC, Philip of Macedon conquered thirty-two Greek states including Olynthus in the Chalcidice peninsula. During this period the orator Demosthenes delivered the first of three speeches calling on the Athenians to form an alliance with the Olynthians against Philip.

It is this speech that Bessarion translated for the first time from Greek into Latin and included as part of his propaganda package delivered to the Italian princes. Bessarion's motive for including the speech was clearly to draw parallels between the Ancient Greek situation and the current one. The Byzantines, represented by the Olynthians, were facing a modern Philip of Macedon in the guise of Sultan Mehmed II. Western Christendom took the role of Athens, with Bessarion as the present-day Demosthenes.

The Cardinal achieved unprecedented exposure for his texts by partnering with Guillaume Fichet (1433–1480), editor of the first Paris printing press. As rector and librarian of the Sorbonne, he had a strong interest in Italian scholarship, and he was instrumental in disseminating it through France. The two men took on the project of printing Bessarion's *Orationes*, a propaganda tract composed for Pope Paul II and for the princes of the Italian states calling for peace in Italy so that a unified resistance to the Ottomans could be launched. Bessarion sent the *Orationes* to Fichet on 14 December 1470 with a letter describing his reasons:

> I undertake to send you the *Orationes* that I have just composed on the subject of the dangers which threaten Italy and all Christians: I am sending them to you, in truth, less for you to look for purity of style in theme or the strength and superior speech, but rather to indicate to you the innumerable evils that menace the Christian world in the lifetime and fortune of her children and to engage you to reveal, to make the king and other important people, who must or could find a solution, really understand the situation.

Although Bessarion did not directly ask Fichet to print *The Orationes*, he knew the Frenchman was closely involved in the printing trade in Paris so anything that he sent him would likely end up in print. The Cardinal had previously harnessed the propaganda power of printing in Italy for a long defence he wrote against some of his Greek critics, and he was shrewd enough to recognise the medium's potential for disseminating his *Orationes* throughout northern Europe. Bessarion and the Pope were engaged in efforts to incentivise Louis XI of France into supporting a Crusade to regain Constantinople. It was in their interest to establish a network of northern leaders, and the mutually beneficial partnership with the Frenchman was a means to this end. Guillaume Fichet was inspired by Bessarion's work and believed that print was the medium to bring about a change in the attitude of the northern princes towards a crusade campaign. Around sixty copies are known, of which twenty survive. Fichet himself spoke of the distribution of Bessarion's text – a feat which would have been much more difficult and expensive without printing: 'Not only have I freely distributed forty-six books containing your *Orationes*, whose cause I was entrusted to defend, in all of France and Germany, but besides I took care that each of my religious brothers at the head of provincial ministries, to whom I offered an exemplaire...'

The publisher's effort to disseminate Bessarion's text extended the Cardinal's sphere of influence – both politically and intellectually – in the West to include northern Europe. Some of the more deluxe editions included a full-page portrait of the Cardinal on the frontispiece. In the copy given to King Edward IV of England, Fichet is depicted on his knees offering the book to the king, who sits under a pink baldaquin. Bessarion stands behind the editor in his Basilian robes and cardinal's hat. A monochrome architectural frame surmounts the scene, and the receding ground draws the viewer in and enhances the air of intimacy. This portrait of Bessarion was a visual mechanism that clearly raised the Cardinal's profile among the northern potentates who received the *Orationes*.

Fichet won the support of Jean Bouchard, confessor of King Louis, and of Cardinal Elie de Bordeilles, both of whom encouraged him to press Bessarion to visit France in person to throw his weight behind the efforts to avert an internal war in the country. It was crucial that domestic peace be attained before a successful campaign could be waged against the Ottomans.

Amplifying Bessarion's exhortations, Pope Paul II addressed the secular rulers of the Italian states and their neighbours, writing to each of them:

> …immediately upon reading the present letter you send us … as your envoy and upright, God-fearing man, who is bent upon preserving the Christian commonwealth, with ample authority to negotiate and conclude a general league in Italy, for as the Italian failure to reach an accord feeds the Turkish tyrant's audacity and encourages his advance, just so will his courage be dispelled when he learns that the armed might of the Italians has been conjoined by common agreement… Beloved sons, there must be no delay, because our enemy, who seems to desire nothing more than bloody extermination of all Christendom [is] already at our throats, grows stronger every day, and fresh from the victory [Negroponte] he has had, he is strengthened in his resolve, so that every slightest delay affords him the opportunity for our common destruction.

This request was made in a series of impassioned letters that the Pope sent to Ludovico Gonzaga of Mantua, Guglielmo Paleologo of Montferrat, King John II of Aragon-Catalonia, Dukes Borso d'Este of Ferrara and Amadeo IX of Savoy. Paul II summoned the representatives of these states to Rome to revive the Italic League that Pope Nicholas V and Bessarion had forged to lead a crusade in the aftermath of Constantinople's demise. Paul's call on the princes of Christendom to set aside their differences had little impact, despite the public celebrations for the renewed League. Amid a three-day fanfare of church bells, parades and bonfires, the League of Lodi was announced in Bologna during a papal visit to the city in 1471. In reality, there was very little to celebrate. Venice was at odds with Hungary and Florence. They accused the latter, along with the Genoese, of tacit support for the Sultan in exchange for favourable commercial arrangements at the expense of Venice. The Pope was engaged in conflict with Florence and Milan, and the northern European princes were too preoccupied with their domestic agendas to contribute to a crusade.

Simultaneously, Paul set up a commission of cardinals charged with raising and administering funds for a military campaign. The commission worked from Bessarion's house and recommended that the Pope allocate a quarter of the annual papal revenue to financing the crusade. This would have amounted to 50,000 ducats per year. The Venetians repeatedly demanded that the Pope contribute more significantly by selling his treasure to raise money and by demanding that his cardinals donate half their revenue. Paul protested that, since his election in 1468, he had allocated 200,000 florins from the treasury to assist the Hungarians, the Morea, Albania and the Arta. Nonetheless, in early 1471, the Pope agreed to the financial request of Bessarion and his commission of cardinals. Rome, Aragon, Venice, Naples and Rhodes joined forces to organise an expedition against the Turks off the coast of Asia Minor. Once again, luck was not with the West; Pope Paul died suddenly and unexpectedly, bringing the plans to a halt.

The Venetians mobilised a campaign to have Bessarion elected as the next pope. They had been infuriated by Paul, convinced that he never supported his crusade rhetoric with realistic financial backing. In their frustration, they had resorted to offering a reward to any assassin who successfully poisoned the Sultan. The Senate seized the opportunity to push for a papal candidate whom they trusted to deliver real support for a military campaign against the Turks, instructing their ambassador to the court of Federico da Montefeltro to urge the Duke to promote Bessarion. The irony would not have been lost on Bessarion. The very Republic that had dragged its feet for decades over launching a crusade to help the Byzantines now sought to lever a Byzantine onto the papal throne, because they needed a tool that would back military intervention.

The Doge's plans were thwarted, and the cardinals elected Francesco della Rovere as Pope Sixtus IV instead. To the relief of Venice and Bessarion, the new Pope recognised the gravity of the Ottoman threat and offered a strong commitment to mounting a vigorous response. He published an encyclical lamenting the advance of the Ottomans through Constantinople, Negroponte, Asia Minor, the Balkans, Hungary and inner Germany. The list was starkly alarming in its geographical scope. Within a few months of his election, he held a secret consistory in which he appointed five legations *a latere*, charged with gaining support for a crusade from the European leaders. The five cardinals fanned out across the continent. Cardinal Bessarion was sent to France, Burgundy and England. Cardinal Rodrigo Borgia went to Spain; Angelo Capranica travelled around Italy; Marco Barbo visited the rulers in Germany, Hungary and Poland; and Oliviero Carafa was sent to the court of Naples.

Despite his advanced years, Bessarion set out on his mission in 1472, travelling to the French court to petition the king for support. Throughout his reign, King Louis XI had shown little interest, bordering on open hostility, to joining the Pope in a military campaign against the Sultan. Bessarion knew the scale of the challenge he faced. On the way he stopped over in Bologna to await Louis' safe-conduct, which took two months to procure. He finally arrived in Lyons, where he was greeted by Guillaume Fichet. Together they met the king at the Chateau Mayenne, in Chateau-Gontier. It was an inauspicious time to be approaching the French monarch to ask him to commit himself and resources to a crusade, since the duke of Burgundy was besieging Louis in an effort to unite Picardy with the Low Countries. Having achieved little, Bessarion turned back for Italy. He was not strong enough for the journey and died at Ravenna in November 1472.

Of the legates commissioned by Sixtus, only Cardinal Carafa achieved tangible results. He persuaded the King of Naples to prepare a fleet which assembled off the coast of Rhodes in 1472. The Venetians joined the Napolitans in furnishing additional ships, and the Pope allocated 144,000 florins to the project. Together, they built a Christian armada of eighty-seven galleys and fifteen transport vessels. The naval expedition achieved a handful of small victories off the coast of Asia Minor. The most notable of these was the attack on the port town of Smyrna in September. The Turkish garrison was destroyed, and the Venetians indulged in a gruesome showcase of their success by festooning their ships with the severed head of 215 Ottomans.

The weakness of the unity between the Italians characterised the nature of the progress that they made against the Ottomans – the results were equally insignificant and short-lived. Relations between Naples and Venice broke down, and the Napolitans withdrew their ships from the fleet. Throughout the 1470s, Pope

Sixtus pursued the Italian princes and other secular leaders to unite against the Turks. The crusade never materialised, and the Ottomans swallowed up the lands of the Byzantine Empire. Less than a decade after Bessarion's death, the warnings that he and Isidore had made throughout their careers came back to haunt the West. 'The Turk thinks he can achieve nothing worthier, nothing which would add more glory to his name, than leading an army into Italy and adding to his dominions a province accustomed to dominating.'

These words, written by Bessarion, seemed prophetic when the Sultan led his forces to victory at Otranto in southern Italy in 1480. The diarist Jacopo da Volterra recorded a searing description of the sacking of the city. The Turks killed the archbishop and his priests, the old were slaughtered and the young enslaved. The soldiers destroyed churches, fed relics to the dogs and raped women on the altars.

Bessarion died after experiencing yet another disappointing response to the plight of Byzantium from the West, which was blind to the existential threat that they themselves faced due to their resolute inaction. The inertia of the western nations and indifference towards their eastern neighbours were tropes that would play out again and again. Bessarion and Isidore had recognised that the Ottoman success in Byzantium had implications for all Christendom, and together they had devoted their lives to the struggle to get the West to set aside short-term internal differences so that they could defend a common culture, religion and way of life.

The alleged decadence and self-absorption of Byzantine society has often been blamed for its ultimate demise. This view is so pervasive that 'byzantine' has become a pejorative adjective for 'excessive, complicated and ineffective'. Quips abound about the Turks being at the gates of Constantinople while the Greeks were too absorbed within the walls of the city by debates over the gender of an angel to notice the threat outside. By judging the victims, the West overlooked how its own failings remarkably mirrored those that they identified in the East. Had the leaders in the East and West been able to put aside their doctrinal differences, a united front might have been sufficient to deter Mehmed.

Was this the end for Byzantium? From the ashes, there were signs of life. Under the Ottomans a policy of religious tolerance enabled the Orthodox Church to flourish; Sultan Mehmed II encouraged the return and prosperous integration of former residents of Constantinople. Those who fled the former empire's lands brought Byzantine literature, language, philosophy, art and culture to their hosts' societies. Bessarion, in particular, was a major contributor to the preservation of the idea of Byzantium. While it is clear that the political geography no longer featured Byzantium as a physical empire, there's no question it still retained a powerful identity for several centuries beyond the crisis of 1453 and the subsequent territorial losses.

9

CHAMPIONING BYZANTIUM: THE LEGACY

For Bessarion and Isidore, the Byzantine Empire was a multifaceted entity encompassing geographical territories unified under a secular ruling family, a religion and a culture. Isidore was singularly focused on preserving territorial integrity, and he pursued a campaign to bring about a military defence of the empire. Bessarion was equally committed to this path, but he had a broader vision of what it meant to save Byzantium. He was convinced that he could preserve the cultural and spiritual identity of the Byzantines outside the physical territories. This mindset was the engine driving all his cultural activities, from assembling an extraordinary library of Greek manuscripts to collecting icons and relics from Byzantine lands. Whether he was teaching the Greek language, mentoring western princes or providing shelter and patronage to exiled Greeks, Bessarion had one goal: the preservation of the intellectual, cultural and spiritual attributes of Byzantium.

He upheld and promoted a narrative of Greek intellectual superiority, which he believed was the engine that drove the Humanist movement in scholarship. Bessarion referred to the Greeks as 'the most celebrated and wisest nation (*praeclarissima et sapientissima*)', and as 'the fount of all wisdom'. When he presented a translation of St Basil, one of the Greek Church Fathers, to King John II of Castile, he wrote in the dedication, 'All knowledge comes [from the Greeks].' From the moment Bessarion set out for the Council of Ferrara-Florence up to his death thirty years later, he brought a passion to this agenda that equalled the energy and commitment to his campaign for a crusade.

This chapter explores the projects that the Cardinal initiated and sponsored to ensure the survival of the Empire as a concept and a culture. He took on the roles of patron, scholar and spiritual leader, pursuing his agenda throughout his Italian career. Indeed, in the early 1450s, the pace of Bessarion's work to preserve Greek culture and spiritual practice intensified, perhaps reflecting a frustration with Pope Nicholas's reluctance to pursue a crusade. While Isidore was shuttling back and forth between Rome and Constantinople, the Pope had appointed Bessarion to deal with the unsettled city of Bologna, removing the Cardinal from the arena of negotiations over the Ottoman threat. Bessarion's cultural focus was comprehensive, reflecting a kaleidoscope of philosophies that ranged from importing technological advances from the West to reviving classical Greece to preserving the unique character of Byzantine spirituality.

Bessarion was cultivating theories for improving and preserving Byzantium long before he visited Italy for the first time to attend the Council of Ferrara-Florence. As a young man, he and his like-minded contemporaries judged Byzantium to be stagnant and lacklustre; a society that was ripe for the revival of its intellectual and practical life. Even though, at this stage, he had not yet travelled outside the Empire, he was convinced that many of Byzantium's solutions lay in embracing the West and collaborating with them in the fields of industry, science and learning. For Bessarion, union with the West was about more than religious doctrinal alignment, it was about a shared culture and social fabric, a mutual catalyst for prosperity in Christendom.

In this spirit, he led a campaign for industrial reform to modernise and strengthen the Empire and advocated action to boost the literacy of the Byzantine population. He proposed that young men be sent to Italy to learn the western canon of ancient texts combined with instruction in recent advances in technology. Once fully trained, Bessarion envisaged that they would return to Constantinople and other imperial territories to teach their new skills to the local population. He stressed the need for innovation in weapon manufacture, ship building, water-driven sawmills and bellows. In his plan, Bessarion even identified four industries for special attention: glass, silk, wool and dye.

Alongside his interest in western technologies, Bessarion became convinced that the survival of the Empire depended on the revival of ancient Hellenic philosophy and learning. Where did such ideas come from? The seeds of his intellectual agenda were planted in the early years of his career. In 1430 Bessarion accompanied his mentor Bishop Dositheos to the Peloponnesian city of Mistra, where he encountered a thriving intellectual community led by the philosopher Pletho, sponsored by Despot Theodore and his wife Cleope. Pletho had an extremely negative viewpoint. He taught that Byzantine society was in freefall and the only way to save it was to restore the customs of Ancient Greece. He blamed the degeneration of the Empire on the parasitical Church and weak secular leaders who were controlled by the monks. He highlighted the sad state of Constantinople as proof of his theory. The poverty level was so high that desperate residents frequently pillaged the grandiose buildings for firewood. Many of the formerly grand churches, such as the Holy Apostles and the Church of the Mother of God, were no longer properly maintained and were becoming increasingly dilapidated. Pletho's ideas were so extreme that he had been exiled from Constantinople and was widely seen by contemporaries as an apocalyptic radical. Bessarion's criticisms of Byzantine society had a more rhetorical nature than those of Pletho. However, he also subscribed to the notion that ancient philosophy could offer radical solutions to bolster the Byzantine Empire. The philosopher's ideas around societal and military reform resonated with Bessarion, and the relationship he forged with Pletho had a profound impact on his development as a scholar and philosopher.

This had been a difficult position to sustain in the face of his Greek peers. Monastic hostility towards secular learning was a deeply embedded tradition in Constantinople, and many of Bessarion's fellow monks were suspicious of the modern intellectual trends which favoured reviving ancient Hellenism. Bessarion and other Greek intellectuals felt stifled by the Constantinopolitan Church, and they believed this disdain for learning was symptomatic of the stagnation that rendered the Empire vulnerable. What a contrast he found in Florence when he arrived for the Council, where patrons commissioned new churches and palaces, and scholars enjoyed financial support and near-idolisation by the princes of the Church and the secular elite. This was fertile ground for Bessarion's intellectual theory that the panacea to the struggling Empire was a reversion to the heyday of Ancient Greece, via their literature and philosophy. The Italian environment seemed to have far more potential than the Constantinopolitan for Bessarion to develop his ideas of restoring the Empire.

Championing Byzantium: The Legacy

How would the revival of Hellenism preserve the Empire? Several Byzantine scholars and philosophers, including Pletho and Bessarion, believed that a superior morality could be found in ancient Greek society and that restoring this would give the imperial citizens the backbone needed to defeat the Ottoman threat. The study of classical literature would energise and inspire the population with themes of civic virtue. Bessarion and his peers called for a return to ancient ethics and logic; from these classical writers they expected to find the means to discipline society so that it would become a coherent force. By highlighting the common cultural identity of the Byzantines, these men harnessed their Greek roots as a rallying point to motivate their fellow citizens in their struggle to maintain independence.

It was under the influence of Pletho that Bessarion began to collect secular classical literature with a particular interest in philosophy and science. This collection and its thematic focus would continue to grow after he came to Italy. His choice of manuscripts reflected his agenda of a Hellenic revival. During this period Bessarion made his own copies of texts by Plutarch, Xenophon, Lucian and Plato.

When Bessarion arrived in Italy with the Greek delegates, he garnered much attention from the Italian court humanists. They were interested in his manuscript collection and saw him as a conduit for ancient Greek texts in their original language. For his part, Bessarion embraced the opportunity to experience the West's stimulating and dynamic cultural environment that Greek scholars had envied for many years. For these scholars, the revival and preservation of ancient Greek literature would happen in Italy and not in Byzantium itself.

Cardinal Bessarion actively collected ancient Greek texts along with Byzantine patristic and spiritual literature and ultimately, he donated these to the Republic of Venice as the founding collection of the state library, the Biblioteca Marciana. There can be no clearer example of the salvation of the Byzantine cultural identity than this repository.

Bessarion pursued a multi-faceted agenda: to transcribe the most important Greek texts; to preserve Greek texts from destruction; to make them more widely known; and to achieve greater Greek penetration of the western European continent. The manuscripts included texts on literature, law, mathematics, science, theology and scripture. This was a very personal collection constructed methodically to reflect Bessarion's narrative of the Byzantine cultural and spiritual identity. His proactive presence is found throughout the collection: a third of the texts are copies that he personally commissioned. Bessarion ran two dedicated teams of copyists located in Rome and Crete. Many manuscripts, especially those on astronomy and philosophy, are heavily annotated in his own hand. He gathered multiple versions of individual texts so that he and his followers could compile collated editions, and by the end of his life Bessarion had amassed a collection of Greek manuscripts that dwarfed those of the most dedicated book collectors of the period. The renowned collections of the humanist Niccolo Niccoli, Federico da Montefeltro, Duke of Ferrara Ercole d'Este, Pope Nicholas V and even that of the Vatican did not match Bessarion's library.

The fall of Constantinople increased the urgency and scope of Bessarion's efforts to collect books. One of his copyists in Crete was the Greek scholar Michael Apostolis, whom Bessarion paid to hunt down and purchase the texts on his wish list. He advised Apostolis to look in Adrianople, Athens, Thessalonica, Constantinople, Ainos, Thrace and Gallipoli, and to focus on classical secular literature. Bessarion sent similar instructions and funds to Theophanes, the bishop of Athens.

Championing Byzantium: The Legacy

Writing to Apostolis shortly after the catastrophe at Constantinople, Bessarion clearly articulated his state of mind and his agenda to salvage Greek literature for the sake of the Byzantines, not for the benefit of the westerners. In his letter he speaks of his drive to acquire copies of their works, not for his own sake,

> ...but so that if there are any Greeks now left and if in the future their fortunes improved, they will have somewhere where the whole of their cultural heritage as it now exists is preserved; they will find it in a safe place and copy it many times and ... not be left without a voice and no different from barbarians and slaves... I ask you to help me, and for the sake of my aim, which you must share, to do all that you can to find and buy everything.

Bessarion chose to donate his book collection to the Republic of Venice, a government with which the Cardinal spent many years discussing a potential crusade. By making Venice the beneficiary of his donation, he was applying political pressure to the Republic. A Venetian initiative was critical to the success of any military campaign. At the Council of Mantua, Pope Pius II appointed Bessarion and Nicholas of Cusa to negotiate a Venetian contribution to a military operation against the Ottomans. In 1463, Pius sent the Cardinal to Venice as apostolic legate, with the mission to muster support for another crusade attempt. Bessarion stayed for a year, consorting with the Venetian notables and exercising his right to vote in an election. He succeeded in persuading the Venetians to go to war as early as 29 July 1463. They embarked on a conflict with the Ottoman Turks which would last until 1479. By donating his library to the Republic, Bessarion was perhaps making a gesture which he hoped would encourage Venice to continue their participation in the war with the Ottomans.

Furthermore, Venice was a location that he felt would suit the agenda of his library. Bessarion identified the Republic as a 'second Byzantium' and, as such, a fitting location to achieve his goal to preserve Byzantine culture. As the Ottomans advanced over the years, Venice became the port of entry for the Greek refugees. This influx became a flood after the fall of Constantinople in 1453. The city took on the role of a haven, and many Greeks settled there in the Greek Quarter. Their presence made Venice a comfortable home where the Byzantines could re-establish their communities in an environment not too dissimilar from their own.

Bessarion was emotionally bound to this 'home from home', and wrote to Doge Cristoforo Moro that, '...the Greeks, who came from their provinces by ship first disembarked in Venice, seem to enter an alternative Byzantium, having been driven to your city and bound by necessity to you moreover.' The Greek community in Venice became the largest in Europe, and the Cardinal was heavily involved with it in his role as Uniate Patriarch, a papal appointment that made him the head of the pro-union Byzantine Church from April 1463.

Bessarion's prominence in the Curia clearly made him a desirable patron, and after settling in Rome he was accepted as an influential person among the local intellectuals. He used this status shrewdly in his campaigns, both to preserve Byzantine culture and to muster a crusade. The Cardinal's circle included powerful and influential men from the secular and ecclesiastical institutions. Francesco della Rovere (the future Pope Sixtus IV) joined Bessarion's entourage during the Cardinal's time in Bologna. The Italian duke, Federico da Montefeltro hired Bessarion to tutor his son, and their close relationship introduced the Cardinal into the sphere of the powerful Sforza family that ruled Milan. King Alfonso V of Aragon and Naples was linked to

Championing Byzantium: The Legacy

Bessarion, who dedicated a translation of Aristotle's *Metaphysics* to him. It was surely not a coincidence that Bessarion praised Alfonso's military prowess, comparing him to Alexander the Great in the dedication to his translation. These leaders were regularly exhorted to support a crusade in the east, and their relationship with Bessarion, along with their interest in Hellenism, would have made them more open to provide finances and military support for such a campaign.

Aside from the scope for political pressure afforded by Bessarion's network, its value lay in its service to the Cardinal's cultural agenda. Local humanists, Greek exiles and members of the papal Curia gathered around Bessarion as his *familiares*. Contemporary descriptions refer to his circle as an academy, and the household became a renowned centre of debate. Scholars like Francesco Filelfo (1398–1481) and Marsilio Ficino (1433–1499) mingled with famous Greek refugees such as George of Trebizond, Theodore Gaza and Janus Lascaris. Bessarion hosted and mentored these men, helping them establish their careers in the West. With the Cardinal's support they were able to secure teaching positions in institutions in Florence, Padua, London and Basel. They taught the next generation of rulers, ensuring that Greek literature in its original language was the cornerstone of a leader's education. Through Bessarion's patronage, Byzantine refugees worked in courts across the West to proselytise his narrative that the Greek language was fundamental to a deeper understanding of Latin. As political power and land were ceded to the advancing Turks, the culture of the Byzantine Empire was being embedded in the thinking of the western elite, where it would be preserved for posterity.

The Cardinal's concept of Byzantium encompassed its unique spirituality, and we shall see how he used his position and influence in Rome to protect this. Ironically, Bessarion and

Isidore were often accused of betraying the Byzantine Orthodox Church, by accepting the Decree of Union and then by joining the papal curia. It is clear, however, that Bessarion believed that Orthodox beliefs and rites could be upheld even in a united Church. The eastern Christian traditions and beliefs were defining and powerful elements in the profile of the Empire, and these were even more at risk of annihilation than ancient Hellenistic literature. After every successful Turkish incursion into Byzantine territory, religious institutions and homes were sacked by the Sultan's troops. Typically, the invaders would desecrate the church altars, strip the gold and precious gems from icons, smash the crosses and destroy holy relics. This was standard practice at the time for a conquering force, especially one fuelled by religious ideology. Motivated by fear for his spiritual heritage, the Cardinal gathered and commissioned Byzantine religious icons and reliquaries that he later donated to institutions in Italy, where they would be honoured and protected.

The icon was a painted devotional object that continued to be produced and consumed in the fifteenth century, primarily by the Byzantines. They were usually portraits of saints or holy figures, deemed to be true likenesses of the subject, copied from 'the archetype', which was the very first depiction of the saint from life. This authenticity was crucial, as it imbued the icon with a divine status of its own, and it explains why the icons retained a highly stylised and unchanging vocabulary over the centuries of artistic production. An icon was an exercise in preservation, in transmitting holiness through the image of the person depicted. Bessarion sought not only to possess this holiness, but also to preserve his spiritual heritage through his collection of devotional objects. The Cardinal actively sourced icons from their original locations in Byzantium and commissioned new images from exiled craftsmen based in Rome, or the territories that had not been conquered by the Turks.

Championing Byzantium: The Legacy

A Vatican inventory lists several donations from the Cardinal, including icons of the Archangel Michael, various other saints and the Crucified Christ. These pieces were decorated with Greek letters and embellished with gold and silver, enamel, precious stones and pearls. The Archangel Michael was a popular subject for icon painters and art collectors. He would be depicted frontally, usually in the attire of an emperor or a soldier against a gold background. His rigid, frontal pose would be combined with a lack of modelling or perspective, and by an absence of emotion, symbolising the immateriality of the subject and his divine status. These icons that Bessarion donated embodied a type of spirituality that was distinctly Byzantine in its character. The image held an almost magical power that it drew from the likeness it shared with the subject, and from the holiness generated by its physical contact (however many times removed) with the sacred original – 'the archetype'. Bessarion was generous with his extensive icon collection, and this made him one of the catalysts of a revived interest in icons in Rome in the fifteenth century. One of his most revered objects was a wooden panel framing a micromosaic of St Demetrios holding an ampulla of holy oil. He gave this highly prized reliquary and icon to his close friend and colleague, Niccolo Perotti.

In a bid to encourage the production of traditional Byzantine devotional objects in the West, Bessarion commissioned Italian painters to create new icons. The most significant of these commissions was for an icon that would sit above the altar in the Cardinal's own burial chapel at his church of Santissimi Apostoli, in Rome. Today, as the visitor enters SS Apostoli, this portrait of the Virgin and Child hangs in the chapel of the Holy Conception (once the chapel of the Archconfraternity of St Anthony of Padua), the first on the right of the nave or on the south wall. The icon depicted the Madonna and Child in a pose known in the Greek Orthodox tradition as the *Hodegetria*. The Madonna and Child sit against a gold background decorated with a foliate pattern painted to look like gold cloth. The portrait of Mary is three-quarter length, her body turned slightly to her left and her head demurely inclined. The Christ Child is seated on her lap, held in her left arm while she gestures to him with her right hand. He is a miniature youth, not an infant, holding a globe in his left hand and making a gesture of blessing with his right. It was painted by the artist Antoniazzo Romano to look like a Greek icon. Antoniazzo was one of the very few native Roman painters in the quattrocento, and he enjoyed papal patronage after Eugenius IV returned to the Vatican from exile in Florence. Bessarion recognised his potential to paint *alla maniera greca* from the rather eclectic and archaic style that differentiated him from his Tuscan and Umbrian contemporaries.

Relics and their reliquaries played a significant role in Bessarion's cultural campaign. His involvement in securing the head of St Andrew cannot be overestimated, nor can the significance of such a relic for all Christians – Orthodox and Roman Catholic. The Cardinal frequently capitalised on the potential religious and political messages embodied in a reliquary. Bessarion owned a *stauroteca*, a reliquary containing parts of the True Cross, that was bequeathed to him by his long-standing friend Gregory, the uniate patriarch of Constantinople (1443–1450) at his death in 1459. Gregory had received the relic from the Byzantine empress Irene at some time when he was her court confessor. During Bessarion's appointment as papal legate to Venice under Pope Pius II, he donated the reliquary to the Scuola di S Maria dei Battuti della Carità, granting the confraternity possession of the reliquary upon the Cardinal's death.

In the albergo of the Scuola della Carità it was locked away behind a panel, which was painted by the fifteenth-century

Venetian painter Gentile Bellini and included a portrait of the Cardinal. This suggests little opportunity for extended contemplation and meditation – it was an object for fleeting display in a procession. Bessarion commissioned a shaft to be attached to the icon so that it could be carried aloft. The reliquary was a rallying point and a trophy reserved for ceremonies, rather than a vehicle for a private dialogue between the viewer and the divine. After Bessarion sent the *stauroteca* to Venice from Bologna in 1472, it was solemnly processed from San Marco to the Scuola di S Maria dei Battuti della Carità.

This hybrid reliquary/icon had a function that was not merely spiritual for the Cardinal. By this time the object had a history as a sort of baton to be passed to the next tireless advocate for Byzantium. As its recipient in 1459, Bessarion was assuming the campaign Irene had entrusted to Gregory: that of persuading the Italians to support a crusade. This donation was also a means to generate public support for the crusade. Undoubtedly choreographed, the Venetians proclaimed their intention to mount a crusade in the Piazza San Marco on the same day that Bessarion made his gift. Could there have been a more fitting gift to those whom Bessarion was trying to persuade to fight the Muslims and defend Christianity? The mother of Constantine, St Helena, found the True Cross in the Holy Land and brought back a piece to Constantinople around the year 400. The True Cross in its entirety was transferred to Constantinople in 635, just before the Holy Land was ceded to Islam. For centuries, the relic of wood from the True Cross had possessed connotations with the defence of the Christian Empire.

As the guardian of Byzantine spirituality, Bessarion did not restrict his activities to conserving religious artefacts and promoting Greek religious art. In church administration and worship, Pius II gave Bessarion the tools to build a legacy that would preserve Byzantine traditions and Greek Orthodox practices. The Pope appointed him as the Cardinal Protector of the Orthodox Basilian monasteries and the commendatory abbot of the Abbey of Grottaferrata outside Rome in 1462, positions the Cardinal held until his death in 1472. These titles provided Bessarion with sufficient authority to protect the monks from potential usurpers and the loss of their treasures. The Basilian monasteries, of which Grottaferrata was the most important, were institutions practising Greek rites. They were clustered in southern Italy, mainly in Apulia and Calabria, where they had been founded for Greek monks several centuries earlier. By the fifteenth century they were in steep decline and desperately needed reform. Bessarion began by writing a Rule for the Order in Greek and Latin, based on the ascetic practices of St Basil. This book was distributed to all the Basilian monasteries and formed the basis of life at Grottaferrata until 1579.

The Grottaferrata abbey had been founded in 1004 by Byzantine monks from Calabria led by St Nilus of Rossano. Like all Basilian monasteries, the monks followed the Byzantine-Greco rite of the *Congregazione d'Italia dei Monaci Basiliani* (which had been established to bring Byzantine monks within the control of the Italian Church). They were given permission by Rome to follow Orthodox rites. When Bessarion was appointed abbot, Grottaferrata was the richest and biggest of the Italo-Greek monasteries, with possessions extending from the Roman Campagna to Rome, Lazio and Calabria. During the ten-year period under Bessarion, the monastery experienced a phase of peace and prosperity. He used these institutions as a haven for Byzantine practice – the crosses were empty unlike the Roman Catholic cross which always included the body of Christ. The monks continued the Orthodox style of signing the cross; they did not kneel to pray; and they cultivated their practice of chanting rather than speaking the prayers. Unleavened bread was supplied for the celebration of the Eucharist, and the clerics wore beards, in the tradition of the Orthodox Church.

Bessarion's formidable reach across all aspects of what defined the Byzantine Empire ensured that it was salvaged beyond its physical and political borders. The Ottomans and the Latins had carved up imperial territory between them; the Palaeologan dynasty had fallen; and efforts to muster a successful military campaign against Mehmed II had come to little. Nonetheless, Bessarion had built a safety net in parallel with his and Isidore's diplomatic and political efforts. The existence of Byzantium as a spiritual, cultural and linguistic body had been preserved and would continue to flourish in its original lands and beyond.

10

REINVENTING THE EMPIRE

Bessarion and Isidore, alongside several popes, pursued a course through the fifteenth century that suggests contemporaries did not believe that the fall of the Byzantine Empire was inevitable and that the situation was irreversible. After the loss of Constantinople, the Greeks and Latins were not the only stakeholders vying for control of an empire. The Greeks no longer ran Byzantium, but over time two rival successors to their empire emerged: the Ottoman Turks and the Russians. Both hankered to be heir to the Roman emperors with their deified status. The Turks and Russians engineered their claims in different ways, aspiring to a different imperial vision. This raises questions about the conclusions drawn by historians who position the period as a trajectory of undeniable decline. Perverse as it might appear, the Russians and Ottomans contributed to the preservation of Byzantium.

If the collapse of Byzantium was so obvious to contemporaries of the fifteenth century, why did everyone want to keep it alive? If the writing was on the wall; if Constantinople was a has-been, a husk of its former glory, why was it so desirable to Mehmed to preserve its Byzantine pedigree? Once he had conquered the city he could take advantage of its strategic value for trade and defence. He could have razed it to the ground and rebuilt his own capital in his own image. We will see in the course of this chapter that he did not do this; he did the opposite. If the Byzantine Empire's political systems, cultural values and spiritual health were so compromised by the time that Constantinople fell, why did the Russians aspire to recreate these on their own territory? They could have definitively split from Byzantine Orthodoxy and hosted their own Church for their own nation. However, as we will see, they wanted to claim an identity as the Third Rome.

After his soldiers breached the walls of Constantinople, the Sultan was obliged to allow them a customary period of three days for unrestricted looting. However, Mehmed called off the pillage after just one day. He wanted to preserve a city that would be fit for an imperial capital – his rampaging troops threatened to reduce Constantinople to an uninhabitable pile of rubble. The Sultan's agenda to establish the seat of the Ottoman Empire in Constantinople would be much harder to achieve in a devastated city. After he entered the walls, Mehmed almost immediately set out on a tour of what remained. He visited Hagia Sofia, kneeling and scooping up handfuls of dust that he poured over his white turban in a demonstration of humility and piety in a house of God. From the very beginning of the occupation, it was clear that Mehmed saw himself as the heir to the Roman Empire. He took the title of Caesar and Ruler of Two Continents and Seas. Through Constantine the Great, the religion of the Roman Empire shifted from paganism to Christianity so it was not unrealistic for him to believe that he could engineer a third incarnation: a Muslim-led Roman Empire.

The name of the city was changed to *Istambol*, meaning 'abounding in Islam'. The authority of the old empire would be harnessed to legitimise the new; the Ottomans would reinvent Constantinople as Istanbul, rather than construct it from scratch. By building literally and metaphorically on the pedigree of Constantinople as the central city of Byzantium, Mehmed sought to elevate the Ottomans from a tribe to an imperial power. In 1466, the Byzantine humanist George Trebizond wrote: 'No one doubts you [Mehmed II] are the Emperor of the Romans. Whoever is legally master of the capital of the Empire is the Emperor, and Constantinople is the capital of the Roman Empire.'

Mehmed identified the importance of the urban spaces to his plan to assume the imperial mantle of Byzantium. The most iconic building, dominating the skyline with its domes and sheer size, was Hagia Sofia. He ordered the transformation of the cathedral into a mosque, but the architectural and decorative changes were minimal to preserve its historical legacy as an endorsement of the new regime. Mehmed hastily added a minaret to make the building fit for Friday prayers, but the Christian paintings and floor plan were left untouched. Here, in a highly symbolic gesture, Mehmed personally led the Friday prayers every week.

Beyond the cathedral, a flurry of construction began. He commissioned a new fortress, Yedikule Hisarï, and repairs to the city walls. Borrowing from Byzantine architectural styles and decorative motifs, the Sultan constructed a palace in the centre where the old forum had stood. A few years later, he decided to build an alternative residence, Topkapı, on the outskirts of the city, echoing the isolationist approach of the Byzantine emperors who had removed themselves physically from the mundane lives of their citizens. Like the Byzantines' Great Palace, Topkapı gave the ruler the tools to cultivate an aura of mystery and otherworldliness by using isolation and cumbersome rituals to restrict access to the sultan. Mehmed chose the site of the old Greek acropolis on the north-eastern tip of the peninsula. The precinct included a mosque that was open to the public, but the Sultan had a private entrance to the building so that he could enter and leave unseen.

Mehmed also pursued a public facilities programme inspired by Byzantine and Roman practices. He constructed a bath house, a concept alien to the Ottomans, using the existing aqueduct infrastructure. These were open to all citizens of Istanbul, regardless of religion. Imperial supervision of commerce and trade was achieved through the construction of a commercial space, the *bedestan*, a 15-domed structure for shops. Here, too, the Sultan celebrated the Byzantine legacy by displaying a large imperial eagle above the entrance, the symbol of the Palaeologan dynastic house.

Without a population, however, this programme of urban renewal would be a hollow gesture of imperial authority. Many Greeks had fled in the run up to the siege of the city, and many more had been enslaved or killed in the assault. To settle the city exclusively with Ottoman subjects would not provide sufficient manpower to ensure a flourishing capital, and Mehmed concluded that he needed the Christian communities to make up the numbers. In addition, his authority was further endorsed by the recognition of his sovereignty by Byzantine citizens. Mehmed's apologist, the Greek writer Kritovoulos, described how the Sultan repopulated Constantinople after 1453, 'from all parts of Asia and Europe, and he transferred them with all possible care and speed, people of all nations, but more especially of Christians. So profound was the passion that came into his soul for the city and its peopling, and for bringing it back to its former prosperity.'

The order was given to deport Greeks from the conquered territories to the imperial city. Over the next few years, they came from the Morea, Phoceas, Lemnos, Lesbos, Mityelene and Euboea. Mehmed gave a property to each household that re-settled in Constantinople, and their members were exempted from taxation for an initial period. Men who had been enslaved by the Turks were provided with a wage in exchange for their work on the Sultan's many construction sites so that they could purchase their freedom and establish themselves in the city as free men. The challenge that Mehmed faced was captured in the text of the Ottoman historian and scholar Aşıkpaşazade:

> And he sent officers to all his lands to announce that whoever wished should come and take possession in Istanbul, as freehold, of houses and orchards and gardens, and to whoever came these were given. Despite this measure, the city was not repopulated; so then the Sultan commanded that from every land families, poor and rich alike, should be brought in by force. And they sent officers with firmans to the cadis and the prefects of every land. And they, in accordance with firman, deported and brought in numerous families, and to these newcomers, too, houses were given; and now the city began to become populous.

In 1477, a census of the citizens residing in Istanbul recorded 8,951 Muslim households and 3,151 Orthodox Greek households. In nearby Galata there were 535 Muslim households and 592 Orthodox Greek households. In comparison, all the other communities combined in Galata and Istanbul – Armenians, Latins and Gypsies – totalled only 3,095. The Greek Orthodox minority was vast and dominated all other cultures, second only to the Muslims. The Byzantine community continued to flourish.

Mehmed preserved the continuity of Byzantium in his choice of title, in his building campaigns, in the population he ruled and even in the government structures that he imposed. He absorbed and perpetuated many of the complex Byzantine court rituals. Many of the offices and their roles were retained: the Grand Duke became the *Kapudan pasha* and the Grand Vizier continued the tradition of the Grand Domestikos. The Sultan was served by offices that bore a striking resemblance to the imperial secretary and *logothetes*, who preserved the Byzantine administrative structure. Military command continued to be split between east and west under the *beglerbergs* of Rumeli and of Anatolia. Even the administrative division of the territory into themes, Byzantine military or administrative districts, was retained under the name of *sancaks*.

The most significant gesture toward the continuity of Byzantium made by Sultan Mehmed was his decision to uphold and promote the institutional framework of the Orthodox Church. He took on the responsibility of appointing a patriarch, thus asserting state control over the religion and imbuing the Church in Istanbul with government-sanctioned authority. This seems at odds with the many statements attributed to him before the sack of Constantinople, in which he spoke of his hatred of Christians and his messianic mission to conquer the 'heretics'. It was a shrewd strategy, reflecting the realpolitik of the situation.

The Sultan selected and appointed the patriarch, and his choice served his strategic aim to nurture the division between the Orthodox and Latin Churches. Gennadios's vehement opposition to the Decree of Union had driven him to renounce his erstwhile friend Bessarion. His argument was that salvation of the Empire lay in the preservation of the integrity of the Greek faith, not in military support from the heretical West. In his mind, the fall of Constantinople was divine retribution for the sin of consorting with the Latins. To encourage the anti-unionists was to perpetuate the conflict and to reduce the risk of the West collaborating with the Byzantines to challenge Mehmed in Istanbul. He chose

George Scholarios, now known as the monk Gennadios, to lead the Church as Patriarch of Constantinople.

Kritovolous wrote that in 1453 Gennadios had been captured in the assault but imprisoned in good conditions in Edirne. He described how the Sultan presided over the consecration and enthronement of Gennadios as Patriarch on 5 January 1454 in the Church of the Holy Apostles. A later survey of the Patriarchs of Constantinople, written in 1527 by the Metropolitan of Naupaktos and Arta in Greece, Damaskenos the Studite, recorded:

> When he [Mehmed] returned to the City he inquired about a patriarch. He ordered them to elect a patriarch and select whomever they wished from their own midst. He did this cunningly, like a fox, so that the Christians everywhere would hear about it and would return to the City. So they elected the philosopher, Lord George Scholarios, who had been an imperial judge; he was a most saintly individual and most pious; they elected him even though he had been reluctant and he was given the name Gennadios. The sovereign gave him with his own hand the crook and he received him in friendship and with grace. He also gave him the famous church of the Holy Apostles for his Patriarchate.

The Sultan expected Gennadios to sustain the loyalty of the Greeks to the Ottoman regime, and to raise money for the Ottoman State from his flock through taxation. In exchange the Patriarch had exclusive control of the Church with its own independent legal system based on the Justinian codes of the Byzantine Empire. Mehmed designated the Christians as a protected religious community, called a *millet*. They were allowed to live according to their own laws and to worship freely. The Sultan had positioned himself and his occupying government as protectors of the Orthodox Church. After a period of relative weakness under the Palaeologans, the Patriarchate's authority among the Greeks soared. Ironically, freed from any need to compromise with the West or submit to a pope, the independence of the Orthodox Church was entrenched.

Both religiously and secularly, the Patriarchate came to embody the preservation of the Greek identity and the Byzantine traditions. The Empire survived in the spiritual body of the Church. Greek citizens of the Ottoman Empire looked to the Patriarch as their religious and secular ruler. Many of the titles that had been used by the government prior to the occupation were preserved and transferred to clerics initially, and later to the lay community: the Grand Logothete, the Protekdikos and Grand Oikonomos, among them.

The resident Greeks of the Ottoman Empire were not the only contenders for the Byzantine legacy. After Constantinople, the Morea and Trebizond had fallen, Moscow considered itself to be the only independent Orthodox state, and its religious and secular leaders began manoeuvring to fill the vacancy that emerged from the loss of Constantinople. At the end of the tenth century, Prince Vladimir of Kiev converted to Christianity in the Byzantine Orthodox Church, but culturally the region looked more to the West than to the East. Only several centuries later did the autocracy of Byzantium appeal to the Russians, specifically to the princes of Moscow who were engaged in establishing a dynasty and a reputation as the champions against the invading Mongols. In 1326, the Metropolitan of Russia, appointed by the patriarch of Constantinople chose Moscow to be the official residence of the officeholder. The Orthodox Church allied itself to Moscow, reinforcing the primacy of the state. The Metropolitan even persuaded the ruling prince to commission a burial church for him and his successors.

Endorsement from the institutional Church gave the secular rulers legitimacy and a growing sense of importance. Religious scribes started to make comparisons between the princes of Moscow and the emperors Constantine the Great, Justinian and Manuel Comnenus. Naturally, this bid for primacy caused increasing friction with Constantinople, with complaints from the Patriarch to the Russians becoming more frequent:

> Once more with grief I have heard that your highness has said certain things about the Emperor in derogation... That is bad. The Emperor is not like local and provincial rulers and sovereigns. The Emperors convoked the ecumenical councils; by their own laws they sanctioned what the divine canons said about the correct dogmas and the ordering of the Christian life; they determined by their decrees the order of the episcopal sees and set up their boundaries. The church ordained the Emperor, anointed him, and consecrated him Emperor and Autocrat of all the Romans, that is, of all Christians. My most exalted and holy autocrat is by the grace of God the eternal and orthodox defender and avenger of the church. It is not possible for Christians to have a church and not to have an Emperor.

When Grand Duke Vassily dismissed and imprisoned Isidore after the Council of Ferrara-Florence, he positioned himself as the champion and defender of the true Greek faith. He replaced Isidore with the local Russian bishop Jonas, and a contemporary panegyric to Vassily compared him to Emperor Constantine the Great. The stage was set for the Russians to interpret the catastrophe in 1453 as divine punishment for the union with the Latin church. Some writers went even further and predicted that the Slavs would restore Constantinople to the Orthodox Church and Byzantines:

If all the predictions of the time of Constantine the Great, such as were made by Methodius of Patara and Leo the Sage, if all the predictions concerning this great city have come to pass, then the ultimate prophecy will come to pass also, for it is said: 'the Russian tribes will battle against the Ismaelites with the help of her erstwhile inhabitants, will conquer the city of the seven hills [Constantinople], and will reign there.'

It was a short step to conclude that Russia was the successor to the Byzantines, and that it was next in line for the *translatio imperium*. The Ottoman successes in Byzantium coincided with a growing national identity among Russians that nurtured a tripartite theory: the fall of the Byzantine Empire was not final; the imperial city of Constantinople would be freed by Russians; and that they were the successors to the Roman Empire. The princes of Moscow vied with Novgorod to be the centre of this new incarnation. In the 1450s, Dimitrij Gerasimov, the translator and companion of Archbishop Gennadi of Novgorod, wrote the story of the white mitre in a bid for primacy. In the tale, Novgorod's claim to succeed Constantinople as the centre of the Orthodox religion was based on the white mitre of faith that Constantine the Great allegedly gave to the pope. Somehow the mitre ended up in the care of the patriarch of Constantinople. The patriarch had a vision of the city's demise and sent the mitre to the archbishop of Novgorod for safe keeping. Its place of honour in the city cathedral symbolised Novgorod's role as the guardian of Christian Orthodoxy. This text was one of the earlier instances in which the term the 'third Rome' appeared to describe a Russian city.

Moscow, however, made a stronger claim through the marriage of Zoe Palaeolinga to Grand Prince Ivan III in 1472. The daughter of Despot Thomas, she converted to Roman Catholicism after her family fled from the Ottoman capture of the Morea to Rome. Bessarion and the popes had supported the last of the Palaeologan dynasty, and Sixtus IV negotiated a marriage for her to Ivan III, providing her dowry. The marriage was a bid to use the obligations of the dynastic bond to leverage practical support from Rus' for a crusade. The Pope expected Zoe to serve as an ambassador for the unification of the East and West Churches so that they could unite against the Turks. Accompanied by an enormous papal retinue led by a prelate carrying a Roman cross, Zoe arrived at her new home. Offended by the heretical display, the Metropolitan of Rus' refused to allow the papal representative to enter Moscow. Shortly after her arrival, Zoe repudiated Roman Catholicism, returning to the Orthodox practices in which she had been raised.

Despite being thwarted in his diplomatic designs, the Pope recognised Ivan III as heir to the Byzantine Empire by marriage, and the Venetian Senate followed suit in 1473. Ivan and Zoe set about cementing their position as the imperial heirs and that of Moscow as the new imperial centre. They commissioned the construction of the Kremlin in emulation of the sacred palace in Constantinople, and they retreated to it to live elevated and apart from their subjects following the ceremonial and court rituals of the Byzantine emperors. Ivan III adopted the title of *samoderzhets*, a transliteration of the Byzantine Greek *autokrator*, and appropriated the Palaeologan double-headed eagle as his emblem. Twenty years later, there was little surprise that Metropolitan Zosimus declared the prince of Moscow to be the 'sovereign and autocrat of all Russia, the new Tsar Constantine of the new city of Constantine, Moscow.'

Until the fourteenth century, Moscow had little significance in the region known as Rus. There was no united Russia yet; only several powerful princedoms centred on large cities: Kiev,

Novgorod, Vladimir, Tver, Ryazan and Rostov. The Grand Principality of Moscow had been founded as recently as 1238, but it had steadily grown in size and power by fostering a mutually beneficial relationship with the Mongol khans who controlled most of what is now western Russia. The grand princes ran a state that was particularly effective at raising taxes for the khans, and in exchange the Mongols favoured the principality over their neighbours. By 1453, after Constantinople fell, Moscow was simply one contender of many to become a replacement centre of Orthodoxy. One of the earliest references to continuity of the Roman lineage came from a monk called Foma, whose eulogy for the Grand Prince of Tver, Boris Aleksandrovič, described the city as the New Israel, referred to the deceased prince as an emperor, and compared him to Tiberius, Augustus, Justinian and Theodosius.

Several elements combined over the centuries since its foundation to give Moscow the edge it needed to prevail over the surrounding princedoms. The Metropolitan appointed by the Patriarch of Constantinople moved his residence from Vladimir to Moscow in 1322, a move that endorsed the principality's spiritual primacy. When Isidore arrived as the Metropolitan of Kiev and Rus' it would have been clear that the grand prince controlled a large area of land. This steady expansion over the years had strengthened the princedom to a point where it could challenge the Mongols on the battlefield. Achieving independence from the khans took about 100 years, but by the time that Constantinople fell, Moscow was on course to definitively defeat the khanate by the late fifteenth century. To the prestige that came with being the spiritual nucleus of the Russian Orthodox Church, Moscow added military success, paving its way to a position of centralised power. By claiming the identity of the Third Rome, Moscow lent authority to its pretensions of dominance. The grand prince, now titled tsar or emperor, was endowed with theocratic powers and had control over ecclesiastical affairs, justifying his colonisation of the surrounding territories. Internationally, he positioned Moscow as the protector of eastern Christians.

As the Third Rome, Moscow's supremacy could not be challenged by other Russians. God had chosen the Third Rome as the stage where His agenda would be implemented. With his wife Zoe's dynastic legacy behind him, Ivan III tripled the size of the Muscovite territory. Historians consider him to have been the founder of the Russian state. His successors would pursue a policy of *pax romana* – world peace under the rule of a universal empire. Ivan IV's coronation documents defined him as a ruler sent and appointed by God. As an absolute monarchy, modelled on the Byzantine political system, Moscow presented itself as a political as well as spiritual heir to Byzantium. The tsar saw himself as the emperor of the Christian world as he recreated the strong link between Church and State that had defined the Byzantine system. Ivan IV successfully campaigned to elevate the Metropolitan of Rus to a Patriarch, and the patriarchate of Moscow was established. In 1510, the monk Filofei wrote to Grand Prince Vassily III:

> I would like to say a few words about the existing Orthodox empire of our most illustrious, exalted ruler. He is the only emperor on all the earth over the Christians, the governor of the holy, divine throne of the holy, ecumenical, apostolic church which in place of the churches of Rome and Constantinople is in the city of Moscow, protected by God, in the holy and glorious Uspenskij Church of the most pure Mother of God. It alone shines over all the earth more radiantly than the sun. For know well, those who love Christ and those who love God, that all Christian empires will perish and give way to the one kingdom of our ruler, in accord with the books of

the prophet, which is the Russian empire. For two Romes have fallen, but the third stands, and there will never be a fourth.

These bids by the Ottoman and Moscow rulers to be the heir to the Roman Empire would not have been acceptable to Bessarion and Isidore, nor would they have been convincing to those who had struggled to save Byzantium. The Ottomans practised a religion that Christians considered heretical and inspired by the devil. The Muslims felt the same about Christianity. Every military conquest of a Byzantine territory witnessed atrocities targeting the religious institutions. It was not just about looting for revenge or for remuneration; it was about desecrating the churches and their relics. Ultimately, Mehmed II established an environment of tolerance and safety for the Byzantine Orthodox citizens in the Ottoman Empire, but they would never be equal to their Muslim peers. Fraternisation and cooperation to that extent required a level of religious tolerance that was unsustainable. A very high number of Christians converted to Islam under the Ottomans to access key posts in the government and military that were only available to Muslims. Mehmed also established the *devishirme* system, which required a tribute of young Christians from the conquered territories to be surrendered to the state so that they could be raised as Muslims. Accepting Mehmed II's rule and his occupation of Istanbul meant giving up on the idea of a crusade to restore Byzantine religious and secular power.

Similarly, to accept Moscow as the Third Rome was to surrender any possibility of a Greek revival in the former Byzantine Empire. It signalled the death knell for unification, that was so important to Bessarion and Isidore, between the East and West Churches. In the absence of a united front against the Ottomans, western Christendom was vulnerable to existential threats. These threats periodically came close to becoming a reality: in 1480 when the Turks took Otranto in Italy; in 1526 when Hungary submitted to the Ottomans after the Battle of Mohacs; in 1571 when the westerners narrowly defeated the Turkish bid to control the Mediterranean; and in 1683, when the dramatic siege and Battle of Vienna left Europeans fearing Muslim occupation in the heart of the continent. These pivotal moments underscored how the failure to unite against the Ottoman threat left Christendom on the defensive, perpetually teetering on the brink of collapse.

EPILOGUE

Did Isidore and Bessarion fail? There is no question that the Byzantine Empire collapsed, but debate revolves around identifying an absolute end. Was it in 1453 when Constantinople fell? Or in 1460 when the Morea was occupied by the Ottomans? Or in 1475 when Trebizond was lost? Or was it a gradual decline over centuries without any discernible moment of complete collapse? These are the discussions that feature across millions of words in thousands of books and articles. The wide-ranging opinions reveal a struggle to define the narrative despite the benefit of hindsight, raising the necessary question of whether Byzantium's demise was inevitable. It was far from a hopeless cause for Isidore, Bessarion and many other contemporaries (both Latin and Greek). Even the inaction of the West demonstrated a confidence, though misplaced, in the endurability of the Empire.

The history of the late years of the Empire grew from the accounts of the fall of Constantinople written by contemporaries. The agony of that event for those who witnessed it or recorded a first-hand account should not be underestimated. A need to explain why and how the trauma of 1453 could have happened motivated these writers, and they described the events through a lens of moral judgement that attributed misfortune to punishment for the sinful acts of their leaders. This tone of just deserts has been adopted by historians and reformulated into a narrative of inevitability.

Approaching the events of the fifteenth century more objectively than the Byzantine writers, historians have constructed a narrative of an inevitable demise driven by the weaknesses and challenges facing Byzantium. They point to the political instability and civil strife endured by generations of Palaeologan emperors. Yet, many of the civilisations that did not fall at this time were also experiencing these problems in the fifteenth century. Warring families in Rome, the epicentre of the western Christian world, drove the popes out from the Vatican. Internal conflict regularly forced Ottoman sultans to abdicate and battle to restore their positions. Other historians argue that imperial military prowess had declined, leaving the Byzantines to rely on expensive mercenaries of questionable loyalty. Like internal discord, this experience was common in the fifteenth century. In fact, the Greeks and the Ottomans were often engaged in a bidding war for the same mercenaries. It is a fallacy that the Byzantine forces were weak and inept; many challenges from the Turks were repelled throughout the territories. Previous sieges of Constantinople had failed, and even in 1453 Mehmed's own generals were advising a retreat.

Could the empire have been saved? In the first half of the fifteenth century was it necessarily apparent that Byzantium could not be preserved for future generations? During the lifetimes of Isidore and Bessarion there were several points when

Epilogue

the fortunes of the Byzantine Empire could have been reversed or mitigated. The first of these was the Council of Ferrara-Florence, at which Isidore and Bessarion worked tirelessly to bring about a union of Christendom to stand as one against the threat posed by the Ottomans. The story might have been very different had this union been a more equitable arrangement between the East and West Churches, and had its spirit been translated into action.

Despite this, there were several military opportunities for Christendom to reverse their losses and to contain the Turks. The campaign that was launched in the 1440s put the Turkish armies under considerable strain before the crusading armies met their unfortunate end at the Battle of Varna. A decade later, when Mehmed II besieged Constantinople, the outcome was far from certain. As Pope Nicholas's legate, Isidore had achieved the implementation of the Decree of Union, unlocking the papal intransigence to send military assistance to Constantinople. The sultan's commanders were pressuring him to retreat in the face of the resilience of the city and the losses incurred on the Ottoman side. They knew that western aid was on its way, and they were not convinced of their chances. Even as the crisis of 1453 unfolded, it was interpreted not as the end, but as a beginning – a wakeup call to the West.

The tragedy had a galvanising effect on Popes Calixtus III and Pius II. The former oversaw several successful campaigns that put pressure on the Turks in the Balkans, and the latter was on the cusp of physically leading a crusade to retake Constantinople. The untimely deaths of the successful commander John Hunyadi and the popes themselves thwarted these plans. Had a crusade been mustered and succeeded, the writings of men like Isidore, who focused their trauma on motivating western leaders to take action, might have carried more weight with future historians than those of contemporaries who used the theme of Constantinople's fall as a rhetorical tool of self-flagellation.

The many reasons that a successful military solution was never realised are well rehearsed by historians of the period, and conceptually they differ little from the reasons behind failures across time and geography. Ill fortune, combined with internal issues that took priority over the plight of the Byzantines, meant that the popes were never able to garner much more than lip service from western leaders to the cause of a crusade. Preoccupation with economic advantages from a weakened Byzantium, and the distraction caused by domestic conflict across the European continent, overshadowed the response of those princes who were not immediately threatened by the Turks.

By the time Bessarion passed away, there was little momentum for a crusade. And yet, while the territory of the empire was being steadily eroded, the efforts of men like the Cardinal to salvage a continuity and Byzantine legacy bore fruit. Eastern Orthodox Christianity flourished in the Slavic lands, with the religious leaders positioning Moscow as the centre of Orthodoxy and the 'Third Rome'. The monastic rule of St Basil, nurtured by Bessarion with papal endorsement, retained a healthy presence in southern Italy and flourished across many Orthodox countries. Today, Grottaferrata oversees the monasteries in southern Italy and Sicily and their practice of the Italo-Greco Rite that Bessarion revived. Byzantine icons and reliquaries maintained their stylistic and symbolic character, eagerly collected and venerated throughout Europe.

The Byzantine identity was preserved in the language and literature that exiled scholars brought with them to the western territories, and men like Bessarion and Isidore played a significant

Epilogue

role in supporting these intellectuals. They offered them a refuge and proactively collected the literature, legal codes, military treatises and religious philosophy that formed the cultural empire of Byzantium. The commitment and dedication of these Greek contemporaries to save the empire ensured that the religious, cultural and political legacies of the Byzantine Empire continued to shape European civilisation for many centuries after the physical territories were lost.

DRAMATIS PERSONAE

Emperor John VIII (1392–1448)
John VIII Palaeologus ruled Constantinople and its surrounding hinterland from 1425. His reign was defined by his struggle to defend the Byzantine Empire's interests and territories from Ottoman encroachment. In his efforts to secure support from the West, he believed, like Bessarion and Isidore, that the two Roman Catholic and Byzantine Orthodox Churches had to be united against the sultans. He agreed to lead the Greek delegation at the Council of Ferrara-Florence, and he invited both Bessarion and Isidore to attend. The two priests enjoyed the Emperor's favour and were highly placed in his court.

Emperor Constantine XI (1404–1453)
Constantine XI Palaeologus was John VIII's younger brother, and he succeeded him as Emperor of Constantinople after John died childless in 1448. Accounts of his career have been drawn from Byzantine chroniclers like George Sphrantzes. Constantine believed himself to be the true emperor of an

empire that stretched back to Constantine the Great, a legacy he never had a chance to develop in the short four years of his rule. He married twice to women from noble Italian families, but both his wives died shortly after marriage without producing an heir. Constantine was close to his brother John, who appointed him as regent for Constantinople while John was in western Europe on a campaign to rally support for the Byzantines against the Turks during the early years of his reign. During his absence, Constantine was forced to conclude a humiliating peace treaty with Sultan Murad who had been besieging Constantinople. John would leave Constantine in charge again in 1430 when he led the delegates to the Council of Ferrara-Florence.

Before becoming emperor, Constantine was a military commander and shared the Despotate of Morea in the Peloponnese with his brothers Theodore and Thomas. Constantine fought campaigns to consolidate their rule throughout the entire peninsula, and, by means of force and diplomacy, recovered territory that had been lost to the Byzantines in the aftermath of the Fourth Crusade of 1204. Constantine's first marriage was part of the negotiations; he married the niece of the Italian Carlo Tocco whose attempts to seize land in the Morea had been repelled by the Palaeologan brothers. In the aftermath of these successes, they restored the Hexamilion wall, a six-mile defensive structure that spanned the Isthmus of Corinth to protect the peninsula from Turkish naval attacks. It was not strong enough to withstand the Ottoman's advanced weaponry and succumbed to their long canons, siege engines and scaling ladders when Sultan Murad besieged the Morea. After five days of fierce fighting the Turks prevailed, and Despots Constantine and Thomas submitted to vassalage following the bloody massacre. In the mid-1440s Constantine led the Byzantine armies into Central Greece and Thessaly, reclaiming territory that had been lost to the Ottomans.

When Emperor John VIII passed away, Constantine inherited the throne. At the time, there was no universally accepted patriarch: Joseph II had died in Florence, and the newly appointed patriarch, Gregory Mammas, was perceived to be a stooge of the pope and therefore not recognised by the majority of Constantinopolitans. Constantine was crowned in a civil ceremony only in Mistra before he arrived in Constantinople to assume leadership over a city that was bitterly divided, with the anti-Unionist faction questioning the legitimacy of his accession. His short rule was marred by toxic internal court politics and the external threat of Sultan Mehmed II. Constantine refused the advice of his courtiers to flee when the Turks besieged Constantinople. He stayed and fought, losing his life in the battle for the city's walls. His body was never recovered, giving rise to legends around the Emperor's heroic death. Some people claimed that he was not actually slain but turned to stone to avoid having to see his city fall. They prophesied that the Marble Emperor would one day return to reclaim Constantinople.

Demetrius, Despot of the Morea (1407–1470)
Son of Emperor Manuel II and one of the brothers of John VIII and Constantine XI, Demetrius was a thorn in the side of his siblings. He was opposed to the union of the Churches, but John felt compelled to take him to the Council of Ferrara-Florence, fearing Demetrius would attempt to usurp the throne in his absence. When Constantine XI became emperor, he appointed Demetrius as a co-despot of the Morea with his younger brother Thomas. The friction between the two despots eventually enabled Mehmed to mount a successful invasion and conquer the Morea

in 1460. Demetrius was captured at Mystra but permitted by the Sultan to live in genteel retirement in Thrace and later in Adrianople where he became a monk after the death of his only child in 1469.

Thomas Palaeologus (1409–1465)
The youngest brother of Emperor John VIII, the despots Demetrius, Theodore and the last emperor, Constantine XI, Thomas was appointed as one of the despots of the Morea by John in 1428. Alongside Constantine, he actively attempted to resist Ottoman advances. Thomas sought western assistance against the Ottomans, representing the Palaeologan dynasty's final efforts to preserve their rule over Byzantium. Invited to settle in Rome after fleeing the Morea, he was the figurehead for the plans to take Constantinople back from the Sultan in the early 1460s.

Patriarch Joseph II (1360–1439)
Joseph II was Patriarch of Constantinople from 1416 to 1439. He was born in Bulgaria, and it is speculated that he was John Asen, an illegitimate son of the last tsar of Bulgaria. Like many well born children in Byzantium, he became a monk, joining the community on Mount Athos, a prestigious and important centre of power in the Orthodox Church. He rose through the church hierarchy and was appointed Metropolitan of Ephesus by Emperor Manuel II Palaeologus before becoming the Patriarch of Constantinople in 1416. Joseph held this position for over two decades and was very elderly when he led the Byzantine clerics to the Council of Ferrara-Florence in the company of Emperor Manuel's successor, John VIII. The journey was gruelling for even the healthiest, and the Patriarch's fragility and ill health took their toll on him. He was pro-Union but had been disappointed that

the Greeks had not persuaded the Latins to hold the council in Constantinople.

To his mind, the union would be easily achieved by a meeting with the pope in person to explain why the Orthodox Church was right and the Roman Catholic Church was wrong on all the issues that divided the two. Joseph believed that the Greeks would simply outline a position that would be obvious and convincing to the Latins. Burdened by such expectations, the Patriarch's experience in Ferrara and Florence must have been deeply disappointing and frustrating. The Pope did not treat him as an equal, and the Emperor clearly dominated the Byzantine contribution to the proceedings. Confined to his chambers due to ill health, the Patriarch was increasingly sidelined. He was not a scholar and seemed to find the extensive and in-depth philosophical and doctrinal discussions at the Council tedious. However, Italian writers lavished much praise on the Patriarch, commenting on his venerable appearance and gentle countenance. Joseph succumbed to illness before the declaration of the Decree of Union. On his deathbed he expressed reluctance to sign the document, but he allegedly left a written record of his acceptance of the decree before passing away. Anti-Unionists would cite this missing signature in their future claim that the Patriarch had not supported the union. In recognition, however, of Patriarch Joseph II's significance, his funeral was widely attended by notable Latins, and he was given a burial place inside S. Maria Novella, one of Florence's largest churches.

Pope Eugenius IV (1383–1447)

Pope Eugenius IV was born in Venice as Gabriele Condulmer and took the name Eugenius as pope. He came from a wealthy family of merchants and was educated in local churches. After inheriting a large fortune at a young age, he distributed his money to the poor and entered a monastery. Condulmer rose rapidly, becoming Bishop of Siena in 1407. The Sienese protested against the appointment, objecting to Condulmer's 'foreign' Venetian origins so he was elevated to a cardinal-priest and given the titular church of S. Clemente in Rome. Pope Martin V recognised Condulmer's skills and promoted him to cardinal-priest of the prestigious basilica of S. Maria in Trastevere. When Pope Martin died, the papal conclave elected Cardinal Condulmer and he became the 207th pope.

Rome became increasingly unstable in the first three years of Pope Eugenius' papacy, ravaged by civil warfare and hostile to a pope who used taxation as a tool to raise money for defence: the citizens were unable to leave the city and no outsiders were able to get in. There were food shortages, crime was rife and poverty was acute. The two rival clans, the Orsini and Colonna families, were fighting each other for dominance, a rivalry that had persisted for centuries and would periodically flare into outright war. The Colonna clan accused Pope Eugenius of favouring the Orsini, motivating them to provoke a rebellion of the citizens to oust the pope from his secular overlordship of the city. The crisis peaked when the pope found himself under siege and had to be smuggled out of Rome dressed in a monk's habit at the siesta hour. This plan nearly failed. His flight was discovered before the Pope had managed to get clear of Rome. Angry Romans chased his boat along the banks of the Tiber as Eugenius fled to a vessel in the Ostia harbour from where he was taken to Pisa and ultimately to Florence. He would not return to Rome for almost ten years.

Simultaneously Church leaders, known as Conciliarists, were challenging the authority of the papal institution. With the backing of the German princes, they convened the Council of Basel to discuss ways to reduce the power of the papacy. Basel was the latest stage of a power struggle that had begun thirty years earlier. By the middle of the fifteenth century, cardinals depended on papal acquiescence for any power that they wielded, and their influence over the direction of the papacy was negligible. The conciliar movement was a thorn in the side of the Pope so Eugenius tried to move the Council from Basel to Italy in the hope that an Italian location would counter the influence of the Germans. His efforts triggered a crisis, and a significant faction de-selected him as pope. Felix V was appointed in his place, and Eugenius was forced to spend the next few years building up a support network of international secular allies and loyal cardinals. This culminated in his triumphant return to Rome in September 1443, effectively eliminating Felix V as a credible threat to Eugenius' position.

Pope Nicholas V (1397–1455)

Pope Nicholas V was born Tommaso Parentucelli in the Ligurian town of Sarzana. His family was not wealthy; his father was a physician whose death forced Tommaso to pause his studies at the University of Bologna and find work as a tutor. He was hired by the Florentine noble families, the Strozzi and the Albizzi. Eventually he was able to return to Bologna to complete a degree in theology. Tommaso entered into service for the bishop of Bologna and stayed with him for more than twenty years. It was during this appointment that he started to collect books and to forge a reputation as a humanist scholar. At the Council of Ferrara-Florence Pope Eugenius noticed Tommaso, and made plans for him to become the bishop of Bologna. Unrest in the city thwarted this agenda, and the Pope sent Tommaso on a round of diplomatic missions throughout Italy and Germany. These were successful, and he was rewarded with a cardinal's hat.

By the time that Eugenius died, Tommaso had established a strong reputation in the papal court and beyond, making him a viable candidate as the Conclave gathered to elect a new pope. On 6 March 1447, he was duly elected and took the name of Nicholas V. Traditionally, he is deemed to have been the first 'Renaissance' pope on account of his extensive literary and artistic patronage. Nicholas committed much energy and money to revitalising the urban centre of Rome, commissioning major architectural and art projects including extensive road and aqueduct repairs, rebuilding of the city's fortifications and a massive renovation project for the Vatican Palace. He supported many humanist scholars and amassed an enormous library numbering some 5,000 volumes.

The conciliar struggles that had blighted Eugenius's pontificate were superficially laid to rest with the Concordat of Vienna in 1448 whereby the papal rights were recognised. He shrewdly capitalised on this *zeitgeist* of renewed papal authority by hosting an extravagant Golden Jubilee in 1450. Not only did this give the Pope the opportunity for an international display of his role as undisputed head of the Church, it was also a major fundraising event. Hordes of Christians descended on Rome to purchase the plenary indulgence that Pope Nicholas offered for those who made the pilgrimage in this special year. At an extra cost, the wealthy who were unable or unwilling to make the long journey to the city could still buy the plenary indulgence. The money that poured into the Vatican in the years around the Golden Jubilee, combined with the economic reforms initiated by the financially astute Pope, meant that Nicholas was the only pope in the fifteenth century who managed to balance the books.

Nicholas's papacy, nonetheless, suffered some major challenges including ongoing unrest in the city of Bologna and a plot in

Rome, where attempts were made to establish a republic. Amidst such challenges, the Pope focused almost exclusively on his efforts to establish the primacy of the Apostolic See in secular governments, by military force where necessary. These distractions prevented him from grasping the severity of the threat facing the Byzantines in 1453, and the fall of Constantinople marred his reputation and legacy.

Pope Calixtus III (1378–1458)

Alfonso de Borgia, later Pope Calixtus III, was born to Juan Domingo de Borgia y Doncel and Francina Llançol in the Valencia municipality of Canals. At the University of Lleida he studied logic, arts and grammar, receiving degrees in canon and civil law. A story circulated later in his life that as a young man he met the famous Dominican Vincente Ferrer at one of his lectures, and that Ferrer had predicted he would be pope one day. As Calixtus III, Alfonso canonised Ferrer, an act that seemed to give substance to the anecdote. He began his career, however, as an administrator, and was appointed to be King Alfonso V of Aragon's confidential royal secretary. Alfonso de Borgia was instrumental in the negotiations to improve the relations between the Aragonese kingdom and the current pope, Martin V. For these services the king rewarded him with the profitable bishopric of the affluent See of Valencia. Impressed by his administrative skills, Eugenius IV conferred a cardinalate on the bishop.

Nicholas V's death provoked an intractable conflict in the 1455 conclave to elect a replacement. The warring clans in Rome, the Orsini and Colonna, were championing candidates who would favour each family over the other, and the sixteen electors who attended the conclave were evenly divided between the two sides. As per tradition, the electors were incarcerated in the Vatican Palace in a common space with no partitions for privacy and only one separate room for the lavatory. There was no natural light source, and their diet was progressively restricted after three days and then again after five days. Three sets of guards made up of ambassadors, Roman citizens and prelates ensured that no outside communication was permitted, and that no one could exit or enter. The guards examined the food that was served to make sure that no messages were smuggled in or out. Cardinals were allowed to bring one attendant each, and these men (known as conclavists) would act as confidants and intermediaries between the electors as they negotiated deals with each other in clandestine meetings before the daily vote. Under such circumstances, illness spread and tempers flared.

In 1455, realising that the tussles between the Roman noble families had brought the conclave to an impasse, the cardinals settled on a compromise by choosing the elderly Alfonso de Borgia as the next pope. As a Spaniard and Catalan, not only was he a neutral candidate, but his advanced age of 77 years reassured the electors that he would not live for much longer, making him an ideal caretaker pope. Alfonso de Borgia took the name of Calixtus III, and in his role pursued an agenda to raise a crusade against the Turks. As anticipated, his papacy was short lived – he died after three years. Although Calixtus had a reputation of piety in comparison to his more worldly predecessor, Nicholas V, he was generally perceived by contemporaries to be a weak and ineffective pope. He is best remembered for his vice of nepotism; he appointed two of his nephews as cardinals and he gave a third the governorship of the Castel Sant'Angelo in Rome.

Pope Pius II (1405–1461)
Born in Corsignano near Siena, Aeneas Silvius Piccolomini was the oldest of eighteen children from a noble but relatively

impoverished family. After studying at the University of Siena, Piccolomini briefly returned home to help his father manage their estate before leaving for Florence, where he continued his studies with the humanists. Eventually, he took a degree in law and began his secretarial career in the service of Bishop Capranica, whom he accompanied to the Council of Basel. Here Piccomolini forged his position as a conciliarist in opposition to Pope Eugenius IV. His oratorical and administrative skills made him an attractive candidate for bishops and cardinals who needed support in their diplomatic missions, and Piccolomini accompanied embassies to Arras in France and to Scotland. He was briefly a secretary to the antipope Felix V but astutely realised that he was backing the wrong horse and looked for a position that would be more beneficial to his career. After Holy Roman Emperor Frederick III crowned Piccolomini as an imperial poet, the Italian found a role for himself in the Emperor's court. This proved to be a long-lasting relationship, and he served Frederick III for many years as an imperial diplomat.

Piccolomini was notorious for his dissolute lifestyle, fathering at least two illegitimate children. It seems, however, that he reached a watershed moment in 1445 when he returned to Rome, becoming reconciled with Pope Eugenius and abandoning the more immoral aspects of his life. He was ordained shortly afterwards, and the newly elected Pope Nicholas V offered Piccolomini the bishopric of Trieste and later that of Siena.

When Calixtus III was elected, he raised Piccolomini to the rank of cardinal, and he became Calixtus's successor. He took the name of Pius II and wrote prolifically, leaving an extensive set of memoirs that have provided historians with a treasure trove of source material. During his papacy, he championed the cause of a crusade and even fantasised about converting Sultan Mehmed to Christianity. His untimely death on the shores of Ancona, where he was about to set off at the head of a crusade, ended the hope of a military response to the Turkish advance in Isidore and Bessarion's lifetimes.

Pope Paul II (1417–1471)

Pietro Barbo was born in Venice to Niccolo Barbo and Polixena Condulmer, the sister of Pope Eugenius IV. He was highly educated and trained for a career as a Venetian merchant. When his uncle became pope, however, Barbo entered the Church so that he could benefit from generous papal patronage. During Eugenius's papacy he served as the archdeacon of Bologna, the bishop of Cervia and then Vicenza, a cardinal-deacon and the archpriest of the Vatican Basilica. Ultimately Barbo was appointed to the cardinalate of S. Marco, Venice, and his influence in Rome continued to grow under the popes Nicholas V and Calixtus III.

In 1464 he succeeded Pius II and was elected as Pope Paul II. By this stage Isidore was dead and Bessarion ageing. The Pope attempted to forge an alliance with the Persians to reduce the power of the Turks, but little came of his diplomatic efforts. He reformed Rome's municipal statutes, organised relief for the poor, and bestowed pensions on some cardinals. The College of Cardinals, however, was increasingly alienated by Paul II as he took various measures to consolidate papal power at the expense of ecclesiastical officials.

He was known to have a generous nature, but his vanity was much mocked by contemporaries and later critics. It was said he wanted to take the name of Formosus II (the handsome) after his election, and his advisors struggled to persuade him not to do this. On other matters Paul II got his way: he commissioned his own papal tiara encrusted with precious stones, and he built the Palazzo di Venezia, where he lived in Rome even as pope, filling it with his extensive collection of antique artefacts. After his death the papal treasury was found to contain 800 gemstones, 54 silver shells filled with pearls, and a giant diamond worth 7,000 ducats. In addition, his papacy was marked by extravagant pageantry that took the form of carnivals, games and banquets.

Pope Paul was learned and engaged with the humanist movement of the times. He issued legislation to protect universities, and he oversaw the introduction of the printing press into the papal states. However, he clashed with the Roman Academy, which he suppressed following accusations that its members were promoting paganism and immorality. After a brief papacy, Paul II died prematurely in 1471.

Pope Sixtus IV (1414–1484)

Francesco della Rovere came from a wealthy northern Italian merchant family, and he was brought up in Celle Ligure near the Ligurian port of Savona. He entered the Franciscan Order from an early age and studied philosophy and theology at the University of Pavia. It became clear that he was a gifted scholar, and he earned himself a reputation as a distinguished orator and theologian, lecturing at many universities throughout Italy. Francesco della Rovere's name was so well known among humanists that Bessarion sought him out when he came to the Council of Ferrara-Florence. By the time he was in his fifties, he had been elected Minister General of the Franciscan Order, and Paul II appointed him to a cardinalate with the titular church of San Pietro in Vincoli. Admired for his piety, Della Rovere was elected pope by the conclave that assembled after the death of Paul II.

He adopted the name of Sixtus, and during his papacy he was a generous and inspired patron of the arts and scholarship. As pope, he re-founded and expanded the Vatican Library, and demonstrated an unusual interest in the sciences when he issued a papal bull allowing bishops to offer the bodies of executed criminals and unidentified corpses for dissection to physicians and artists.

Sixtus IV initiated a programme of urbanisation that continued the work Nicholas V had started. He restored Rome's aqueducts, repaired around thirty dilapidated churches, commissioned a major new road as well as another bridge over the River Tiber. His plans included the widening of existing streets, the clearing of passageways to facilitate traffic flow, and the first campaign of street paving since Roman times.

The Pope's foreign and domestic relationships were less effective than those he forged with scholars and artists. After promising to launch a crusade, he failed to make anything happen, and his attempts to reinvigorate the union of the East and West churches came to nothing. Sixtus IV claimed the dubious achievement of establishing the Spanish Inquisition in the kingdom of Castile in 1478, but this was not his idea. Threatened with the withholding of military support for Sicily by King Ferdinand of Aragon, who used the campaign of papal persecution to weaken his enemies in Castile, Sixtus was forced to declare an Inquisition.

The papacy was blighted by various scandals, including conspiracy to murder. In addition, his overt and unrepentant nepotism marred his reputation. His treatment of his nephew, Pietro Riario was typical. Promoted to Cardinal, bishop of Florence, Patriarch of Constantinople, and showered with no fewer than forty-five additional benefices, Riario became one of Rome's wealthiest and most influential men.

In August 1484, Pope Sixtus IV fell ill and within a few days passed away. He had made poor political alliances, exhausted the papal coffers and failed to launch a promised crusade. Bessarion and Isidore had died without witnessing the failures of this papacy.

Sultan Murad II (1404–1451)

Murad II was the eldest of five brothers and five sisters, and he inherited the sultanate after his father Mehmed I died in 1421. He was groomed for rulership from a very young age, assuming the governorship of the provinces of Amasya and north-central Anatolia when he was only twelve years old. Murad reigned twice; his first sultanate ended when he abdicated the throne in favour of his twelve-year-old son, named Mehmed after his grandfather. The Janissaries, the elite military caste, disapproved of his decision, and rose up against Mehmed to demand the return of Murad. This second period of rule lasted until the Sultan's death in 1451.

He faced many challengers to his position, including his uncle and a younger brother, who had the support of the Byzantine emperor. During his reign he dealt with a power struggle over the kingdom of Hungary, which the Ottomans coveted in a bid for the expansion of their empire further west. To complicate the matter further, Pope Eugenius IV was committed to a crusade to push the Turks back from the Byzantine territories. After suppressing these threats, he successfully consolidated Turkish power in the Balkans and forced the Byzantines to pay tribute. Murad II led the Ottoman army to victory against the Christian armies in the Battle of Varna, ending Pope Eugenius's aspirations to drive the Ottomans out.

Despite the turbulence that he faced, the Sultan preferred to negotiate peace treaties rather than to wage war. When he was able to contain the military threats, he invested time and money into developing key Ottoman cities, especially the capital, Edirne, through an extensive programme of urbanisation. He commissioned the construction of bridges, mosques and palaces. After conquering the Greek city of Thessaloniki, Murad began a campaign to rebuild the walls that had been damaged in the battle. He was also a committed patron of Turkish arts and literature.

Murad II was reputed to be generous and kind to his subjects. His legacy was the consolidation of the empire's territories and the reestablishment of the centralised government that his grandfather and father, Bayezid I and Mehmed I, had struggled to sustain.

Sultan Mehmed II (1432–1481)

Mehmed II was born on 30 March 1423 in the Ottoman capital city, Edirne. His father was Sultan Murad II and his mother was a slave called Huma Hatun. As a child, Mehmed was sent to govern the province of Amasya, in the tradition of training future sultans. He was accompanied by tutors who embedded strong Muslim beliefs and planted the seed that the ultimate fulfilment of his Islamic duty would be to overthrow the Byzantine Empire. After his father abdicated in 1444, the twelve-year-old Mehmed experienced a short-lived reign as sultan – his father returned to the throne to deal with the military threats facing the empire at the time.

After Murad I died in 1451, Mehmed's agenda to conquer Constantinople defined the early period of his thirty-year rule. He assumed the title of Caesar of Rome, symbolising the Turkish conquest of the Eastern Roman Empire, and he launched a campaign to make the city his imperial capital. This involved repairing the damaged walls, constructing a citadel, a large hospital, barracks for the janissaries and a new palace. Mehmed deported residents from the territories he vanquished and forcibly relocated them to Constantinople so that he could repopulate the city that he now called Istanbul. He incentivised commerce and heralded an era of religious tolerance, re-establishing the Greek Orthodox Patriarchate, and appointing a Jewish grand rabbi and an Armenian apostolic patriarch. Under Mehmed II the seeds were sown for Istanbul to become the largest city in Europe within a mere fifty years.

His success was followed by military campaigns that seized a series of Greek cities, the western coastal towns of the Black Sea, Serbia, Bosnia, Trebizond, Wallachia and Albania. In 1480, his Ottoman armies even invaded Italy, occupying Otranto and sending Rome into a panic that it would be next. A year later Mehmed died, and the ensuing internal quarrels over the successor weakened the Ottoman sultanate so that the army was forced to withdraw from Otranto after King Ferdinand I of Naples prosecuted a successful siege.

Mehmed was celebrated, during and after his lifetime, as a great military commander and scholar. Reputed to speak seven languages fluently, he filled his library with books in Greek, Persian and Latin. Alongside establishing a university and building magnificent mosques, he patronised Italian artists, humanists, Greek scholars and Muslim scientists at his court.

Mark Eugenicus (1392–1444)

A Greek Orthodox bishop and theologian who strongly opposed the union with the Roman Catholic Church, Mark Eugenicus was born in Constantinople and studied with leading academics in the city before being elected Metropolitan of Ephesus. He was appointed by Emperor John VIII to represent Antioch at the Council of Ferrara-Florence, but was not persuaded by the debates, particularly on the issue of the *Filioque*. He refused to attend many of the sessions and withheld his signature from the Decree of Union in 1439. Back in Constantinople, he began a successful campaign against the union, and was arrested on the island of Lemnos where he was imprisoned for two years.

Revered as a defender of Orthodoxy, he continued to mobilise resistance to the union after his release and persuaded George Scholarios to continue his work on his death bed.

George Scholarios (c. 1400–c. 1473) (Gennadios II)

Scholarios was appointed as a theological advisor by John VIII and, initially, supported the union: he gave four speeches at the Council of Ferrara-Florence in favour of conciliation. He collaborated with Bessarion to draft arguments on doctrinal disputes between the two Churches that would be vague enough to facilitate agreement on both sides. However, as time passed, he became disillusioned with the Council, and Mark Eugenicus harnessed his ambivalence on his return to Constantinople, ahead of the Emperor and Bessarion. The growing local hostility to the Decree of Union combined with Mark's convictions, led Scholarios to take up the cause and become a staunch anti-unionist and campaigner for the theological and cultural independence of the eastern Orthodox Church. He advocated the survival of Orthodoxy under Ottoman governance, securing his position as a key figure in post-Byzantine religious history when Sultan Mehmed II appointed him as the Patriarch of the Orthodox Church in Istanbul after Constantinople fell.

John Hunyadi (1407–1456)

John Hunyadi was a Hungarian nobleman who rose to prominence in the army and government, becoming regent of the kingdom during the minority of Ladislaus V. He honed his military prowess defending the southern border of Hungary against Ottoman incursions, and his reputation earned him the nickname of the 'Turk-Buster'. His successful campaigns were the first led by Europeans to defeat the large Turkish armies that became the norm under Mehmed II. Hunyadi amassed enormous wealth from land acquisition and he sustained his influence at the court and in domestic politics up until his death.

Grand Prince Vassily (r. 1425–1462)

Vassily II became Grand Duke of Moscow at the age of 10 years. His mother acted as regent during his minority, and several decades of turmoil ensued with rival internal claimants and the menace of the Tatars on the borders Muscovy. Vassily was forced to flee Moscow in 1439 after the Tatar siege, and his cousin, Dmitry Shemyaka was appointed to govern in his place. Dmitry recalled Vassily to Moscow to appease the former duke's supporters, but had him blinded to prevent any challenge. The infirmity did not stop Vassily and his followers from mounting a successful coup to regain the throne. From 1450 until his death in 1462, Vassily worked tirelessly to expand the size of this territory, declaring himself sovereign of all Rus' and positioning himself and his kingdom as the defenders of the Orthodox Church in the aftermath of Constantinople's demise.

Appendix

A BRIEF SURVEY OF THE BYZANTINE EMPIRE

Christianity and the Roman Empire in the Fourth Century
Constantine the Great's conversion to Christianity and his adoption of it as the formal imperial religion put the Roman Empire on a lengthy but ultimately inevitable path to universal conversion. Although Christianity was by no means an exclusive religion under Constantine, the Emperor positioned himself as head of the Church, setting an important precedent of cooperation between Church and State that would be both a benefit and a burden for the rulers throughout the life of the Empire that we describe as Byzantine. Orthodox Christianity developed in a very distinct way in the east, compared to its evolution in the west where it became Roman Catholicism. Imperial and church powers were inextricably entwined in Byzantium, and conflict between the two institutions was as frequent as mutual endorsement. Eventually, the secular and religious spheres fused into a single entity, with the emperor and patriarch essentially co-ruling the Empire.

The Collapse of the Empire in the West: Fifth Century

During the fifth century, the Roman Empire collapsed in the West under the pressure from the increasingly powerful tribes such as the Goths, Visigoths, Alarics, Lombards and others. The papacy was threatened, and the Church sought allies from among the warring groups to preserve their power and control of western Christendom. Ultimately, the plight of the western Church would have a major impact on the development of the split between Roman Catholic and Orthodox. By the end of the 400s, the demise of the West threatened to spread to the East. Byzantium faced pressures ranging from mass migratory movements of hostile tribes to extreme poverty, frontier pressures and internal conflict. Its internal structures were unable to withstand the cumulative effect of these, and the eastern Empire descended into a series of revolts and civil wars that erupted periodically, causing great damage to the state, until the accession of Emperor Justinian in 527.

Emperor Justinian, the Sixth-Century Recovery and the Spread of Christianity

When Emperor Justinian came to the throne, the western territories of the Roman Empire had been overrun by barbarians in the west. In his determination to restore a single frontier that stretched from the west to the east, he directed his two renowned generals, Belisarius and, later, Narses to reconquer the lost lands. They fought the Vandals in Africa; the Ostrogoths in Italy; and the Visigoths in Spain. While virtually all the military might of the Empire was directed against the threats in the west, Justinian tried to keep Persians at bay in the east with treaties and expensive tribute payments. The Emperor's military campaigns, combined with the cost of peace in the east and extravagant building projects in Constantinople, depleted the imperial treasury and put huge strain on the imperial subjects.

Despite the financial constraints, Justinian successfully codified Roman law and implemented it throughout Byzantium. His reforms were a major contribution to the Empire's unity, synthesising Greek customs and Christianity to facilitate an agenda to impose the monotheistic religion throughout the Empire.

Seventh-Century Crises
In the hands of Justinian's successors, the Empire's expanded western frontiers contracted again. They lost Italy to the Lombards in 568; Spain was back in the hands of the Visigoths by 584; and the situation in the east became acute as the Persians and Byzantines went to war over Armenia. In the Balkans, the Avar and Slav raids increased in both frequency and ferocity putting these territories at risk. Strained on every frontier, the court collapsed internally after the military leader General Phocas staged a coup and purged the aristocracy in Constantinople. He presided over a reign of terror until 610 when the ruler of Carthage, Heraclius, led a successful campaign to depose Phocas. As emperor, Heraclius (610–641) led the Byzantine armies in a struggle for existence. He founded the Heraclian dynasty, during which ultimately the Persians and Avars were defeated, but much territory was lost to the Arabs. The Avars, a powerful tribe that controlled the Slavs in the Balkans, began to permanently occupy Byzantine territory in and around Thessalonica. Macedonia, Thrace, Dalmatia and the Greek islands. Around the same time, in 613, the Persians defeated the imperial army at Antioch and went on to take Damascus and to occupy Armenia, Jerusalem and almost the entire Near East.

The Rise of Arab Islam in the Seventh and Eighth Centuries
With all the focus on the Persians, little attention was paid to the Prophet Mohammed, who was laying the foundations in Medina

for an Islamic-Arab state. He began to expand into Byzantine and Persian territory by sending out raiding parties into regions scattered throughout Asia Minor. Simultaneously, the Heraclian rulers oversaw the evolution of Byzantium into a more compact collection of central lands, and they presided over a period of reform and restructure from which the Empire emerged stronger. The military was reorganised in a move away from mercenaries, whom the impoverished state could no longer afford, to compulsory military service imposed on small landowners. A new peasant class evolved that cultivated the land and generated some of the tax revenue that had been lost when the Empire had contracted. Emperor Heraclius and his descendants also initiated a period of Hellenization, and as a result Greek became the official language of the Empire.

By the middle of the same century, the Arabs developed maritime capability, giving them access to Cyprus, Rhodes and even Constantinople. In 674 they attempted to besiege the city, but the superior Byzantine weaponry and more seasoned military resulted in a major defeat and a thirty-year peace treaty. The respite was short-lived as a new threat emerged in the early eighth century with the rise of the Bulgar Kingdom.

Taking advantage of the new pressure on Byzantium with the rise of the Bulgars, the Arabs resumed hostilities, and once again besieged Constantinople. It was the Emperor Leo III (c.685–741) who saw off the Bulgars and Arabs in a series of military campaigns that succeeded in pushing back these challengers.

The Iconoclast Movement: The First Iconoclasm (c.726-787) and the Second Iconoclasm (c.814-842)

Although the immediate threats were contained, there is no question that the quality of life for the Empire's citizens was diminished. Constantinople had been under threat multiple times in a generation, and the imperial cities throughout the Empire were impoverished. Leo and the leading clergy came to the conclusion that the Byzantines had angered God and were being punished. They identified the communal sin as that of idolatry, and initiated the Iconoclast movement, with an edict to destroy all religious images. Byzantine society was deeply divided over the issue, and it deepened the ever-widening gulf between the Roman Catholic and Orthodox Churches.

The Eighth-Century Wars with Bulgaria
Leo III's son, Constantine V (718–775) faced a challenger for the throne at his accession. As a stellar military leader, like his father, he decisively overthrew the usurper. Leo had left a relatively stable situation on the eastern frontier, but the Bulgarians resumed hostilities in response to a provocative frontier wall that Constantine constructed. A series of wars broke out, led by the Bulgarian Khan, who was finally defeated by Constantine in 763 at Anchialus, on the shores of the Black Sea in Thrace. The Emperor's success against the Arabs and Bulgarians came at the expense of the Byzantine foothold in the Italian peninsula. The pope had traditionally relied on Byzantine support here to keep his enemy, the Lombards, from incursions into Italy. When Byzantine Ravenna finally fell to the Lombards in 751, the papacy turned to the increasingly powerful Frankish kingdom for protection. Divided spiritually from the eastern empire by the Iconoclast movement that Rome bitterly opposed, the papacy preferred to forge alliances with the emerging western powers rather than with Byzantium.

As Rome turned away from the East, the Byzantines lost much of their territory in the Mediterranean, further severing their ties in the west. Only Greece, its islands, southern Italy and Sicily remained under the jurisdiction of the Patriarch of

Constantinople, and in the early decades of the ninth century the Arab Caliphate captured Sicily and Crete, leaving Byzantium with a much-reduced presence in the west.

Emperor Nicephorus and Bulgaria in the Ninth Century

Shortly after Charlemagne was crowned, a more effective emperor came to the Byzantine throne, Nicephorus (802–811). His taxation and administrative reforms increased the revenue for the imperial treasury. He also addressed recruitment issues in the army, substantially increasing the pool of citizens eligible for compulsory military service.

Nicephorus established the conditions to reconsolidate Byzantine control in the Balkans, and by the middle of the ninth century Macedonia, Thrace, Cephalonia and the Ionian islands, Thessalonica and Dalmatia were all returned to Byzantine rule after a period of occupation by the Slavs. The Emperor's reforms were soon put to the test after he acceded to the throne when a new Bulgar ruler appeared on the scene. Krum was a battle-hardened chieftain who relished the challenge posed by the Byzantine fortifications that kept the Bulgarian kingdom from encroaching on imperial territory. Nicephorus intervened forcefully after Krum attacked the fortress of Sardica in 809, and he followed up with an offensive campaign against the aggressors. His intention was to destroy the kingdom, and he rejected Krum's request for a peace treaty after his army ravaged the Bulgar capital and incinerated the ruler's palace. Nicephorus pursued the fleeing Bulgars into the mountains where his army was unexpectedly ambushed, surrounded and massacred. Nicephorus was slain – the first Byzantine emperor to lose his life in battle for over five hundred years. The catastrophe provoked a crisis in Constantinople, and several decades of internal conflict and civil war ensued.

A new emperor, Theophilus (c.812–842), came to the throne in 829 and began a programme of rebuilding Constantinople and its defensive structures. He led armies to success on the eastern frontier and reorganised the Byzantine provinces on the Black Sea coast. However, yet another new enemy emerged – this time in the north, the Rhos, Slavs of Scandinavian origin. They threatened to take the kingdom of Bulgaria, which was an important buffer zone for the Byzantines. It was Theophilus's son, Emperor Michael III (840–867), who led an army into Bulgaria and forced its ruler to be baptised, thus converting its citizens into subjects of the Patriarchate of Constantinople.

Reform and Conquest: The Macedonian Dynasty in the Tenth Century

The losses incurred to the Byzantine territories over the centuries reduced the state's revenue from taxation, and the Empire could no longer afford to pay mercenaries. To survive the external challenges, the court cultivated a native army and this, combined with a growing landed aristocracy in the new agricultural centres of Constantinople's hinterlands, gave rise to a class of provincial militarised landowners. This group made a bid for power under the leadership of Basil the Macedonian (811–886), and in 867 he staged a coup, establishing the Macedonian dynasty which lasted nearly two centuries.

These centuries were a period in which Byzantium reasserted its military and political powers as it gradually recovered some of its former territories in Italy and Dalmatia. A programme to build fortifications and to establish new centres of administration made these conquests permanent. However, it was not all plain sailing. The Bulgarians became problematic again in the first two decades of the tenth century under the charismatic leadership of Symeon. Raids and external threats to Constantinople, combined with a series of controversies over the imperial succession, destabilised the empire. The Bulgarian problem was ultimately solved by diplomacy. After Symeon (c.864–927) unexpectedly died, his successor Peter I (r.927–969) was persuaded to marry a Byzantine princess, rendering Bulgaria a benign protectorate of Byzantium.

The Macedonian emperors continued their military campaigns, expanding the empire in the east to stretch from Armenia to Mesopotamia. In the early 960s, they reconquered Crete, which ended the frequent Arab raids in the Aegean. By 1025 they had ejected the Arabs from Italy, and they ruled from the Straits of Messina to the Tigris and from the Danube to Syria.

The last effective Macedonian emperor was Basil II (958–1025) who died without an heir in December 1025. He left the Empire with settled borders and an unprecedented state of peace. Sadly, his successors failed to capitalise on the breathing space and squandered the opportunity to strengthen the Byzantine state. Under their watch the feudal aristocracy's thirst for power went unchecked, and the imperial court became a tool for their personal gain. A period of conflict, manifested in complex court intrigue between the military and landed aristocracy, paralysed the state. The civil nobility prevailed at the expense of the Empire's military strength. Feudal landowners had unfettered capacity to increase the size of their estates and to pressure the central government for privileges in the form of tax exemption. Any taxes imposed on the peasants were collected by the landowners, bypassing the imperial treasury.

The inevitable drop in revenue provoked an economic crisis that was compounded by a significant debasement in the coinage. One of the consequences of these changes to the economic and social structure of the Empire was the weakening of the army. The numbers of native troops declined dramatically and, once again, the state had to rely on mercenaries it could ill afford. Inevitably, the period of calm that had been established under Basil II came to an end as new enemies emerged. In the east, the Seljuk Turks replaced the threat of the contained Arabs; in the north, the tribes of the Steppes became an increasingly severe threat to Byzantium; and the Normans applied pressure from the west.

The Rise of the Comnenian Dynasty in the Eleventh Century
The eleventh century was not a positive period for Byzantium. It was characterised by internal dynastic quarrels and military revolts. The Arabs recaptured parts of Sicily; the Normans encroached on their territory in southern Italy; and the Seljuk Turks grew increasingly powerful. Assailed by these internal and external challenges, the Macedonian hold on Byzantine power was slipping. In 1057, a highly placed commander Isaac Comnenus (c.1007–1059), whose father had served Emperor Basil II, instigated a military revolt in Asia Minor. He ousted the current emperor, Michael VI (r.1056-1057), triggering a civil war in Constantinople. Once again, the external enemies of the Byzantines took advantage of their domestic weakness. The Seljuks expanded their territory; the Bulgarians revolted; and the Norman nobleman Robert Guiscard seized Bari, the last Byzantine possession in Italy.

As emperor, Isaac led military expeditions in vigorous defence of the imperial territories, however, after a sudden illness he abdicated and retired to a monastery. His nephew Alexios I (c.1057–1118) succeeded him and over the next century, Byzantium was ruled by the Comnenian dynasty. The imperial family consolidated and stabilised their powerbase.

In the meantime, the Seljuk Turks had seized control of most of Asia Minor, and they systematically converted their citizens to Islam. In 1091 they forged an alliance with the Pechenegs, who came from the plains of Ukraine and Wallachia, to besiege Constantinople. Emperor Alexios dealt with the crisis by agreeing a treaty with the Turks, giving respite to him and an Empire that faced threats on all sides.

Internal Collapse in the Twelfth Century

The rise of the Muslim states inspired a reaction from beyond the eastern Christian lands, and the era of the Crusades began. Relations between the Crusaders and the Byzantines were strained, and the emperors who ruled during these campaigns were uneasy to have large numbers of ill-disciplined, armed crusaders gathering in Constantinople as they awaited transport to the Holy Land. Tension arose between the foreign crusaders and the locals, who were suspicious of armed foreigners who practised, in their minds, a heretical form of Christianity. The war aims of both groups were not aligned. The Byzantines wanted help to weaken the Turks and to restore their political control of the region. The crusaders were driven by religious fervour to wrest the Holy Land from the occupation of the Muslims. As the Turks were defeated, disputes arose over the ownership of the recaptured territories. The westerners were reluctant to return the recovered lands to the Byzantines, treating the local population with contempt as they plundered their land.

The latter half of the twelfth century was marked by the corruption practised by the Byzantine feudal aristocracy that played an increasingly powerful role in the government of the state. The mismanagement was on both provincial and central levels, characterised by the sale of offices and unrestrained venality. External foes put additional pressure on the Empire, with more revolts in Bulgaria; a series of wars with the Normans that resulted in the loss of Thessalonica; and an uprising of the Serbian states.

In the aftermath of the Third Crusade, Richard the Lionheart (1157–1199) took Cyprus and imprisoned its Byzantine ruler. Tensions continued to rise with the German Holy Roman emperors, and they reached a crisis point when Henry VI (1165–1197) succeeded his father, Frederick I Barbarossa. Emperor Henry had aspirations of world domination, and Byzantium was in his sights, a threat that became closer to a reality after he inherited the throne of Sicily in 1194.

The Venetian doge Enrico Dandolo was also plotting the downfall of Byzantium for economic reasons. He wanted Venice to have a maritime monopoly, and Constantinople stood in the way of the Republic's hegemony of the seas. In Rome, Pope Innocent III wanted to launch a crusade led by a united Church; he envisaged a union between East and West that would bring the schismatic Orthodox Church to heel in an acknowledgement of papal supremacy. The planning of the Fourth Crusade presented an opportunity for collective western hostility to the Byzantine Empire to solidify into a plan of conquest. The vested interests of the participating states resulted in the crusade being hijacked by an alternative objective: the conquest of the Christian East.

The Latin Occupation of Constantinople in the Thirteenth Century

In Constantinople, the government was in crisis and weakened by internal conflict. Emperor Isaac II (1156–1204) lost his throne to an imperial usurper who blinded him and imprisoned him with his son, Alexius. The young man managed to escape and made his way to Venice where he asked the Venetians and crusaders to help him restore his father to the throne. He promised money to Venice and to the crusaders for their onward campaigns in the Holy Land, and he committed to delivering a union of the Churches to the pope.

Saving Byzantium: The Struggle to Salvage an Empire

The crusaders stormed Constantinople on 17 July 1203 and restored Isaac II to the throne alongside Alexius, who became co-Emperor. Alexius was unable to fulfil the financial promises he had made to the crusaders and the Venetians. His subjects turned on him and his father for inviting the Latins into Constantinople. They rose up in rebellion against Alexius, slaughtering him and imprisoning his father. A new emperor, Alexius V Ducas Murtzuphlus, was appointed without the consent of the crusaders and Venetians. Within a few months, the western forces regrouped and took Constantinople again. This time, however, they did not even appoint a puppet Byzantine emperor, they simply installed a Latin ruler of Constantinople under a total occupation that would last for the next fifty years. The victorious westerners were brutal, pillaging and massacring the local population without mercy for a period of three days. They destroyed and looted religious treasures that they shipped back to Venice and elsewhere. The trauma of the event would linger for centuries and influence the resistance of the Constantinopolitans to the union of the Churches proposed over two hundred years later.

In the aftermath of the bloodshed, the Venetians and Franks set up an electoral college to appoint a new emperor. They chose Count Baldwin of Flanders (1171-1206), who was crowned in Hagia Sofia on 16 May 1204, and they appointed the Venetian Thomas Morosoni to be Latin Patriarch of Constantinople. The entire Empire was divided between Baldwin, the Franks and the Venetians. The latter, who probably did best out of the conquest, took the most important harbour cities and islands to achieve their goal of maritime monopoly. Constantinople itself was also partitioned between Baldwin and Venice.

The occupiers made little effort to win over the local population, and many feudal lords left the conquered territories for areas that were still independent of the West. The empires of Nicaea and Epirus were established, and here the rulers preserved the Byzantine religion, culture and way of life. For a time, the Empire of Trebizond also thrived outside the imperial Latin grasp. Epirus and Nicaea were rivals, and eventually the latter prevailed to forge a new Byzantine state in Asia Minor that rallied around the leadership of Theodore I Lascaris (c.1175–1221). After Theodore was crowned as emperor, a stalemate evolved in which both Theodore and the Latin emperor ruled separate, recognised realms.

The stalemate ended when Nicaea's most important statesman, John III Vatazes (1222-1254) became emperor, and eclipsed Epirus on the international stage. Vatazes forged an alliance with Bulgaria against the Latin Empire, which was an increasingly weak institution suffering from poor finances and resistance from the local population. He seized Thrace, areas of Macedonia and Thessalonica, doubling the size of the Nicaean territories. With astute diplomatic skills, Vatazes also cultivated advantageous relations with both the Holy Roman Emperor, Frederick II Hohenstaufen, and the ruling Pope, Innocent IV (c.1195–1254).

The Emperor's domestic reforms were as successful as his international achievements. By reinstating compulsory military service in exchange for land, the native soldier numbers began to climb, reducing the need for mercenaries. Vatazes initiated a programme to reinforce the frontier defences. He aspired to economic self-sufficiency and invested time and funds into improving agricultural techniques, even leading by example with husbandry that he personally supervised on the imperial estates. The period saw the rise of the Mongols and the devastation that they wreaked on their neighbours. Nicaea, with its thriving exports of excess harvest, indirectly benefited from the suffering.

With their fields and economies destroyed, these regions looked to Nicaea for supplies, enriching Vatazes's citizens.

The Rise of the Palaeologans and the Expulsion of the Latins

After Vatazes passed away, his son ruled briefly as Theodore II, dying at an early age and leaving a seven-year-old successor. Michael Palaeologus (1224–1282), a leading aristocrat at the imperial court with pretensions to the throne, became regent during the minority of Emperor John IV. The military and clergy admired Michael, eventually supporting his elevation to co-emperor. He was crowned as Michael VIII in 1258 with the expectation that he would restore Constantinople to the Empire. In pursuit of this goal, Michael had to eliminate a hostile alliance between Manfred of Sicily, the Despot of Epirus and William of Villehardouin of Achaia, who ruled over the Latin duchy of Athens and Euboea. Aware of the Latin Empire's frailty, these major powers united against the Nicaeans. Michael led an army to a resounding victory over the alliance at the battle of Patagonia in 1259. This left no major power, other than Venice, to challenge the Nicaean bid for Constantinople.

To deal with the Venetian threat, Emperor Michael forged a treaty with the Republic of Genoa, granting them all sorts of maritime privileges in exchange for military support if Venice launched an attack. The actual recovery of Constantinople ended up being an underwhelming event. In the summer of 1261, when one of Michael's imperial commanders was on his way to the Bulgarian frontier with his army, he discovered by chance that Constantinople had been left undefended while the Venetian navy dealt with a threat elsewhere. Michael seized the opportunity, and the imperial army entered the city at dawn on 25 July 1261 as the Latin rulers and courtiers fled.

A Brief Survey of the Byzantine Empire

After receiving the imperial insignia of the defeated Baldwin, the Emperor proceeded to the city. The Constantinopolitans were euphoric. The intensity of the celebrations to welcome Michael VIII to Constantinople reflected the depth of the trauma that the Byzantines had experienced under the Latin occupation. The Emperor was greeted by a parade led with the city's most precious icon, the Madonna and Child (Hodegetria) believed to have been painted by St Luke. In a display of humility that reinforced his image as a Christian saviour, Michael proceeded on foot to Hagia Sofia where the patriarch crowned him again as emperor and his son as heir. Simultaneously, Constantinople was reborn just as the emperor gave birth to a new ruling dynasty, the Palaeologue.

The Palaeologan Emperor spun a complex web of diplomatic alliances and treaties over the next twenty years of his rule. For several years he dangled the prospect of church union before Rome to mitigate any potential papal hostility to the restored empire. To reclaim the islands that had been lost to the Latins, Michael initiated military campaigns using the support of Seljuk mercenaries and the Genoese navy. Marriage alliances brought Epirus under imperial rule, and calmed tensions with the Bulgarians, Russian Tatars and the Mamluks. In the west, Michael forged separate treaties with Venice and Genoa, protecting the Empire's maritime interests.

A major threat, backed by the papacy, arose from Sicily which was now ruled by the militant and expansionist Charles of Anjou. Recognising Michael's exposure, the Pope gave him an ultimatum – the Greeks must agree to a union of the churches or he would give Anjou free rein to attack Byzantium. Against the wishes of the clergy, Michael submitted to the Pope, and the union was ratified in 1274. This provoked internal resistance to the Emperor, and both the clergy and the population repudiated the union. The elevation of Martin IV to the papal throne caused further problems for Michael. He was a stooge of Charles of Anjou, who still aspired to acquire the Byzantine Empire, and he persuaded the Pope to declare the Byzantine Church to be schismatic and to depose Michael. The Angevins were on the cusp of seizing Byzantium when the Emperor forged a pact with King Peter III of Aragon (the son-in-law of Sicily's previous ruler, Manfred) to stir up a revolt and to overthrow Charles in Sicily in 1282. The Angevin kingdom in southern Italy collapsed and Michael's diplomacy saved his empire.

Internal Crises and the Partitioning of the Empire during the Fourteenth Century

Michael had been an extremely astute statesman as well as a strong military leader. Unfortunately, his dynastic successors were not so gifted and were far less well equipped to handle the challenges that faced them. The struggle to consolidate the Empire was ongoing and a perpetual drain on the court finances. Several Greek states continued to resist Palaeologan unification: Thessaly, Epirus, Aetolia and Acarnania. The Balkan and frontier wars had exhausted the Byzantines.

As with the third century crisis, the emperors turned to partitioning and decentralisation to manage the state's affairs. Although the divisions were made between imperial siblings, the ties between the centre and provinces unravelled under the arrangement. The strong centralised administration established by Emperor Michael VIII slowly disintegrated under the mismanagement of his descendants. Ruling power became dependent again on the large landowners, who demanded privileges in the form of tax relief and the enlargement of their estates. The consequence for the government was a dwindling treasury, and ultimately they were forced to debase the currency.

For the citizens, the consequences were high prices and famine. Squabbling over power between Palaeologan family members escalated into a long period of civil wars from 1321 to 1328, further weakening the Empire and leaving it exposed to the next external threat.

The Rise of the Ottomans
The rise of the Ottoman Turks began to take its toll on Byzantium from the mid-thirteenth century when the Mongol invasions drove several Turkish tribes into Asia Minor. The displaced tribesmen raided and pillaged the Byzantine border territories, which were virtually undefended after years of neglect. The Palaeologan restoration had focused almost exclusively on the hostilities with the West, diverting funds and troops away from the eastern frontiers. By 1300 the Turks had captured most of Asia Minor, apart from a handful of Byzantine fortresses in places like Nicaea, Nicomedia, Heraclea and Smyrna.

By the 1350s, these Turkish tribes, the Ottoman Seljuks, the Aydins and the Karamans, were occupied with enlarging their power bases as they vied for dominance amongst themselves. It was the Ottoman tribe that caused most concern to the Byzantines, as they were developing a power base along the Dardanelles and Bosporus Straits. Their proximity to Christian territories gave them a strong position from which to launch small incursions that succeeded in establishing a handful of footholds on the European side of the Dardanelles.

The Palaeologan emperors John V (1332–1391) and Manuel II (1350–1425) deemed it prudent to accept a system of vassalage to the Ottomans throughout the 1370s and 1380s, by which they agreed to restrictions on their power and to pay a tribute in exchange for peace. This system broke down during the rule of Bayezid I (c.1360–1403), a sultan with a mission to take

Saving Byzantium: The Struggle to Salvage an Empire

Constantinople. He besieged the port city for several years but failed to breach the walls. Emperor Manuel II appealed to France, Burgundy, Venice, Hungary and England for military support, and a crusade was launched and led by Sigismund of Hungary in 1396. The crusaders were defeated at Nicopolis by the Ottomans. But it was not the end of the story for Constantinople.

A respite for the Byzantines came in the form of inter-tribal conflict among the Turks. A rival tribe seized Ottoman lands in Asia Minor, and Bayezid's retaliatory response provoked the Mongols. Led by Timur of Samarkand, they defeated the Ottoman forces and captured Sultan Bayezid. Unable to sustain a fight on multiple fronts, his successor Suleyman ended the siege, returning the lands surrounding Constantinople and Thessalonica that his father had seized.

The Empire enjoyed a relatively peaceful period for a few years. Not only were the Turks distracted by their own internal wars, but the Balkan states that had also once been a threat to the Byzantine empire splintered into a medley of small vassalages and lordships. Physically, the emperors and despots from Thessalonica to Mistra were well protected by manmade or natural defences. The iconic city of Constantinople was encircled by multiple rings of fortified walls with nearly 200 towers for archers. The Bosporus with its prevailing currents made landing impossible beyond the Golden Horn, which itself was protected by a large chain that could block access to the harbour.

With fewer external threats, Byzantium was an entirely viable empire made up of lands that held immense economic potential. The high fertility of the soil in the Peloponnese provided vineyards, olive trees, orchards, honey, wax and grain. The residents sold surplus crops to the Venetians for additional revenue. There were natural sources of timber and marble, and Thessalonica was a renowned exporter of cotton. Constantinople

A Brief Survey of the Byzantine Empire

and its residents continued to profit as a pilgrimage centre, whilst all the territories of Byzantium benefited economically from their ideal position as a natural centre point for the trade of commodities between Europe and Asia. Without the benefit of hindsight, it would be entirely reasonable to conclude that Byzantium had all the elements required to thrive and prosper.

GLOSSARY

Antipope A claimant to the papacy in opposition to the recognised pope, often supported by dissenting factions within the Church. Antipopes were prominent during times of church division, particularly in the western Schism, reflecting disputes over papal authority and influencing Byzantine-Western relations.

Augousteion An important public square in Constantinople, named after the Emperor Augustus. Situated near the Hagia Sofia, it served as a ceremonial space where imperial events, religious processions and public gatherings occurred. It was an epicentre of Byzantine power and displayed the fusion of Roman heritage with Greek culture.

Glossary

Autocephalous — Describes a church that governs itself independently, without external oversight from a higher ecclesiastical authority. In the eastern Orthodox tradition, autocephalous churches appoint their own leaders and make decisions autonomously, reflecting Byzantine and post-Byzantine concepts of religious self-governance.

Bailo — A Venetian diplomatic and commercial representative stationed abroad, especially in Byzantine and Ottoman territories. *Baili* negotiated trade agreements, represented Venetian interests and maintained political relations, often playing a crucial role in diplomacy.

Beglerbegs — Ottoman provincial governors overseeing large administrative regions (beylerbeyliks). They held military and civil authority, collecting taxes, maintaining order and leading provincial armies, crucial to the Ottoman administrative and military system post-1453.

Biremes — Ancient and medieval galleys with two rows of oars on each side, used for naval warfare and trade in the Mediterranean. Biremes were essential for Byzantine and later Ottoman naval fleets, combining speed and manoeuvrability in battle.

Bull (Papal) — An official papal decree or letter, sealed with a lead 'bulla', used for formal pronouncements on doctrine, church policy or political matters. Bulls were influential tools in medieval diplomacy, often used to communicate papal decisions regarding eastern and western Church relations.

Church Fathers — Influential early Christian theologians whose writings shaped Christian doctrine and practice, particularly in interpreting scripture and defining orthodoxy. Figures like Augustine, Athanasius and Gregory the Great profoundly impacted both Roman Catholic and Greek Orthodox theological traditions, including Byzantine theological debates.

Co-Emperor — A junior emperor or heir appointed to share Byzantine rule, often to ensure smooth transitions, govern distant territories or prepare a successor. Common in Byzantine dynasties, co-emperorship stabilised governance but sometimes fuelled conflicts over imperial succession and power-sharing.

College of Cardinals — The body of Roman Catholic cardinals responsible for advising the pope and electing his successor. The College played a significant role in church governance and political decisions, often interacting

Glossary

	with Byzantine and other European leaders on church unification and defence matters.
Commendatory Abbot	A layman or cleric appointed to oversee a monastery's income and properties without residing there. Commendatory abbots often managed resources while benefiting from monastery revenues, a common practice in the later medieval Church amid financial and administrative changes.
Conciliarism	A reform movement in the fourteenth- to fifteenth-century Catholic Church asserting that ecumenical councils held supreme authority, even over the pope, especially during times of papal crisis or corruption.
Consiliarius	A counsellor or advisor, especially within church or royal courts. In Byzantine and Renaissance contexts, *consiliarii* advised rulers on policy, diplomacy and ecclesiastical matters, serving as key figures in governance and negotiations.
Consistory	A formal assembly of the pope and cardinals in the Roman Catholic Church, convened to discuss church matters, make appointments or issue decrees. Consistories were particularly important for decisions affecting diplomacy and church governance, including relations with the eastern Church and political alliances.

Council of Basel	A Roman Catholic council (1431–1449) addressing church reform and authority. It became a conciliarism milestone, advocating council supremacy over the pope. The council's debates on unifying the eastern Orthodox and Catholic Churches were a preliminary step in setting the stage for the Council of Ferrara-Florence.
Curia	The central governing body of the Roman Catholic Church, managing ecclesiastical matters under the pope's authority. In the fifteenth century, the Curia included departments like the Secretariat of State and various congregations. It was instrumental in coordinating western support for Byzantium and handling Catholic diplomatic efforts.
Deacon	A rank within the Christian clergy, just below that of priest. In the eastern Orthodox Church, deacons assist bishops and priests in liturgical services and may take on other roles such as charity work or administrative duties. The deaconate is significant in Orthodox tradition for its ceremonial functions and representation of humility and service.

Glossary

Despot A noble title in the Byzantine Empire, used to designate rulers of semi-autonomous regions, especially in the later stages of the empire. It was commonly granted to members of the imperial family who governed territories like the Despotate of the Morea. The despot wielded considerable local authority while acknowledging the Byzantine emperor's sovereignty.

Devshirme The Ottoman practice of collecting Christian boys from the Balkans, converting them to Islam, and training them for military or administrative service, notably as elite Janissary soldiers.

Ducat A gold coin used widely in medieval Europe, particularly by Venice. The ducat facilitated trade and financial transactions across the Mediterranean, including commerce with the Byzantine Empire and the Ottoman Turks.

Eastern Church Refers to the Orthodox Christian Church, which developed distinct theological, liturgical and administrative traditions separate from the Roman Catholic Church. The eastern Church, led by the Patriarch of Constantinople, upheld doctrines and practices rooted in Greek heritage and resisted western influence, especially after the Great

	Schism of 1054. The divide between the eastern and western Churches remained a key issue throughout Byzantine history, affecting political alliances and responses to external threats like the Ottomans.
Encyclical	A papal letter or formal statement sent to bishops or the faithful, addressing significant theological or social issues. Encyclicals often guided church doctrine or policy in the fifteenth century and influenced discussions on church unity, as in the context of East-West church relations.
Filioque	A Latin word meaning 'and from the Son', added by the western Church to the Nicene Creed to state that the Holy Spirit proceeds from both the Father and the Son. This addition triggered a significant doctrinal dispute between the eastern Orthodox and Roman Catholic Churches, hindering church unity.
Florin	A gold coin first minted in Florence, known for its consistent weight and purity. The florin became a standard currency for international trade in fifteenth-century Europe, widely accepted in commerce between Italian states, Byzantium and the Ottomans.

Glossary

Grand Domestikos — The highest-ranking military officer in the Byzantine Empire, responsible for commanding the army. The Grand Domestikos played a key role in defending the empire during the later centuries, particularly against Ottoman advances.

Grand Oikonomos — A high-ranking Byzantine official responsible for overseeing the financial and administrative affairs of churches and monasteries. The Grand Oikonomos managed property, revenue and expenditures, ensuring the economic stability of ecclesiastical institutions.

Grand Vizier — The chief minister in the Ottoman Empire, acting as the sultan's principal advisor and head of the government. The Grand Vizier wielded significant political and administrative power, overseeing state affairs and representing the sultan's authority.

Greco-Slav — Refers to the cultural and religious synthesis between Greek (Byzantine) and Slavic traditions, especially within the eastern Orthodox Church. This term encompasses the shared heritage that developed through missionary work and political alliances, binding Byzantium with Slavic regions like Bulgaria and Serbia and later influencing the culture of Muscovite Rus.

Greek Orthodox Church   The eastern Christian Church, distinct from Roman Catholicism in doctrine and liturgy, centred in Constantinople. It emphasised theological independence, mystical worship and upheld unique beliefs like the Holy Spirit's procession from the Father alone. Tensions with Rome fuelled East-West religious and political divides.

Greek Rites   Liturgical practices and rites of the Greek Orthodox Church, rooted in the Byzantine tradition. Conducted in Greek, the rites involve elaborate liturgies, icons and mysticism. Their divergence from Latin rites underscored the theological and cultural divides between the eastern and western Churches.

Hagia Sofia   A monumental church in Constantinople, initially built under Emperor Justinian I, and one of the greatest architectural achievements of the Byzantine Empire. Hagia Sofia served as the main cathedral of the eastern Orthodox Church, symbolising Byzantine religious, political and artistic identity. It was converted into a mosque after the Ottoman conquest in 1453, further underscoring its status as a powerful symbol across different empires.

Glossary

Hellenism — The spread and influence of Greek culture, language and ideas, particularly in regions under Byzantine and later Ottoman control. Hellenism influenced eastern Orthodox Christianity and Byzantine intellectual life, preserving Greek philosophy and arts during periods of both independence and Ottoman rule.

Humanism — A Renaissance intellectual movement focusing on classical Greek and Roman texts, promoting human potential and emphasising secular studies alongside Christian teachings. Humanism fostered East-West cultural exchange, as Greek scholars from Byzantium brought classical knowledge to Italy, fuelling the Renaissance.

Indulgence (Papal) — A remission of temporal punishment for sins, granted by the Pope. Indulgences were often issued for specific actions, like participation in crusades. They were instrumental in mobilising Christian support for defensive campaigns against the Ottomans and other non-Christian forces.

Islam — The monotheistic religion founded by the Prophet Muhammad in the seventh century, emphasising submission to God (Allah) and following the Quran. The rapid spread of Islam significantly impacted Byzantine territories, especially with the rise of the Ottoman Empire, which challenged Byzantium's Christian strongholds.

Italic League — A fifteenth-century alliance among Italian city-states, formed to maintain regional stability and counter external threats, including the Ottomans. The league fostered political cooperation and helped balance power among Italy's leading states, supporting their diplomatic and military strategies.

Janissaries — Elite Ottoman infantry recruited primarily from Christian youths through the *devshirme* system. Trained as loyal soldiers, the Janissaries were a key force in Ottoman military successes, playing major roles in battles against Byzantium and European powers.

Khan — A title for a ruler of the Mongol and Turkic peoples, signifying a leader of a tribe or confederation. In the fifteenth century, khans governed territories that influenced trade and political relations with Byzantium, the Ottomans and eastern Europe.

Knights Hospitaller — A Christian military and hospitaller Order initially founded to protect pilgrims and provide medical care. The Order later defended Christian territories, especially in the Mediterranean, and became a

Glossary

	key military force resisting Ottoman expansion into Europe.
Comnenoi Dynasty	A prominent Byzantine ruling family from the eleventh to the twelfth centuries. The Comnenoi restored and stabilised the empire following a period of military and political instability, marking a resurgence in Byzantine power. This dynasty, especially under emperors like Alexios I and Manuel I, maintained Byzantium's influence and defended its territories against external threats, setting the stage for the later Palaeologan period.
Latin Rites	The Roman Catholic Church's liturgical practices, traditionally performed in Latin and centred on structured, formal liturgies. Latin rites include the Roman Rite and others that define western Christian worship. Distinctions from Greek rites deepened East-West divisions, complicating church union efforts.
Logothetes	Byzantine officials responsible for various aspects of state administration, such as finance, military logistics or correspondence. The *logothetes* played a crucial role in maintaining the empire's bureaucratic structure and managing resources during times of crisis.

Macedonian Dynasty (867–1056)	A Byzantine ruling family known for military expansion, cultural revival and stability, beginning with Basil I. This era, termed the 'Macedonian Renaissance', saw territorial gains and flourishing art and theology, strengthening Byzantium's political and religious influence.
Metropolitan	A high-ranking bishop within the eastern Orthodox Church, overseeing a metropolitanate or ecclesiastical province. Metropolitans held significant authority and were often involved in both ecclesiastical and political matters, especially during the Byzantine period when church leaders played vital roles in state affairs.
Millet	An administrative system in the Ottoman Empire that allowed religious communities (such as Christians or Jews) to govern themselves under their own laws. Each millet managed its internal affairs, preserving religious autonomy under Ottoman rule.
Mongols	A nomadic empire originating from Central Asia, known for their expansive conquests in the thirteenth and fourteenth centuries under leaders like Genghis Khan. The Mongols influenced many regions, including the Byzantine Empire and the Rus territories, disrupting trade and

Glossary

	altering political landscapes. Their arrival indirectly contributed to the destabilisation of eastern Europe and Anatolia, impacting Byzantine strategies and alliances.
Muscovite Rus	The early Russian principality centred around Moscow, which rose to prominence after the decline of Kievan Rus and later came to view itself as the successor to the Byzantine Empire, especially after Constantinople's fall. Muscovite Rus adopted eastern Orthodox Christianity and Byzantine customs, aspiring to preserve the spiritual legacy of Byzantium as the 'Third Rome'.
Nicene Creed	A foundational Christian statement of faith formulated at the First Council of Nicaea (325), affirming belief in the Trinity and Jesus's divinity. Central to both eastern and western Christianity, the creed's wording – especially the addition of the *Filioque* – became a source of major East-West doctrinal conflict.
Order of St Basil	A monastic order within eastern Orthodoxy, based on the Rule of St Basil. It emphasised asceticism, community life and charity, with monasteries often serving as cultural and educational centres, preserving Byzantine traditions and resisting Latin influences.

Ottoman Turk	A member of the Ottoman Empire, founded by Turkish tribes and expanding into Byzantine territories by the fourteenth century. The Ottoman Turks under leaders like Mehmed II eventually captured Constantinople, bringing about the fall of the Byzantine Empire and reshaping eastern Europe.
Palaeologan Dynasty (1261–1453)	The final Byzantine ruling dynasty, responsible for restoring Constantinople to the Greeks after Latin occupation. The Palaeologans faced internal conflicts and Ottoman threats, attempting western alliances through proposed church union. The dynasty's rule ended with Constantinople's fall.
Patriarch	The senior bishop and leader of an autocephalous church within eastern Orthodoxy. In Byzantium, the Patriarch of Constantinople held significant influence as both a religious and political figure, often aligning or clashing with imperial policy. Following the Ottoman conquest, the patriarchate continued under Ottoman rule, maintaining Orthodox religious identity and autonomy.
Pentarchy	The five early Christian patriarchal sees – Rome, Constantinople, Alexandria, Antioch, Jerusalem –

Glossary

	representing the highest church authority. The Pentarchy's governance reflected early Christian unity, but Rome's claims to primacy led to tensions with eastern sees, affecting Byzantine church politics and provoking doctrinal conflicts.
Protekdikos	A Byzantine legal official who acted as a defender or advocate in ecclesiastical courts. The *protekdikos* represented individuals or groups in legal disputes, particularly within the complex legal structure of the Byzantine Church.
Roman Catholic Church	The western Christian Church based in Rome, led by a pope, emphasising papal supremacy and distinct doctrines like the *Filioque*. Differences with the eastern Orthodox Church culminated in the 1054 East-West Schism, which, even centuries later, strangled attempts to unite the Churches against common Ottoman threats.
Spahis	Ottoman cavalry units, whose members were typically granted land in exchange for military service. The *spahis* served as provincial forces, playing a critical role in Ottoman conquests and maintaining control over territories. Alongside the Janissaries, they formed the backbone of the Ottoman military.

Synod	A council or assembly of church officials convened to discuss and decide on ecclesiastical matters. In the eastern Orthodox Church, synods held substantial power over theological and administrative decisions, and they were crucial for maintaining doctrinal unity, especially during periods of theological controversy or political change.
Titular Church	A church assigned to a cardinal in Rome, symbolising his participation in the clergy of Rome while holding administrative duties elsewhere. Titular churches were part of the cardinal's title and role in the Curia, reflecting his authority within the Catholic ecclesiastical hierarchy.
Turcoman	Nomadic Turkic tribes inhabiting Anatolia and the Middle East. In the fifteenth century, Turcomans played significant roles as frontier warriors, often serving as mercenaries or vassals for the Ottomans, while sometimes resisting centralised Ottoman control to maintain their autonomy.
Uniate Patriarch	A patriarch aligned with the Roman Catholic Church while leading an eastern Christian community. Uniate patriarchs maintained eastern rites but recognized papal authority, typically in regions where political alliances favoured Catholic-Orthodox cooperation, often sparking internal divisions.

Glossary

Vassalage — A system where a ruler pays tribute to a more powerful overlord for protection and autonomy. As Byzantine emperors faced external threats, they often became vassals to Ottoman sultans, retaining varying degrees of independence in exchange for allegiance, particularly during the empire's decline.

Venetian-Ottoman Wars — A series of conflicts between Venice and the Ottoman Empire, fought for control over trade routes, territories and maritime dominance in the Mediterranean. These wars highlighted the shifting power balance as Venice defended its commercial interests against Ottoman expansion.

NOTES

Prologue

For general surveys of the Byzantine period, *The Cambridge History of the Byzantine Empire c.500–1492*, edited by Jonathan Shepard (Cambridge: Cambridge University Press, 2008) is a good starting point. Other surveys include Warren Treadgold, *A History of the Byzantine State and Society* (Stanford: Stanford University Press, 1997); George Ostrogorsky, *History of the Byzantine State* (New Brunswick and New Jersey: Rutgers University Press, 1969); and Anthony Kaldellis, *The New Roman Empire: A History of Byzantium* (Oxford: Oxford University Press, 2024).

Introduction: The Historians

Several scholars have looked at the concept of historical writing and its purposes in the classical and Byzantine worlds. These include Leonora Neville, 'Why did Byzantines Write History?', *Proceedings of the 23rd International Congress of Byzantine Studies* (The Serbian National Committee of AIEB and the contributors, 2016); and Ingela Nilsson, 'To Narrate the

Notes

Events of the Past: On Byzantine Historians, and Historians on Byzantium', *Byzantine Narrative: Papers in Honour of Roger Scott* (Australian Association for Byzantine Studies, 2006). For a useful introductory survey to contemporary Byzantine writers of history, see Leonora Neville, *Guide to Byzantine Historical Writing* (Cambridge: Cambridge University Press, 2018). I have used the following translations in English of the four texts quoted in this chapter. Harry Magoulias (ed.), *Decline and Fall of Byzantium to the Ottoman Turks, by Doukas. An Annotated Translation of 'Historia Turco-Byzantina'* (Detroit: Wayne State University Press, 1975); Marios Philippides (ed.), *The Fall of the Byzantine Empire: A Chronicle by George Sphrantzes* (Amherst: University of Massachusetts Press, 1980); Anthony Kaldellis (ed.), *The Histories by Laonikos Chalkokondyles*, Vols I and II (Massachusetts: Dumbarton Oaks Medieval Library, 2014); and Charles T. Riggs (ed.), *A History of Mehmed the Conqueror by Michael Kritovoulos* (Connecticut: Greenwood Press, 1970). Translations of Bessarion's comments on Trebizond come from Bessarion, 'Encomium on Trebizond', edited and translated by Scott Kennedy in *Two Works on Trebizond* (Massachusetts: Dumbarton Oaks Medieval Library, 2019)

1 *The Champions of Byzantium: Isidore and Bessarion*

Until very recently the only monographs on Bessarion have been in German, French and Italian. However, an accessible and thorough publication in English is now available. Michael Malone-Lee, *Cardinal Bessarion (1403-1472)* (London: Routledge, 2024). Sources and information about Isidore are scarce, but Marios Philipppides and Walter K. Hanak published a short survey of what is known about him, alongside translations of his writings in their work, *Cardinal Isidore, c. 1390-1462: A Late Byzantine Scholar, Warlord, and Prelate*

(London: Routledge, 2018). The translations of Isidore's texts throughout are drawn from this source. Mistra's importance as an urban cultural centre for Byzantium in the fifteenth century is examined in Steven Runciman's *Lost Capital of Byzantium: The History of Mistra and the Peloponnese*, (London: Thames & Hudson, 1980). The leading authority on Byzantine monasticism, Alice-Mary Talbot, has published an introduction to the topic, *Varieties of Monastic Experience in Byzantium, 800-1453* (Indiana: Notre Dame Press, 2019). A translation of Pero Tafur's travels and account of Constantinople can be accessed in a digitised form from *The Broadway Travellers* series, edited by Sir E. Denison Ross and Eileen Power, see *Pero Tafur: Travels and Adventures (1435-1439)*, translated and edited with an introduction by Malcolm Letts (New York, London: Harper & brothers 1926). Sphrantzes on Emperor Manuel's concerns about his son John are translated by Marios Philippides in *The Fall of the Byzantine Empire: A Chronicle by George Sphrantzes*. John Kananos is quoted in Bartusis, Mark, C., *The Late Byzantine Army: Arms and Society, 1204-1453* (Philadelphia: University of Pennsylvania Press, 1992).

2 Emperor John VIII, Sultan Murad II and the Byzantine Empire in the Fifteenth Century

Survey histories of Byzantium are plentiful – one of the most solid is Warren T. Treadgold's *A History of the Byzantine State and Society* (Stanford: Stanford University Press, 1997). For equally scholarly and captivating publications see Judith Herrin, *Byzantium: The Surprising Life of a Medieval Empire*, (NJ: Princeton, 2008) and more recently, Jonathan Harris, *The Lost World of Byzantium* (New Haven and London: Yale University Press, 2016). For a more in-depth discussion of the differences between the East and West Churches, see

Joan Mervyn Hussey, *The Orthodox Church in the Byzantine Empire* (Oxford: Clarendon Press, 1986). To understand the complexities of the main contention between the Byzantines and the Roman Catholics read Donald Nicol, 'The Byzantine View of Papal Sovereignty', in *The Church and Sovereignty, c.590-1918: Essays in Honour of Michael Wilks*, ed. Diana Wood (Oxford: Blackwell's, 1991), and Henry Chadwick, *East and West: The Making of a Rift in the Church. From Apostolic Times until the Council of Florence* (Oxford: Oxford University Press, 2003).

3 Salvation through Spiritual Union

The letter from Bessarion to Francesco Foscari, Doge of Venice, quoted at the start of the chapter, can be found in Bruce, James and McLaughlin, Mary (eds), *The Portable Renaissance Reader* (London: Penguin Publishing Group, 1968). For more on Eugenius IV and the Council of Basel see Morimichi Watanabe's chapter, 'Pope Eugenius IV, the Conciliar Movement, and the Primacy of Rome' in *The Church, the Councils and Reform: The Legacy of the Fifteenth Century*, ed. Gerald Christianson, Thomas Izbicki and Christopher Bellitto (Washington: Catholic University of America Press, 2008). For the Council of Ferrara-Florence I have drawn heavily on the contemporary account of Sylvester Syropoulos in his memoirs. A translation of his text is printed in the appendix of *The Memoirs of Sylvester Syropoulos*, Section IV, edited by Fontini Kondyli, Vera Andriopoulou, Eirini Panou and Mary B. Cunningham, *Sylvester Syropoulos on Politics and Culture in the Fifteenth-Century Mediterranean* (Birmingham: Birmingham Byzantine and Ottoman Studies, 2014), vol. 16. For an overview of the issues involved in the Council of Florence see Giuseppe Alberigo (ed,), *Christian Unity: The Council of Ferrara-Florence 1438/39-1989* (Leuven:

Peeters Publishers, 1991); and Deno J. Geanakoplos's chapter, 'An Orthodox View of the Councils of Basel and Florence', in *Constantinople and the West: Essays on the Late Byzantine (Palaeologan) and Italian Renaissances and the Byzantine and Roman Churches* (Madison: University of Wisconsin Press, 1989). I used the excellent discussion of the experiences of the Greek delegates in Italy in the chapter by Nicholas Constas, '"Tongues of Fire Confounded"': Greeks and Latins at the Council of Florence (1438-1439)', in *Conciliation and Confession: The Struggle for Unity in the Age of Reform, 1415-1648*, edited by Howard P. Louthan and Randall C. Zachman (Indiana: University of Notre Dame Press, 2004). The best source of information about Isidore's role in the Council of Ferrara-Florence is the monograph written by Marios Philippides and Walter K. Hanak, *Cardinal Isidore, c. 1390-1462: A Late Byzantine Scholar, Warlord, and Prelate* (London: Routledge, 2018). The translations of Isidore's speeches are drawn from this source. Many historians have discussed Bessarion's involvement in the council, and further reading can be found in Joseph Gill's article, 'The Sincerity of Bessarion the Unionist', *Journal of Theological Studies* XXVI (1975) and his *Personalities of the Council of Florence and Other Essays* (Oxford: Blackwell, 1964); as well as in Ihor Sevcenko's article, 'Intellectual Repercussions of the Council of Florence', *Church History*, 24 (1955).

4 Saving Byzantium as the Pope's Man

Once again, the most comprehensive account (and the source of the translated quotes in this chapter) of Isidore's papal mission to the Slavic lands can be found in *Cardinal Isidore, c. 1390-1462: A Late Byzantine Scholar, Warlord, and Prelate* (London: Routledge, 2018) by Marios Philippides and Walter K. Hanak. For a detailed examination of Isidore's journey to Russia to deliver the Decree of Union, see Anna A. Hlaváčová, 'The Return of the Russian Delegation from the Council of Florence Through the Medieval Kingdom of Hungary', *Slovak Studies, Rivista dell'Istituto Storico Slovacco*, 1-2 (2019). The prince of Rus's letter to the emperor is printed in A.G., Welykyi, 'Isidore's Encyclical Letter from Buda', in *Analecta Ordinis S. Basilii Magni. Miscellanea in Honorem Cardinalis Isidore (1463–1963)*, 4/1–2 (Rome, 1963). To learn more about Bessarion's relationship with Pope Eugenius and his position in Rome as a cardinal see Joseph, S.J. Gill, *Personalities of the Council of Florence and Other Essays* (Oxford: Blackwell, 1964). Bessarion's choir books are discussed in Roberto Weiss's article, 'Two Unnoticed "Portraits" of Cardinal Bessarion', *Italian Studies*, vol. 2 (1967). Fra Bartolomeo de Giano's letter is translated by W.L. North from the edition of the letter in J.P. Migne (ed.), *Patrologia Graeca* 158, cols. 1055-1068. Eugenius's efforts to raise a crusade are examined by Thaddeus V. Tuleja, 'Eugenius IV and the Crusade of Varna', *The Catholic Historical Review*, vol. 35, no. 3 (1949). And for a forensic description of the Battle of Varna, see Alexander Zakrzewski, 'The Battle of Varna: "Let Us Fight with Bravery"', *Military Heritage*, vol. 20, no. 5 (2019).

5 Greek Hawks in the Sacred College

For more detail on Nicholas V's position and approach to diplomacy see Hanak's article, 'Pope Nicholas and the Aborted Crusade of 1452-1453 to Rescue Constantinople from the Turks', *Byzantinoslavica: Revue Internationale des Etudes Byzantines*, 65 (2007). Mehmed's poem is translated and published by Avni, 'Imtisal-I Jahidu' fi-'llah olup dur niyyetim', in *Ottoman Literature: The Poets and Poetry of Turkey*, translated by E.J.W. Gibb (New York: M. Walter Dunne, 1901). Other primary sources used in this chapter include Melissenos

[Melissourgos], Makarios, 'The chronicle of the siege of Constantinople April 2 to May 29 1453', in *The Fall of the Byzantine Empire. A Chronicle by George Sphrantzes 1401-1477*, translated by Marios Philippides (Amherst: University of Massachusetts Press, 1980). The Emperor's concerns are printed in Antonio Ivani da Sarzana's *Expugnatio Constantinopolitana* (composed in the winter of 1453/1454). Scholarios's rant to Constantine is translated in his *Apologia pro vita sua*. The text can be found in *Oeuvres complètes de Gennade Scholarios*, edited by L. Petit, X.A. Sidéridès and M. Jugie, 4 vols (Paris: Maison de la bonne presse, 1930–1935), vol 4. For more information on Mehmed II and the rise of the Ottomans in the Mediterranean, see Freely, John, *The Grand Turk* (New York: Overlook Press, 2009); and Kate Fleet, 'The Ottomans in the Mediterranean in the Later Fifteenth Century: the Strategy of Mehmed II', *Storja* (2015).

6 The Battle for Constantinople

About the Fall of Constantinople see Steven Runciman, *The Fall of Constantinople* (Cambridge: Cambridge University Press, 1965); Jonathan Harris, *The End of Byzantium* (New Haven & London: Yale University Press, 2010); and Marios Philippides and Walter K. Hanak, *The Siege and Fall of Constantinople* (London: Routledge 2011). The near-contemporary account written by Henry of Soemmern is the main source that I used for Isidore's involvement in the siege of Constantinople and his escape after the Ottomans broke through the walls. Henry [Heinrich] of Soemmern, 'Codice diplomatico delle colonie Tauro-Liguri durantela signoria dell'Ufficio di S. Giorgio (MCCCCLIII–MCCCCLXXV).' A translation of Soemmern has been included in Marios Philippides' *Mehmed II the Conqueror and the Fall of the Franco-Byzantine Levant to the Ottoman*

Turks: Some Western Views and Testimonies (Tempe: Arizona Center for Medieval and Renaissance Studies, 2007). Translations of Isidore's letters to Pope Nicholas, Bessarion and various secular princes are printed in Marios Philippides and Walter K. Hanak, *Cardinal Isidore, c. 1390-1462: A Late Byzantine Scholar, Warlord, and Prelate* (London: Routledge, 2018). For an assessment of Isidore's letters following his escape from Constantinople, see the article by Marios Philippides, 'The Fall of Constantinople 1453: Classical Comparisons and the Circle of Cardinal Isidore', *Viator*, vol. 38, 1 (2007).

7 A Call to Arms

Nicholas V's belated efforts to raise a crusade and his justifications for not having responded in time to save Constantinople can be found in the article by John B. Toews, 'Formative Forces in the Pontificate of Nicholas V, 1447-1455', *The Catholic Historical Review*, vol. 54, no. 2 (1968). For a description and analysis of Lampo Birago's *Strategicon*, see Damian Iulian M., 'From the "Italic League" to the "Italic Crusade": Crusading under Renaissance Popes Nicholas V and Pius II', in *Italy and Europe's Eastern Border, 1204-1669. Conference proceedings – Rome, 25-27 November 2010*, edited by Alexander Simon, Julian Mihai Damian and Mihailo Popovic (Lausanne: Peter Lang Verlag, 2012). The accusation that Isidore and the Decree of Union were responsible for Constantinople's fall can be found in the text by an anonymous Russian, *Slovo izbranno na latynju*, translated by W.L. North from the Italian translation by A. Danti in A. Pertusi, *La Caduta di Costantinopoli. II. L'Eco nel Mondo.* (Milan: A. Mondadori 2003). The extract from the letter Calixtus wrote to the secular rulers shortly after his election is reprinted by Norman J. Housley in his chapter, 'Giovanni da Capistrano and the Crusade of 1456', in *Crusading in the Fifteenth Century*, edited by Norman J. Housley (London: Routledge, 2004). The source for Pius II's statements are drawn from his commentaries, *The Commentaries of Pius II*, translated by Florence Alden Gragg with notes and introduction by Leona C. Gabel (Northampton, Massachusetts: Smith College, 1957). A useful survey of Aeneas Sylvius Piccolomini's career can be found in the introduction to selected letters written by Pius II, *Reject Aeneas, Accept Pius: Selected Letters of Pope Pius II*, translated and edited by Thomas M. Izbicki, Gerald Christianson and Philip D. W. Krey (Washington: The Catholic University of America Press, 2006). For more detail on Pius II's attempts to lead a crusade, see Nancy Bisaha's chapter, 'Pope Pius II and the Crusade', in *Crusading in the Fifteenth Century*. Bessarion's involvement in Mantua and the aftermath are covered in Norman Housley's introduction to *Crusading in the Fifteenth Century*. The translation of St Andrew's head to Rome is extensively examined by Maya Maskarinec, 'Mobilizing sanctity Pius II and the head of Andrew in Rome', in *Authority and Spectacle in Medieval and Early Modern Europe. Essays in Honor of Teofilo F. Ruiz*, edited by Yuen-Gen Liang and Jarbel Rodriguez (London: Routledge, 2017).

8 Byzantium at the Crossroads

A good overview of both the events in Trebizond and in Negroponte can be found in Kenneth Setton's second volume of *The Papacy and the Levant, 1200-1571* (Philadelphia: American Philosophical Society, 1976). Franz Babinger's book, *Mehmed the Conqueror and His Time* (Princeton: Princeton University Press, 1978) includes extensive descriptions of the Ottoman campaigns against the Comnenoi and the Venetians. Guy Le Strange's translation of Ruy González de Clavijo's description of Trebizond can be found in *Clavijo. Embassy to Tamerlane 1403-1406* (New York and London: Harper, 1928). The surrender terms issued by Mehmed II to Emperor David of Trebizond were recorded by the contemporary writer Doukas in *Historia Turco-Byzantina*. The Venetian merchant Malpiero's letter warning the Republic of Mehmed's naval build up is quoted by Margaret Meserve in her article, 'News from Negroponte: Politics, Popular Opinion, and Information Exchange in the First Decade of the Italian Press', *Renaissance Quarterly* 59 (2006). Fra Jacopo dalla Castella's description of the Venetian fleet anchored off Negroponte and Giacamo Rizzardo's account of the brutality of the invading Ottomans are translated in *Mehmed II the Conqueror and the Fall of the Franco-Byzantine Levant to the Ottoman Turks: Some Western Views and Testimonies*, edited and translated by Marios Philippides (Arizona: ACMRS, 2007). Bessarion's letter to the abbot of San Severino, recording his reaction to the loss of Negroponte is quoted in Mohler, *Kardinal Bessarion als Theologe, Humanist, und Staatsmann: Funde und Forschungen*. And the extract from one of the letters that Paul II wrote to the princes of Italy is a translation of the text to Ludovico Gonzaga published in Kenneth Setton, *The Papacy and the Levant*. Quotes from the correspondence between Bessarion and Fichet can be found in Legrand (ed.), *Cent-Dix Lettres Grècques* (Paris: Hachette Livre Bnf, 1892).

9 *Saving Byzantium: The Legacy*

For more on Bessarion's admiration for the western intellectual movement see A. G. Keller's article, 'A Byzantine Admirer of "Western" Progress: Cardinal Bessarion', *The Cambridge Historical Journal*, XI, no.3 (1955). For a detailed examination of Pletho's life and his philosophies see C. M. Woodhouse, *George Gemistos Plethon: The Last of the Hellenes* (Oxford:

Oxford University Press, 1986). There is not much literature in English about Bessarion's book collection and donation to Venice. The best and most readable source is Michael Malone-Lee's monograph on Cardinal Bessarion, *Cardinal Bessarion (1403-1472)* (London: Routledge, 2024). For more on the symbolism and nature of the icon, see Gary Vikan's article, 'Ruminations on Edible Icons: Originals and Copies in the Art of Byzantium', *Studies in the History of Art*, 20 (1989) and Henry Maguire, *The Icons of their Bodies* (New Jersey: Princeton University Press, 1996). Bessarion's own writings are drawn from translations printed in *Greek Emigres in the West 1400-1520* (Camberley: Porphyrogenitos, 1995) by Jonathan Harris; and in Lotte Labowsky, *Bessarion's Library and the Biblioteca Marciana: Six Early Inventories* (Rome: Edizioni di storia e letteratura, 1979).

10 Reinventing Byzantium

The quotations from Kritovoulos's work in this chapter are drawn from Charles T. Riggs's translation of the *History of Mehmed the Conqueror*. For an exploration into Mehmed II's efforts to establish the former glory of Constantinople in its new guise as Istanbul, see Marios Philippides's introduction and commentary in *Emperors, Patriarchs, and Sultans of Constantinople, 1373–1513: An Anonymous Greek Chronicle of the Sixteenth Century* (Brookline MA: Hellenic College Press, 1990). This book also includes the quotation from *A History of the Patriarchs of Constantinople*, composed by Damaskenos the Studite from Thessalonica, Metropolitan of Naupaktos and Arta in 1527. Ashiqpashazade's observations about the repopulation of the occupied city are quoted in Halil Inalcik's article, 'The Policy of Mehmed II Toward the Greek Population of Istanbul and the Byzantine Buildings of the City', *Dumbarton Oaks Papers*, 23/24 (1969). To read more about the Muscovite bid to be the third Rome, see volume III of

The Papacy and the Levant (1204-1571) by Kenneth M. Setton; and Robert Lee Wolff's article, 'The Three Romes: The Migration of an Ideology and the Making of an Autocrat', *Daedalus*, 88 (1959). A fascinating comparison between Putin's Russia and the nascent nationalism of the sixteenth century is presented by Irina Papkova in 'Saving the Third Rome. "Fall of the Empire", Byzantium and Putin's Russia', *Junior Visiting Fellow Conferences Vol. 24*, Insitut für die Wissenschaften vom Menschen (no date). The letter from the patriarch of Constantinople complaining about the Russians is reprinted in F. Miklosich and I. Muller, *Acta et Diplomata Graeca Medii Aevi II* (Vienna, 1862). Dimitri Strémooukhoff quotes the prediction that the Slavs would restore Constantinople to the Christians in his article, 'Moscow the Third Rome: Sources of the Doctrine', *Speculum*, 28, no. 1 (1953); and the monk Filofei's letter is printed in Alars Laats's article, 'The Concept of the Third Rome and its Political Implications', *Kaitseväe Ühendatud Õppeasutused*, 12 (2009).

Epilogue

The contemporary writers who analysed the fall of Constantinople include Doukas, *Decline and Fall of Byzantium to the Ottoman Turks, An Annotated Translation of 'Historia Turco-Byzantina'*, edited by Harry J. Magoulias (Detroit: Wayne State University Press, 1975). *Laonikos Chalkokondyles: A Translation and Commentary of the 'Demonstrations of Histories'*, Books I-III, translated by Nicolaos Nicoloudis (Athens: Historical Publications St. D. Basilopoulos, 1996). George Sphrantzes, *The Fall of the Byzantine Empire: A Chronicle*, translated by Marios Philippides (Amherst: University of Massachusetts Press, 1980). Kritovoulos, *History of Mehmed the Conqueror* translated by Charles T. Riggs (New Jersey: Princeton University Press, 1954).

Appendix

For monographs on Constantine the Great and Emperor Justinian, see Timothy Barnes, *Constantine: Dynasty, Religion and Power in the Later Roman Empire* (Chichester: Wiley-Blackwell, 2011). Peter Sarris, *Justinian: Emperor, Soldier, Saint* (London: John Murray Press, 2023), wrote a definitive study of the Roman emperor drawing on sound scholarship to tell the story in an engaging and readable manner. To understand more about the relationship between the Persians and the Roman Empire, see Beale Dignas and Englebert Winter, *Rome and Persia in Late Antiquity* (Cambridge: Cambridge University Press, 2007). This study lends itself to both specialists and non-specialists on the topic of Persia's relations with the late Roman Empire. For an in-depth study on the Bulgarian threat, see Steven Runciman's *A History of the First Bulgarian Empire* (1930), which has been published in many editions, a testament to its gripping narrative and academic accuracy. The rise of Islam and the Arab Wars are covered in Robert G. Hoyland, *In God's Path: The Arab Conquests and the Creation of an Islamic Empire* (Oxford: Oxford University Press, 2014), a useful contextualisation of early Arab conquests in the empire and their religion in the ancient Near East. For more on the Macedonian period, see Norman Tobias, *Basil I, Founder of the Macedonian Dynasty: A Study of the Political and Military History of the Byzantine Empire in the Ninth Century* (Lewiston, New York: Edwin Mellen Press, 2007). More detail on the Comnenian period can be found in Michael Angold, *The Byzantine Empire 1025–1204* (Harlow Essex: Longman, 1984). Much has been written about the crusading period. A good overview of the impact on the Byzantines has been covered by Jonathan Harris in *Byzantium and the Crusades*, 2nd edition (London: Bloomsbury, 2014). The Fourth Crusade and the Latin occupation of Constantinople is considered from the Byzantine perspective in Michael Angold, *The Fourth Crusade* (London: Routledge, 2003) and from the Latin perspective in Jonathan Phillips, *The Fourth Crusade and the Sack of Constantinople* (London: Pimlico, 2005). Emperor Michael's entry into Constantinople described by Georgios Akropolites in his *History* is printed in Ruth Macrides, *George Akropolites: The History, Translated with an Introduction and Commentary* (Oxford: Oxford University Press, 2007). For more on the rise of the Ottoman Empire, Heath Lowry's book is an interesting revisionist study that counters the traditional theory that the primary motivation for expansion was religious. See Heath W. Lowry, *The Nature of the Early Ottoman State* (Suny Series in Social and Economic History of the Middle East: State University of New York Press, 2003).

BIBLIOGRAPHY

Alberigo, Giuseppe (ed.), *Christian Unity: The Council of Ferrara-Florence 1438/39-1989* (Leuven: Leuven University Press, 1991).

Alexander, J.J.G., 'Patrons, Libraries and Illuminators in the Italian Renaissance', *Studies in Italian Manuscript Illumination*, ed. J.J.G. Alexander (London: Pindar, 2002).

—, *Federico da Montefeltro and his Library* (Milan: Foundation for Italian Art & Culture, 2007).

Andaloro, Maria, 'L'Icona della Vergine "Salus Populi Romani"', *La Basilica Romana di Santa Maria Maggiore*, ed. Carlo Pietrangeli, (Nardini: Florence, 1987).

Antoniutti, Arianna (ed.), *Pio II e Sant'Andrea Apostolo: Le ragioni della devozione* (Rome: Comitato Nazionale Renascentes Arte, 2004).

Aretino, Leonardo Bruni, *Humanistisch-philosophische Schriften mit einer Chronologie seiner Werke und Briefe*, ed. Hans Brown (Leipzig: Teubner, 1928).

Bibliography

D'Ascia, Luca, *Il Corano e la tiara: L'epistola a Maometto II di Enea Silvio Piccolomini (papa Pio II)* (Bologna: Pendragon, 2001).

Babinger, Franz, *Mehmed the Conqueror and His Time* (Princeton: Princeton University, 1978).

Bacchelli, Franco, 'La legazione del cardinale Bessarione (1450-1455)', *Bessarione e l'umanesimo* (Naples: Vivarium, 1994).

Baiardi, Giorgio Cerboni, Giorgio Chittolini and Piero Floriani, *Federico di Montefeltro*, 3 volumes (Rome: Bulzoni Editore, 1986).

Bandini, Aloysius, *Commentarius*, reprinted in Migne, J.-P., (ed.), *Patrologiae Graecae: Cursus Completus*, 161 (Paris, 1866).

Barbier, Frédéric, 'La ville, le prince et la bibliothèque: Espaces, savoirs et pouvoirs dans l'Europe de la Renaissance', *Le Pouvoir des Livres à la Renaissance*, ed. Dominique de Courcelles (Paris: Ecole nationale de Chartres, 1998).

Beierwaltes, Werner, *Agostino e il Neoplatismo cristiano* (Milan: Vita e Pensiero, 1995).

Belting, Hans, *Likeness and Presence: A History of the Image before the Era of Art*, trans. Edmund Jephcott (Chicago and London: University of Chicago Press, 1994).

Bertelli, Carlo, 'Icone di Roma', *Stil und Überlieferung in der Kunst des Abendlandes*, 1 (Berlin: Gebr. Mann, 1967).

Bessarion, Cardinal Iohannes, *Oratio dogmatica de Unione*, ed. Emmanuel Candal (Rome: Pontificium Institutum Orientalium Studiorum), 1958.

—, *Encyclica ad Graecos*, reprinted in Migne, J.-P. (ed.), *Patrologiae Graecae: Cursus Completus*, 161 (Paris, 1866).

Bianca, Concetta, 'La formazione della biblioteca latina del Bessarione', *Scrittura, Biblioteche e Stampa a Roma nel*

Quattrocento (Vatican City: Scuola Vaticana di Paleografia, Diplomatica e Archivistica, 1980).

—, 'La biblioteca romana di Niccolò Cusano', *Scrittura, Biblioteche e Stampa a Roma nel Quattrocento* (Vatican City: Scuola Vaticana di Paleografia, Diplomatica e Archivistica, 1982).

—, 'Auctoritas et Veritas: il Filelfo e le dispute tra platonici e aristotelici', *Francesco Filelfo nel quinto centenario della morte* (Padua: Atti del convegno di studi maceratesi, 1986).

—, 'L'Abbazia di Grottaferrata e il Cardinale Bessarione', *Fatti, Patrimoni e Uomini Intorno All'Abbazia di San Nilo Nel Medioevo*, Atti del I Colloquio internazionale, Grottaferrata, 26-28 April 1985 (Grottaferrata. 1988).

—, *Da Bisanzio a Roma. Studi sul cardinale Bessarione* (Rome: Roma nel Rinascimento, 1999).

Bilderback, Loy, 'Eugene IV and the First Dissolution of the Council of Basel', *Church History*, 36 (1967).

Black, Anthony, *Council and Commune: The Conciliar Movement and the Fifteenth-Century Heritage* (London: Burns & Oates, 1979).

Blum, Paul Richard, 'George Gemistos Plethon; George of Trebizond; Cardinal Bessarion: The Controversy between the Platonists and Aristotelians in the Fifteenth Century', in *Philosophers of the Renaissance* (Washington: Catholic University of America Press, 2010).

Bond, H. Lawrence, 'The "Icon" and the "Iconic Text" in Nicholas of Cusa's *De Visione Dei* I-XVII', in *Nicholas of Cusa and His Age: Intellect and Spirituality*, ed. Thomas M. Izbicki and Christopher M. Bellitto (Leiden, Boston, Cologne: Brill, 2002).

Bracciolini, Poggio, *Lettere*, ed. Helene Harth (Florence: Olschki Editore, 1984-87).

Braschio, Johannes Baptista, *Memoriae Caesenates Sacrae et Profanae* (Rome: Ansillioni, 1738).

Bresc, Henri, *Livre et société en Sicile (1299-1499)* (Palermo: Palermo Luxograph, 1971).

Bruni, Leonardo, *Humanistisch-philosophische Schriften mit einer Chronologie seiner Werke und Briefe*, ed. Hans Baron (Leipzig: Teubner, 1928).

Burckhardt, Jacob, *The Civilization of the Renaissance in Italy*, trans. S.G.C. Middlemore, 2 volumes (New York: New American Library, 1958).

Burkle-Young, Francis A., *Passing the Keys: Modern Cardinal, Conclaves, and the Election of the Next Pope* (Lanham: Madison Books, 1999).

Bussi, Giovanni Andrea, *Prefazioni alle edizioni di Sweynheym e Pannartz Prototipografi romani*, ed. Massimo Miglio (Milan: Il polifilo, 1978).

Caciorgna, Maria Theresa (ed.), *Santa Maria di Grottaferrata e il Cardinale Bessarione: Fonte e Studi sulla Prima Commenda* (Rome: L'Erma di Bretschneider, 2005).

Campbell, Caroline, 'Cardinal Bessarion and Two Members of the Scuola della Carità in Prayer with the Bessarion Reliquary', *National Gallery Review*, April 2001-March 2002.

Candal, Emmanuel, 'Bessarion Nicaenus in Concilio Florentino', *Orientalia Christiana Periodica*, 6 (1940).

Canova, Giordana Mariani, 'Una illustre serie liturgica ricostruita: I corali del Bessarione già all'Annunziata di Cesena', *Saggi e memorie di storia dell'arte*, 11 (1977).

Carosi, Gabriele Paolo, *Subiaco e l'introduzione della stampa in Italia* (Milan: U. Hoepli, 1972).

Cattapan, Mario, 'Nuovi Elenchi e Documenti dei Pittori in Creta dal 1300 al 1500', *Thesaurismata*, 9 (1972).

Cavallaro, Anna, 'Il rinnovato culto delle icone nella Roma del Quattrocento', *L'Arte di Bisanzio e l'Italia al tempo dei Palaeologi, 1261-1453*, ed. Antoni Iacobini and Mauro della Valle (Rome: Edizioni dell'Elefante, 1999).

Cawkwell, George, *Philip of Macedon* (London: Faber & Faber, 1978).

Cecchini, Giovanni, 'Evoluzione architettonico-strutturale della Biblioteca pubblica in Italia dal secolo XV a XVII', *Accademie e Biblioteche d'Italia*, 35 (1967).

Chacon, *Vitæ et res gestæ summorum pontificum et S.R.E. cardinalium ad Ciacconii exemplum continuatæ, quibus accedit appendix qua vitas cardinalium perficit à Guarnaccio non absolutas*, volume 2 (Rome: Pagliarini, 1787).

Chambers, David S., 'The Earlier "Academies" in Italy', *Italian Academies of the Sixteenth Century*, ed. David S. Chambers and Francois Quiviger, volume 1 (London: The Warburg Institute, 1995).

Charlet, J.L., *Deux pièces de la controverse humaniste sur Pline: N. Perotti, Lettre à Guarnieri. C. Vitelli, Lettre à Partenio di Salò* (Sassoferrato: Centro Studi Sassoferrato, 2003).

Chatzidakis, Nano (ed.), *Da Candia a Venezia: Icone Greche in Italia XV-XVI Secolo* (Venice and Athens: Olkos, 1993).

Christianson, Gerald, 'Annates and Reform at the Council of Basel', *Reform and Renewal in the Middle Ages and the Renaissance*, ed. Thomas Izbicki and Christopher Bellito (Leiden: Brill, 1999).

Clark, M.T., 'The Role of Neoplatonism in St Augustine's Civitate Dei', *Neoplatonism and Early Christian Thought: Essays in Honour of A. H. Armstrong*, ed. H. Blumenthal and R.A. Marks (London: Variorum, 1981).

Claudin, Anatole, *The First Paris Press: An Account of the Books Printed for G. Fichet and J. Heynlin in the Sorbonne, 1470-1472* (London: Bibliographical Society, 1878).

Clough, Cecil H., 'Bessarion and Greek at the Court of Urbino', *Manuscripta*, 8 (1964).

—, 'The Library of the Dukes of Urbino', *Librarium*, 9 (1966).

Coccia, Antonio, 'Il Cardinale Bessarione ed il suo sepolcro nella basilica dei SS. Apostoli', *Almananacco dei Bibliotecari Italiani* (1972).

—, 'Vita e Opere del Bessarione', *Miscellanea Francesca*, 73 (1973).

Colliard, L.-A., *Un ami savoyard du cardinal Bessarion: Guillaume Fichet, Ancien recteur de l'Université de Paris* (Paris: Honoré Champion, 2004).

Coluccia, Giuseppe, *Basilio Bessarione: Lo spirito Greco e l'Occidente* (Florence: Leo S. Olschki, 2009).

Connell, Susan, 'Books and their Owners in Venice: 1345-1480', *Journal of the Warburg and Courtauld Institutes*, 35 (1972).

Creighton, Mandell, *Historical Essays and Reviews* (London and New York: Longmans, Green and Co., 1902).

Crouzet-Pavan, Elisabeth, *Espaces, pouvoir et société à Venise à la fin du moyen-age*, volume II (Rome: École Française de Rome, 1992).

Crowder, C.M.D., *Unity, Heresy and Reform, 1378-1460: The Conciliar Response to the Great Schism* (New York: St. Martin's Press, 1977).

Cutler, Anthony, 'From Loot to Scholarship: Changing Modes in the Italian Response to Byzantine Artefacts, ca. 1200-1750', *Dumbarton Oaks Papers*, 49 (1995).

Damerini, Gino, *L'Isola e il cenobio di San Giorgio Maggiore* (Venice: Istituto Veneto di Scienze, Lettere ed Arti, 1956).

Davies, Martin, 'Juan de Carvajal and Early Printing: The 42-line Bible and the Sweynheym and Pannartz Aquinas', *The Library*, series 6, vol. 18, no. 3 (1996).

De Benedictis, Angela, *Repubblica per contratto: Bologna: una città europea nello Stato della Chiesa* (Bologna: Il Mulino, 1995).

De Margerie, B., 'Vers une relecture du concile de Florence grâce à la reconsidération de l'Ecriture et des Pères grecs et latins', *Revue Thomiste*, 94 (1986).

Demosthenes, *The Orations of Demosthenes*, ed. and trans. Charles Rann Kennedy, volume 1 (London: George Bell and Sons, 1897).

Dennis, George T., 'Death in Byzantium', *Dumbarton Oaks Papers*, 55 (2001).

Derbes, Anne and Amy Neff, 'Italy, the Mendicant Orders, and the Byzantine Sphere', *Byzantium: Faith and Power*, ed. Helen C. Evans (New York: Metropolitan Museum of Art, 2004).

Devoti, Luigi, *L'Abbazia di Santa Maria di Grottaferrata dalla fine del medioevo al secolo XX* (Rome: Istituto storico italiano per il Medioevo, 1997).

Doukas, *Decline and Fall of Byzantium to the Ottoman Turks, An Annotated Translation of 'Historia Turco-Byzantina'*, ed. Harry J. Magoulias (Detroit: Wayne State University Press, 1975).

Duchesne, ed., *Liber Pontificalis*, second edition (Vatican City: Vatican Press, 1955).

Duits, Rembrandt, '"Una Icona Pulcra". The Byzantine Icons of Cardinal Pietro Barbo', *Mantova e il Rinascimento italiano: studi in onore di David S. Chambers*, ed. Philippa Jackson and Guido Rebecchini (Mantua: University of Mantua, 2011).

—, 'Byzantine Icons in the Medici Collection', *Byzantine Art and Renaissance Europe*, ed. Angeliki Lymberopoulou and Rembrandt Duits (London: Routledge, 2013).

Dunston, A.J., 'Pope Paul II and the Humanists', *The Journal of Religious History*, 7, no. 4 (1973).

Dvornik, Francis, *The Idea of Apostolicity in Byzantium and the Legend of the Apostle Andrew* (Cambridge, Mass.: Harvard University Press, 1958).

—, *Byzance et la primauté romaine* (Paris: Editions Montaigne, 1964).

Esposito Aliano, Anna, 'Testamento e inventari per la ricostruzione della biblioteca del Cardinale Gugliemo d'Estouteville', *Scrittura, Biblioteche e Stampa a Roma nel Quattrocento, Atti del seminario*, 1-2 July 1979 (Vatican City: Biblioteca Apostolica Vaticana, 1980).

Eubel, Conradum, *Hierarchia catholica medii aevi: sive Summorum pontificum, S.R.E. cardinalium, ecclesiarum antistitum series ab anno 1198 usque ad annum 1431 perducta e documentis tabularii praesertim Vaticani collecta, digesta edita*, 2 volumes (Regensburg: Monasterii Regalis Typis Bibliopolii, 1898-).

Evans, Helen C., *Byzantium: Faith and Power (1261-1557)* (New York: Metropolitan Museum of Art, 2004).

Every, George, *Misunderstandings between East and West* (London: Sheed & Ward, 1965).

Fantaguzzi, Giuliano, *Caos: Cronache Cesenati del Sec. XV*, ed. Dino Bazzochi (Cesena: Tipografia Nazionale, 1915).

Farenga, Paola, 'Il sistema delle dediche nella prima editoria romana del Quattrocento', *Il libro a corte*, ed. Quondam Amadeo (Rome: Bulzoni Editore, 1994).

Feld, M.D., 'Sweynheym and Pannartz, Cardinal Bessarion, Neoplatonism: Renaissance Humanism and Two Early Printers' Choice of Texts', *Harvard Library Bulletin*, 30, no. 3 (1982).

Fiaccadori, Gianfranco, and Paolo Eleuteri, *I Greci in Occidente: La Tradizione filosofica, scientifica e letteraria dalle raccolte della Biblioteca Nazionale Marciana* (Venice: Biblioteca Nazionale Marciana, 1966).

Ficino, Marsilio, *Opera omnia. Con una lettera introduttiva di Paul Oskar Kristeller e una premessa di Mario Sancipriano* (Basel: Henricus Petrus, 1576; facsimile, Torino: Bottega d'Erasmo, 1962).

Fink, K.A., 'Eugene IV and the Council of Basel-Ferrara-Florence', *Handbook of Church History*, ed. H. Jedin, volume 4 (New York: Herder and Herder, 1970).

Fogolari, Gino, 'La teca di Bessarione e la croce di San Teodoro di Venezia', *Dedalo*, 3 (1922).

—, 'La Chiesa di Santa Maria della Carità di Venezia', *Archivio Veneto-Tridentino*, 5 (1924).

Franceschini, Adriano, 'Codici e libro a stampa nella società e nelle biblioteche private ferraresi del secolo XV', *La Bibliofilia*, 85 (1983).

Franceschini, Gino, 'Violante Montefeltro Malatesti Signora di Cesena', *Studi Romagnoli*, I (1950).

Frantz, Alison, 'Byzantine Illuminated Ornament: A Study in Chronology', *Art Bulletin*, 16 (1934).

Freedberg, David, *The Power of Images: Studies in the History and Theory of Response* (Chicago: University of Chicago Press, 1989).

Frolow, A., *La Relique de la Vraie Croix: Recherches sur le développement d'un culte* (Paris: Institut Français d'Archéologie Orientale, 1961).

Fuessel, Stephan, *Gutenberg and the Impact of Printing*, trans. Douglas Martin (Aldershot: Ashgate, 1999).

Furlan, Italo, *Codici greci illustrati della Biblioteca Marciana* (Padua: CEDAM, 1988).

Garin, E., *Le traduzioni umanistiche di Aristotele nel secolo XV* (Florence: Accademia Fiorentina, 1950).

Gaspare de Verona and Michele Canensi, *Le vite di Paolo II*, ed. Giuseppe Zippel (Città di Castello: Tipografia S. Lapi, 1904).

Geanakoplos, Deno J., *Byzantine East and Latin West: Two Worlds of Christendom in the Middle Ages and Renaissance. Studies in Ecclesiastical Church History* (Oxford: Basil Blackwell, 1966).

—, 'An Orthodox View of the Councils of Basel and Florence'. *Constantinople and the West: Essays on the Late Byzantine (Palaeologan) and Italian Renaissances and the Byzantine and Roman Churches* (Madison, WI: University of Wisconsin Press, 1989).

Gersh, Stephen, *Middle Platonism and Neoplatonism: The Latin Tradition*, 2 volumes (Notre Dame: University of Notre Dame Press, 1986).

Gesamtkatalog der Wiegendrucke, volume 1 (Leipzig-Stuttgart-Berlin: Hiersemann, 1925-).

Ghirardacci, Cherubino, *Della historia di Bologna*, 4 volumes (Bologna: Rossi, 1596-1657).

Ghisalberti, Alberto M., *Dizionario biografico degli italiani* (Rome: Istituto della Enciclopedia Italiana, 1960-).

Giannini, Romano, 'Vita della Theotocos di Grottaferrata: una luminosa presenza plurisecolare'. *Bollettino della Badia Greca di Grottaferrata* 42 (Rome: Badia Greca di Grottaferrata, 1988).

Gill, Joseph, *Council of Florence* (Cambridge: Cambridge University Press, 1959).

—, *Eugenius IV: Pope of Christian Union* (London: Oxford University Press, 1961).

—, *Personalities of the Council of Florence and Other Essays* (Oxford: Basil Blackwell, 1964).

—, 'East and West in the Time of Bessarion'. *Rivista di studi bizantini e neoellenici* 5 (Rome: Istituto per l'Oriente, 1968).

—, 'The Sincerity of Bessarion the Unionist'. *Journal of Theological Studies* 26 (Oxford: Oxford University Press, 1975).

Ginzburg, Carlo, *The Enigma of Piero: Piero della Francesca: the Baptism, the Arezzo cycle, the Flagellation* (London: Verso, 1985).

Giovenale, G.B., *La basilica di S. Maria in Cosmedin* (Rome: Tipografia Regionale, 1927).

Glaser, Tamas, 'The Remnants of the Hellenes: Problems of Greek Identity after the Fall of Constantinople'. *Der Beitrag der Byzantinischen Gelehrten zur Abendlaendischen Renaissance des 14. und 15. Jahrhunderts*, ed. Evangelos Konstantinou (Frankfurt: Peter Lang, 2006).

Goff, Frederick, *Incunabula in American Libraries: A Third Census of Fifteenth-Century Books Recorded in North American Collections* (New York: Bibliographical Society of America, 1964).

—, *Indice generale degli incunaboli delle biblioteche d'Italia*, ed. T. M. Guarnaschelli, E. Valenziani, and E. Cerulli, 4 volumes (Rome: Istituto Poligrafico dello Stato, 1943-65).

Gruppo Archeologico Latino Colli Albani 'Bruno Martellotta', *L'Abbazia Greca di Grottaferrata* (Rome: Edizioni Archeoclub d'Italia, 2006).

Guerrini, Paola, 'Il Bessarione a Grottaferrata: un'ipotesi sulla donazione dell'icona'. *Studi Medievali* 32, ser. 2 (Spoleto: Fondazione Centro Italiano di Studi sull'Alto Medioevo, 1991).

Guarino Veronese, *Epistolario di Guarino Veronese*, ed. R. Sabbadini (Venice: Istituto Veneto di Scienze, Lettere ed Arti, 1915-19).

Hall, Edwin, *Sweynheym and Pannartz and the Origins of Printing in Italy* (McMinnville, Oregon: Collegium Graphicum, 1991).

Hankins, James, *Plato in the Italian Renaissance* (Leiden and New York: E.J. Brill, 1990).

—, 'Renaissance Crusaders: Humanist Crusade Literature in the Age of Mehmed II'. *Dumbarton Oaks Papers* 49 (Washington, D.C.: Dumbarton Oaks Research Library and Collection, 1995).

—, *Humanism and Platonism in the Renaissance* (Rome: Edizioni di Storia e Letteratura, 2003-04).

Harris, Jonathan, *Greek Emigres in the West 1400-1520* (Camberley: Porphyrogenitus, 1995).

—_, 'Being a Byzantine after Byzantium: Hellenic Identity in Renaissance Italy'. *Kampos: Cambridge Papers in Modern Greek* 8 (Cambridge: University of Cambridge, 2000).

Helmrath, Johannes, *Das Basler Konzil, 1431-1449: Forschungsstand und Probleme* (Koln: Böhlau Verlag, 1987).

Hirsch, Rudolph, 'Early Printed Latin Translations of Greek Texts'. *The Printed Word: Its Impact and Diffusion*, ed. Rudolph Hirsch (London: Variorum Reprints, 1978).

—, 'The Size of Editions of Books Produced by Sweynheym and Pannartz between 1465 and 1471'. *The Printed Word: Its Impact and Diffusion,* ed. Rudolph Hirsch (London: Variorum Reprints, 1978).

Hoeniger, Cathleen, *The Renovation of Paintings in Tuscany, 1250-1500* (Cambridge: Cambridge University Press, 1995).

Housley, N., *Religious Warfare in Europe, 1400-1536* (Oxford: Oxford University Press, 2002).

Howe, Eunice D., 'The Miraculous Madonna in Fifteenth-Century Roman Painting'. *Explorations in Renaissance Culture* 8-9 (New York: AMS Press, 1982-83).

Hussey, Joan Mervyn, *The Orthodox Church in the Byzantine Empire* (Oxford: Clarendon Press, 1986).

Indice generale degli incunaboli delle biblioteche d'Italia, ed. T. M. Guarnaschelli, E. Valenziani, and E. Cerulli, 4 volumes (Rome: Istituto Poligrafico dello Stato, 1943-65).

Infessura, Stefano, *Diario della Città di Roma*, ed. Oreste Tommasini (Rome: Forzani e C., 1890).

Janin, R., *La géographie ecclésiastique de l'empire byzantin. Le siège de Constantinople et le patriarcat oecuménique. Les églises et les monastères* (Paris: Institut Français d'Études Byzantines, 1953).

John of Damascus, *Three Treatises on the Divine Images*, trans. Andrew Louth (New York: St Vladimir's Seminary Press, 2003).

Jones, Howard, *Printing the Classical Text* ('t Goy-Houten: Hes & De Graaf, 2004).

Kalra, Vrinder, Raminder Kaur, and John Hutnyk, *Diaspora and Hybridity* (London and New Delhi: Sage Publications, 2005).

Karahan, Anne, *Byzantine Holy Images: Transcendence and Immanence: The Theological Background of the Iconography and Aesthetics of the Chora Church* (Leuven, Paris, and Walpole, Mass.: Peeters, 2010).

Kenney, E.J., 'The Character of Humanist Philology'. *Classical Influences on European Culture, AD 500-1500* (Cambridge: Cambridge University Press, 1971).

Krautheimer, Richard, *Corpus Basilicarum Christianarum Romae: Le basiliche cristiane di Roma*, volume 1 (Vatican City: Pontificio Istituto di Archeologia Cristiana, 1937).

Kraye, Jill, 'Philologists and Philosophers'. *The Cambridge Companion to Renaissance Humanism*, ed. Jill Kraye (Cambridge: Cambridge University Press, 1996).

Kristeller, Paul, 'Neoplatonismo e Rinascimento'. *Il Veltro* 35, no. 1-2 (Rome: Il Veltro Editrice, 1991).

Kruger, Klaus, 'Medium and Imagination: Aesthetic Aspects of Trecento Panel Painting'. *Italian Panel Painting of the Duecento and Trecento*, ed. Victor M. Schmidt (New Haven and London: Yale University Press, 2002).

Labowsky, Lotte, 'An Unknown Treatise by Theodorus Gaza'. *Medieval and Renaissance Studies* 6 (London: Warburg Institute, 1968).

—, 'An Unnoticed Letter of Bessarion to Lorenzo Valla'. *Medieval Learning and Literature: Essays Presented to Richard William Hunt*, eds J.J.G. Alexander and M.T. Gibson (Oxford: Clarendon Press, 1976).

—, *Bessarion's Library and the Biblioteca Marciana: Six Early Inventories* (Rome: Edizioni di Storia e Letteratura, 1979).

Laurent, V., 'La Succession épiscopale de Trébizonde'. *Archeion Pontou* 21 (Athens: Society of Pontic Studies, 1956).

Lee, Egmont, *Sixtus IV and Men of Letters* (Rome: Edizioni di Storia e Letteratura, 1978).

Le Grand, Emile, *Cent-dix lettres grecques de François Filelfe: publiées intégralement pour la première fois d'après le Codex Trivulzianus 873*, trans. and ed. Emile Legrand (Paris: E. Leroux, 1892).

Levi, Anthony, 'Ficino, Augustine and the Pagans'. *Marsilio Ficino: His Theology, His Philosophy, His Legacy*, eds. Michael J.B. Allen and Valery Rees (Leiden/Boston/Cologne: Brill, 2002).

Lollini, Fabrizio, *Il Cardinale Bessarione e le arti figurative*, PhD diss., University of Bologna, 2 volumes (Bologna: University of Bologna Press, 1986-87).

—, 'Bologna, Ferrara, Cesena: 'I corali del Bessarione tra circuiti umanistici e percorsi di artisti'. *Corali Miniati del Quattrocento nella Biblioteca Malatestiana*, ed. Piero Lucchi (Milan: Skira, 1989).

—, 'Volumi Liturgici miniati nel territorio Cesenate'. *Storia della chiesa di Cesena*, ed. Marino Mengozzi (Cesena: Stilgraf Editrice, 1998).

Lowry, Martin, 'Aldus Manutius and Benedetto Bordon: In Search of a Link'. *Bulletin of the John Rylands University Library of Manchester* 66 (Manchester: Manchester University Press, 1983).

—, 'Diplomacy and the Spread of Printing'. *Bibliography and the Study of Fifteenth-Century Civilization*, British Library Occasional Papers 5 (London: British Library, 1987).

Ludovici, Sergio Samek, 'La introduzione della stampa in Italia: Sweynheym, Pannartz, Bussi e Nicolo Cusano'. *Italia grafica* 19 (Milan: Istituto di Studi sul Rinascimento, 1964).

Lymberopoulou, Angeliki, *The Church of the Archangel Michael at Kavalariana: Art and Society on Fourteenth-Century Venetian-Dominated Crete* (London: Routledge, 2006).

—, 'Audiences and Markets for Cretan Icons'. *Viewing Renaissance Art*, eds. Kim Woods, Carol M. Richardson, and Angeliki Lymberopoulou (New Haven and London: Yale University Press, 2007).

Maguire, Henry, 'Style and Ideology in Byzantine Imperial Art'. *Gesta* 28 (Chicago: University of Chicago Press, 1989).

Malvasia, Bonaventura, *Compendio Historico della Ven. Basilica di SS. Dodeci Apostoli sua Fondatione, Origine, Nobilita, Sito...Descritto dal P.F. Bonaventura Malvasia da Bologna* (Rome: Stamperia di Giovanni Francesco Buagni, 1655).

Mango, Cyril, 'Byzantinism and Romantic Hellenism'. *Journal of the Warburg and Courtauld Institutes* 28 (London: Warburg Institute, 1965).

—, *The Art of the Byzantine Empire, 312-1453* (New Jersey: Prentice Hall, 1972).

Marcon, Susy, 'La Miniatura nei codici del cardinale Bessarione'. *I luoghi della memoria scritta: manoscritti, incunaboli, libri a stampa di biblioteche statali italiane*, ed. Guglielmo Cavallo (Rome: Bulzoni Editore, 1994).

—, 'Miniatures in Latin Manuscripts Commissioned by Cardinal Bessarion'. *Bessarione e l'Umanesimo* (Naples: Istituto Italiano per gli Studi Filosofici, 1994).

Marti, Susan, Till-Holger Borchert, and Gabriele Keck, *Charles le Téméraire: faste et déclin de la cour de Bourgogne* (Bruges: Ludion, 2008).

Martin, Jacquilyne E., *Cardinal Bessarion, Mystical Theology and Spiritual Union between East and West*, PhD diss. (Winnipeg: University of Manitoba, 2000).

Masai, François, *Pléthon et le Platonisme de Mistra* (Paris: Klincksieck, 1956).

Masini, Nicolo, *Vita Malatestae Novelli Caesenae Principis, et Bibliothecae huius eximiae conditoris*, transcribed from the Eccles. Signor Dottore Giovanni Ceccaroni Legista, 1584.

Medica, Massimo, 'Alcune considerazioni per una presenza bolognese del "Maestro del Breviario Francescano"', *Quaderno di studi sull'arte lombarda dai Visconti agli Sforza*, ed. Maria Teresa Balboni Brizza (Milan: Cisalpino, 1990).

Melograni, Anna, 'Un Antifonario Ricomparso. Nuove Proposte per il Catalogo del Terzo Maestro del Bessarione', *Arte Bollettino*, 124 (2003).

Mercati, Giovanni, *Ultimi contribute alla storia degli umanisti, Fasc. 1: Traversariana* (Città del Vaticano: Biblioteca Apostolica Vaticana, 1939).

Meserve, Margaret, 'Patronage and Propaganda at the First Paris Press', *Papers of the Bibliographical Society of America*, 97 (2003).

—, 'Italian Humanists and the Problem of the Crusade' *Crusading in the Fifteenth Century: Message and Impact*, ed. Norman Housley (Basingstoke: Palgrave Macmillan, 2005).

Michelini Tocci, Luigi, 'La formazione della biblioteca di Federico da Montefeltro: codici contemporanei e libri a stampa', in *Federico da Montefeltro: lo stato, le arti, la cultura*, eds. Giorgio Berboni Baiardi, Giorgio Chittolini and Pietro Floriani, volume 3 (Rome: Bulzoni Editore, 1986).

Migne, J.-P., ed., *Patrologia Latina*, 144 (Paris: J.-P. Migne, 1853).

—, *Patrologiae Graecae: Cursus Completus*, 161 (Paris: J.-P. Migne, 1866).

Miller, William, *Trebizond: The Last Greek Empire* (London: Society for Promoting Christian Knowledge, 1926).

Minisci, Teodoro, *Santa Maria di Grottaferrata* (Grottaferrata: Abbazia di Grottaferrata, 1966).

Mioni, Elpidio, 'Bessarione Bibliofilo e Filologo', *Rivista di studi bizantini e neoellenici*, n.s. 5 (1968).

—, *Cento Codici Bessarionei: Catalogo di Mostra* (Venice: Comune di Venezia, 1968).

—, 'Bessarione scriba e alcune suoi collaboratori', *Miscellanea Marciana e studi bessarionei*, 24 (1976).

Modigliani, Anna, *Tipografi a Roma prima della stampa: due società per fare libri con le forme (1466-1470)* (Rome: Istituto Grafico Tiberino, 1989).

Moffitt Watts, Pauline, *Nicolaus Cusanus: A Fifteenth-Century Vision of Man* (Leiden: Brill, 1982).

Mohler, Ludwig, *Kardinal Bessarion als Theologe, Humanist, und Staatsmann: Funde und Forschungen* (Paderborn: Schöningh, 1923-41).

Monfasani, John, *George of Trebizond: A Biography and a Study of his Rhetoric and Logic* (Leiden: Brill, 1976).

—, 'Bessarion Latinus', *Rinascimento*, ser. 2, 21 (1981).

—, *Il Perotti e la controversia platonici ed aristotelici* (Lawrence: University Press of Kansas, 1981).

—, 'Still More on Bessarion Latinus', *Rinascimento*, ser. 2, 23 (1983).

—, 'The Byzantine Rhetorical Tradition and the Renaissance', *Renaissance Eloquence*, ed. J.J. Murphy (Los Angeles: University of California Press, 1983).

—, 'Alexius Celadenus and Ottaviano Ubaldini: An Epilogue to Bessarion's Relationship with the Court of Urbino', *Bibliothèque d'Humanisme et Renaissance*, 46 (1984).

—, 'The First Call for Press Censorship: Niccolò Perotti, Giovanni Bussi, Antonio Moreto and the Editing of Pliny's Natural History', *Renaissance Quarterly*, 41, no. 1 (1988).

—, 'Bessarion, Valla, Agricola, and Erasmus', *Rinascimento*, ser. 2, 28 (1988).

—, 'Testi inediti di Bessarione e Teodoro Gaza', *Dotti bizantini e libri greci nell'Italia del secolo XV: Atti del Convegno international, Trento 22-23 ottobre 1990* (Naples: Istituto Universitario Orientale, 1992).

—, 'Platonic Paganism in the Fifteenth Century', *Byzantine Scholars in Renaissance Italy: Cardinal Bessarion and Other Emigres* (Aldershot: Variorum, 1995).

—, 'Giovanni Gatti of Messina: A Profile and an Unedited Text', *Filologia umanistica per Gianvito Resta*, eds. V. Fera and G. Ferraù, 3 volumes (Padua: Antenore, 1997), II:1315-38.

—, 'Marsilio Ficino and the Plato-Aristotle Controversy', *Marsilio Ficino: His Theology, His Philosophy, His Legacy*, ed. Michael J.B. Allen and Valery Rees (Leiden/Boston/Cologne: Brill, 2002).

—, 'A tale of two books: Bessarion's In Calumniatorem Platonis and George of Trebizond's Comparatio Philosophorum Platonis et Aristotelis', *Renaissance Studies*, 22, issue 1 (February 2008).

—, 'Two Fifteenth-Century "Platonic Academies": Bessarion's and Ficino's', *On Renaissance Academies. Proceedings of the International Conference 'From the Roman Academy to the Danish Academy in Rome'* (Rome: Edizioni di Storia e Letteratura, 2011).

—, *Bessarion Scholasticus: A Study of Cardinal Bessarion's Latin Library* (Turnhout: Brepols, 2012).

Moreau, J., 'De la concordance d'Aristote avec Platon', *XVIème Colloque International de Tours, Platon et Aristote à la Renaissance* (Tours: Centre National de la Recherche Scientifique, 1976).

Mouriki, Doula, 'The Wall Paintings at Mistra: Models of a Painters' Workshop in the Fifteenth Century', *The Twilight of Byzantium: Aspects of Cultural and Religious History in the Late Byzantine Empire*, eds. Slobodan Curcic and Doula Mouriki (Princeton: Princeton University Press, 1989).

Muccioli, Giuseppe Maria, *Catalogus codicum manuscriptorum Malatestianae Caesenatis Bibliothecae Fratrum Minorum Conventualium fidei custodiaeque concreditae historica praefatione, variisque adnotationibus illustratus*, II (Cesena: Tipografia Pio, 1784).

Muntz, Eugène, *Les Arts à la Cour des Papes pendant le VXème e le XVIème siècle, II: Paul II (1464-1471)* (Paris: Didron, 1879).

Muntz, Eugène and Paul Fabre, *La Bibliothèque du Vatican at XV Siècle d'après des documents inédits* (Paris: E. Leroux, 1887).

Nasalli Rocca di Corneliano, Emilio, 'Il Card. Bessarione: Legato Pontificio in Bologna', *Atti e memorie della R. Deputazione di Storia Patria per le Romagne*, ser. 4, 20 (Bologna: Deputazione di Storia Patria per le Romagne, 1931).

Negri Arnoldi, Francesco, 'Madonne giovanili di Antoniazzo Romano', *Commentari*, 15 (Bologna: Istituto per i Beni

Artistici, Culturali e Naturali della Regione Emilia-Romagna, 1964).

Nelson, Robert S., 'The Italian Appreciation and Appropriation of Illuminated Byzantine Manuscripts, c. 1200-1450', *Dumbarton Oaks Papers*, 49 (1995).

Nicholas de Cues, 'Le Tableau ou la vision de Dieu', introduced and translated by Agnès Minazzoli (Paris: Éditions du Cerf, 1986).

Nicol, Donald, *Byzantium and Venice: A Study in Diplomatic and Cultural Relations* (Cambridge and New York: Cambridge University Press, 1988).

—, 'The Byzantine View of Papal Sovereignty', *The Church and Sovereignty, c. 590-1918: Essays in Honour of Michael Wilks*, ed. Diana Wood (Oxford: Clarendon Press, 1991).

O'Daly, Gerard, *Platonism Pagan and Christian: Studies in Plotinus and Augustine* (London: Bristol Classical Press, 2001).

Oakley, Francis, *The Conciliarist Tradition: Constitutionalism in the Catholic Church, 1300-1870* (Oxford: Oxford University Press, 2003).

Oikonomides, Nicolas, 'The Holy Icon as an Asset', *Dumbarton Oaks Papers*, 45 (1991).

Ousterhout, Robert G., *The Architecture of the Kariye Camii in Istanbul* (Washington: Dumbarton Oaks Research Library and Collection, 1987).

Pace, Valentino, 'Presenze e Influenze Cipriote nella Pittura Duecentesca Italiana', in *Corso di Cultura sull'Arte Ravennate e Bizantina*, 32 (Ravenna: Accademia di Belle Arti, 1985).

Palermino, R., 'The Roman Academy, the Catacombs and the Conspiracy of 1468', *Archivium Historiae Pontificiae*, 18 (1980).

Partner, Peter, *The Papal State under Martin V: The Administration and Government of the Temporal Power in the Early Fifteenth Century* (London: Macmillan, 1958).

Papadakis, Aristeides (in collaboration with John Meyendorff), *The Christian East and the Rise of the Papacy: The Church 1071-1453 A.D.* (Crestwood, N.Y.: St. Vladimir's Seminary Press, 1994).

Pastor, Ludwig von, *The History of the Popes, From the Close of the Middle Ages*, 8 volumes (London: Kegan Paul, Trench, Trübner, 1899-1908).

Pera, Loredana, 'La Platea del Bessarione: Un patrimonio ricomposto', *Santa Maria di Grottaferrata e il Cardinale Bessarione: Fonti e Studi sulla Prima Commenda*, ed. Maria Teresa Caciorgna (Rome: Edizioni di Storia e Letteratura, 2005).

Peruzzi, Marcella, 'The Library of Glorious Memory: History of the Montefeltro Collection', *Federico da Montefeltro and his Library*, ed. J. Alexander (Italy: Edizioni di Storia e Letteratura, 2007).

Petrucci, Armando, *Writers and Readers in Medieval Italy*, trans. and ed. Charles M. Radding (New Haven: Yale University Press, 1995).

Petta, Marco, 'L'Inventario degli Oggetti del Monastero di Grottaferrata nel 1462', *Bollettino della Badia Greca di Grottaferrata*, 42 (1988).

Pettegree, Andrew, *The Book in the Renaissance* (New Haven and London: Yale University Press, 2010).

Philippe, Jules, *Guillaume Fichet: Sa Vie et Ses Oeuvres* (Annecy: G. et D. Poyet, 1892).

Piazzoni, Ambrogio M., *La Bibbia di Federico da Montefeltro*, 2 volumes (Vatican City: Biblioteca Apostolica Vaticana, 2005).

Piccolomini, Silvius Aeneas, *The Commentaries of Pius II*, eds. W.D. Gray and H.U. Underwood, trans. Florence Alden Gragg (Northampton, Mass.: Smith College Studies in History, 1951).

—, *Reject Aeneas, Accept Pius: Selected Letters of Aeneas Sylvius Piccolomini (Pope Pius II)*, introduced and translated by Thomas M. Izbicki, Gerald Christianson, and Philip Krey (Washington: The Catholic University of America Press, 2006).

Pius II, *Commentaries*, eds. M. Meserve and M. Simonetta (Harvard and London: Harvard University Press, 2003).

Platina, Bartolommeo, *The Lives of the Popes from the Accession of Gregory VII to the Death of Paul II*, trans. Rev. W. Benham (London: George Bell and Sons, 1888).

Pletho, George Gemistos, *Traité des lois ou recueil des fragments, en partie inédits, de cet ouvrage, texte revu sur les manuscrits, précédé d'une notice historique et critique, et augmenté d'un choix de pièces justificatives, la plupart inédites*, ed. C. Alexandre (Amsterdam: A. Swets & Zeitlinger, 1967).

Polacco, Renato, 'La Storia del reliquario Bessarione dopo il rinvenimento del verso della croce scomparsa', *Saggi e Memorie di storia dell'arte*, 18 (1992).

Pseudo-Dionysius, *The Complete Works*, ed. John Farina (New York: Paulist Press, 1987).

Quirini, A.M., *Liber singularis de optimorum scriptorum editionibus quae Romae primum prodierunt post divinum typographiae inventum* (Lindau: K. V. M. Braumüller, 1761).

Richardson, Brian, 'The Debates on Printing in Renaissance Italy', *La Bibliofilia*, 100 (Florence: Leo S. Olschki, 1998).

—, *Printing, Writers and Readers in Renaissance Italy* (Cambridge: Cambridge University Press, 1999).

—, *Manuscript Culture in Renaissance Italy* (Cambridge: Cambridge University Press, 2009).

Richardson, Carol M., *Reclaiming Rome: Cardinals in the Fifteenth Century* (Leiden and Boston: Brill, 2009).

Ringbom, Sixten, *Icon to Narrative: The Rise of the Dramatic Close-Up in Fifteenth-Century Devotional Painting*, Acta

Academiae Aboensis, ser. A, 31 (Åbo: Academia Aboensis, 1965).

Robertson, Ian, 'Paul II: Zentihomo de Venecia e Pontifico', *War, Culture and Society in Renaissance Venice*, ed. David S. Chambers, Cecil H. Clough and Michael E. Mallett (London and Ohio: Centre for Renaissance and Baroque Studies, 1993).

—, *Tyranny under the Mantle of St Peter: Pope Paul II and Bologna* (Turnhout: Brepols, 2002).

Rocchi, A., *La Badia di Grottaferrata* (Rome: Tipografia della R. Accademia dei Lincei, 1904).

Ross, James Bruce and Mary Martin McLaughlin, *The Portable Renaissance Reader* (London: Penguin Books, 1968).

Rouse, Mary A. and Richard H. Rouse, 'Nicolaus Gupalatinus and the Arrival of Print in Italy', *La Bibliofilia*, 88 (Florence: Leo S. Olschki, 1986).

Rubinstein, R. O., 'Pius II's Piazza S. Pietro and St Andrew's Head', *Essays in the History of Architecture Presented to Rudolf Wittkower* (London: Allen & Unwin, 1967).

Runciman, S., *The Fall of Constantinople* (Cambridge: Cambridge University Press, 1965).

Saffrey, H. D., *Recherches sur quelques autographes du Cardinal Bessarion et leur caractère autobiographique* (Rome: Edizioni di Storia e Letteratura, 1964).

Safran, William, 'Diasporas in Modern Societies: Myths of Homeland and Return', *Diaspora*, 1, no. 1 (1991).

Saint Basil, *Saint Basil: The Letters*, trans. and ed. Roy J. Deferrari, Loeb Classical Library (Cambridge, Mass.: Harvard University Press, 1961).

Saraco, Alessandro, *Il Cardinale Capranica (1400-1458) e la riforma della chiesa* (Rome: Edizioni di Storia e Letteratura, 2004).

Schioppalalba, Johannes Baptista, *In Perantiquam Sacram Tabulam Graecam Insigni Sodalitio Sanctae Mariae Caritatis Venetiarum ab Amplissimo Cardinali Bessarione Dono Datam Dissertatio* (Venice: Nella Stamperia di Giambattista Albrizzi, 1767).

Schirò, Giuseppe, 'Il Bessarione e la Cultura Classica e Bizantina d'Occidente', *Miscellanea Francesca*, 73 (1973).

Schmitt, Charles, *Aristotle and the Renaissance* (Cambridge, Mass.: Harvard University Press, 1983).

Scholarios, George, *Oeuvres complètes*, ed. Louis Petit, X. A. Siderides, Martin Jugie (Paris: Éditions de la Librairie Philosophique J. Vrin, 1928-36).

Scholderer, Victor, 'Printers and Readers in the Fifteenth Century', *Fifty Essays in Fifteenth- and Sixteenth-Century Bibliography* (Amsterdam: The Hague, 1966).

—, 'The Petition of Sweynheym and Pannartz to Sixtus IV', *Fifty Essays in Fifteenth- and Sixteenth-Century Bibliography*, ed. Dennis Rhodes (Amsterdam: The Hague, 1966).

Schulz, Peter, 'George Gemistos Plethon (ca.1360-1454); George of Trebizond (1396-1472); Cardinal Bessarion (1403-1472): The Controversy between the Platonists and the Aristotelians in the Fifteenth Century', in *Philosophers of the Renaissance*, ed. Richard Blum (Washington D.C.: The Catholic University of America Press, 2010).

Setton, Kenneth, *The Papacy and the Levant, 1204-1571*, 4 volumes (Philadelphia: The American Philosophical Society, 1976-1984).

Sevcenko, Ihor, 'Intellectual Repercussions of the Council of Florence', *Church History*, 24 (1955).

—, 'The Palaeologan Renaissance', *Renaissances before the Renaissance: Cultural Revivals of Late Antiquity and the*

Middle Ages, ed. Warren Treadgold (Stanford: Stanford University Press, 1984).

Sorbelli, Albano (ed.), *Corpus chronicorum bononiensium*, 4 volumes (Città di Castello: R. Giuffrè Editore, 1906-).

Spatharakis, Ioannis, *The Left-Handed Evangelist: A Contribution to Palaeologan Iconography* (London: Hellenic College Press, 1988).

Staikos, Konstantinos Sp., *The History of the Library in Western Civilization: From Constantine the Great to Cardinal Bessarion* (Delaware: Goy-Houten Press, 2007).

Stieber, Joachim W., *Pope Eugenius IV, The Council of Basel and the Secular and Ecclesiastical Authorities in the Empire: The Conflict over Supreme Authority and Power in the Church* (Leiden: E.J. Brill, 1978).

Stormon, E.J., 'Bessarion before the Council of Florence: A Survey of his Early Writings (1423-1437)', *Byzantina Australiensia*, 1 (1981).

Syropoulos, Sylvester, *Les Mémoires de Sylvestre Syropoulos sur le concile de Florence (1438-1439)*, ed. V. Laurent (Paris-Rome: Institut de France, 1971).

Taft, Robert F., *The Byzantine Rite: A Short History* (Minnesota: The Liturgical Press, 1992).

Tatakis, Basil, *Byzantine Philosophy*, trans. Nicholas Moutafakis (Cambridge: Cambridge University Press, 2003).

Thomson, John A.F., *Popes and Princes, 1417-1517: Politics and Polity in the Late Medieval Church* (London: The Bodley Head, 1980).

Tiberia, Vitaliano, *Antoniazzo Romano per il Cardinale Bessarione a Roma* (Todi: [Publisher not provided], 1992).

Toews, John B., 'Pope Eugenius IV and the Concordat of Vienna (1448) – An Interpretation', *Church History*, 34 (1965).

Trapp, Erich, 'Lateinische Humanistenbriefe zu Bessarions Schrift "In Calumniatorem Platonis"', *Jahrbuch der Östereichischen Byzantinischen Gesellschaft*, 28 (1979).

Tsirpanlis, Constantine, *Mark Eugenicus and the Council of Florence: A Historical Re-Evaluation of his Personality* (Thessalonike: Kentron Byzantinon Ereunon, 1974).

Turner, C.J., 'The Career of George Gennadius Scholarius', *Byzantion*, 34 (1969-70).

Underwood, Paul, *The Kariye Djami*, vol. 1 (New York: Houghton Mifflin, 1966).

Uspensky, Boris, *The Semiotics of the Russian Icon* (Ghent: E. Story-Scientia, 1976).

Vacalopoulos, Apostolos, *Origins of the Greek Nation: The Byzantine Period, 1204-1461* (New Jersey: Rutgers University Press, 1970).

Vast, Henri, *Le cardinal Bessarion (1403-1472): étude sur le chrétienté et la renaissance vers le milieu du XVe siècle* (Paris: Éditions A. et J. Picard, 1878).

Vaughan, Richard, *Charles the Bold: The Last Valois Duke of Burgundy* (London: Eyre & Spottiswoode, 1973).

Verde, Armando F., *Lo Studio fiorentino 1473-1503: ricerche e documenti*, 4 volumes (Florence: Olschki, 1973-85).

Veronese, Guarino, *Epistolario di Guarino Veronese*, ed. Remigio Sabbadini (Venice: Nella Stamperia di Alvisopoli, 1915).

Vespasiano da Bisticci, *Le Vite: edizione critica con introduzione e commento di Aulo Greco* (Florence: Edizioni del Galluzzo, 1970-76).

Vikan, Gary, 'Ruminations on Edible Icons: Originals and Copies in the Art of Byzantium', *Studies in the History of Art*, 20 (1989).

Walbeck, Osten, 'The Concept of Diaspora as an Analytical Tool in the Study of Refugee Communities', *Journal of Ethnic and Migration Studies*, 28, no. 2 (2002).

Walsh, R.J., *Charles the Bold and Italy: Politics and Personnel 1467-1477* (Liverpool: Liverpool University Press, 2005).

Ware, Kallistos, 'Scholasticism and Orthodoxy: Theological Method as a Factor in the Schism', *Eastern Churches Review*, 5.1 (1973).

Watanabe, Morimichi, 'Pope Eugenius IV, the Conciliar Movement, and the Primacy of Rome', *The Church, the Councils and Reform: The Legacy of the Fifteenth Century*, ed. Gerald Christianson, Thomas Izbicki and Christopher Bellito (Washington: The Catholic University of America Press, 2008).

Weiss, Anton, *Aeneas Sylvius Piccolomini als Papst Pius II: sein Leben und Einfluss auf die literarische Cultur Deutschlands* (Graz: Akademische Druck- und Verlagsanstalt, 1897).

Weiss, Roberto, *Un umanista veneziano: Papa Paolo II* (Rome: Edizioni di Storia e Letteratura, 1958).

—, 'Two Unnoticed "Portraits" of Cardinal Bessarion', *Italian Studies*, 22 (1967), 1-5.

Wilson, Nigel, 'The Libraries of the Byzantine World', *Greek, Roman and Byzantine Studies*, 8 (1967).

—, 'Books and Readers in Byzantium', *Byzantine Books and Bookmen*, Dumbarton Oaks, Harvard (Washington D.C.: Dumbarton Oaks Research Library and Collection, 1975).

—, 'The Book Trade in Venice, ca. 1400-1515', *Venezia: Centro di Mediazione tra Oriente e Occidente (Secoli XV-XVI). Aspetti e Problemi*, ed. Hans-Georg Beck, Manoussos Manoussacas and Agostino Pertusi, volume II (Florence: Olschki, 1977).

—, *From Byzantium to Italy: Greek Studies in the Italian Renaissance* (Alessandria: Edizioni dell'Orso, 1992).

Wolff, Robert Lee, 'The Latin Empire of Constantinople and the Franciscans', *Traditio*, 2 (1944).

Woodhouse, C.M., *George Gemistos Plethon: The Last of the Hellenes* (Oxford: Clarendon Press, 1986).

Zacour, Norman, 'The Cardinal's View of the Papacy, 1150-1300', *The Religious Role of the Papacy: Ideals and Realities 1150-1300*, ed. Christopher Ryan (Toronto: University of Toronto Press, 1989).

Zazzeri, R., *Sui codici e libri a stampa della biblioteca Malatestiana di Cesena. Ricerche e osservazioni* (Cesena: Azzali, 1887).

Zorzi, Marino, 'La circolazione del libro a Venezia nel Cinquecento: biblioteche private e pubbliche', *Ateneo veneto*, 177 (1990).

—, 'Bessarione e Venezia', *Bessarione e l'umanesimo: Catalogo della mostra*, ed. Gianfranco Fiaccadori (Naples: Electa, 1994), 197-228.

—, 'Il Cardinale Bessarione e la sua biblioteca', *I Luoghi della Memoria Scritta: Manoscritti, incunaboli, libri a stampa di Biblioteche statali Italiane*, ed. Gugliemo Cavallo (Rome: Edizioni di Storia e Letteratura, 1994).

—, 'Bessarione e i codici greci', *L'Eredità Greca e L'Ellenismo Veneziano*, ed. Gino Benzoni (Venice: Edizioni di Storia e Letteratura, 2002).

INDEX

Note: Numbers in italics refer to plate numbers.

Adrianople (Edirne)   26, 106, 160, 180, 195, 213, 224, 225
Aegean Sea   17, 54, 112
  defence of   140, 145
  Ottoman aggression in   37, 127, 130, 162, 236
Albania   54, 95, 100, 103, 104, 139, 141, 170, 226
Alexandria   62–3, 262
Alfonso V, King of Naples and Aragon   103, 108, 118, 140, 182–3, 218
ancient Greek   19, 35, 45, 167, 177, 178, 179
Ancona   16, 147, 152, 220
Andrew, Apostle   *18*, 61
  relic of   147–51, 186
anti-unionist   78–81, 86, 107, 110–11, 113–15, 136, 195, 212, 214

Apostolis, Michael   180–1

Balkans   12, 18, 207, 246, 253
  Ottoman advances in   28, 171, 224
  relationship with Byzantium   43, 107, 231, 234
  strategic importance of   142, 244
Bayezid I, Sultan   44, 225, 245–6
Belgrade, siege of   17, 140
Bessarion, Cardinal Iohannes   *5*, *6*, 210, 221–3, 227
  acceptance of cardinalate   82, 83, 89–92
  Byzantine culture, preservation of   175–7
  Byzantine spirituality, preservation of   183–9, 208

Index

career in Orthodox
  Church 55, 57, 65
champion of Thomas
  Palaeologus 147–8, 149
collector of Greek
  manuscripts 179–81
commission of choir
  books 92–4
Council of Ferrara-Florence,
  participation in 70–2, 74,
  75, 76–7
early years 39, 40–51
efforts to raise a crusade 96,
  99, 100, 101, 133–4, 135–6,
  140, 143, 147, 151–3, 170
Eugenius IV, relationship
  with 83
Orationes, author of 166–9
papal legate 147, 171–2, 181
patronage and cultural
  network 182–3
Paul II, relationship with 161,
  169–70
Pius II, relationship with 141,
  143–4
receiving of St Andrew's
  head 148–50
return to
  Constantinople 78–81
revival of ancient
  Hellenism 177–9
Strategicon adversus Turcos,
  authorship of 137–8
Venice, role in 171, 181–2
Bianca, Duchess of Milan 147
Birago, Lampo 137–9
Black Sea 40, 94, 156, 157, 233,
  235

battle of Varna 99
maritime trade 106, 112
Ottoman expansion 60, 226
Bulgaria (Bulgarian) 95, 213–36,
  237, 238, 241, 242, 243, 255
battle of Varna 98–9
Bull of Union *see* Decree of Union
Byzantine empire (Byzantium) 2,
  14, 18, 19, 20, 21, 22, 229–
  46
after the Fall of
  Constantinople 190–1,
  199–201, 203
cultural concept 174, 175–9,
  183, 189, 209
definition and history 18–21,
  22
demise of 24, 55, 100, 113,
  129, 174, 205
Doukas 26–9
failure of the West to
  support 96, 101, 109, 115,
  147, 154, 173, 208
George Sphrantzes 29–32
historians of 22–6, 29
in the late fifteenth
  century 54, 175
Laonikos
  Chalkokondyles 32–5
Michael Kritovoulos 35–8
Ottoman threat to
  existence 66, 116, 173
revival 157, 203
saving of 41, 50, 51, 56, 66,
  70, 77, 81, 82, 83, 92, 97, 99,
  103, 134, 136, 155, 156, 178,
  189, 207–9
Troy, comparison with 34

Western aid, appeals for 56, 64, 69, 142
Byzantine exiles (refugees) 129, 142, 153 175, 182, 183, 184, 208

Calixtus III, Pope 16, 139–41, 149, 218–9, 220, 221
   commitment to crusade 139–40, 207
Candia *see* Crete
Cesarini, Cardinal Giuliano 73, 76
Chalkokondyles, Laonikos 24, 32–4
Charlemagne, Holy Roman Emperor 20, 21, 234
Chios 54, 107, 112, 128
church council 66, 68, 69, 70, 85, 109, 251, 261, 264
   Basel, Council of 50, 53, 68–70, 96, 103, 215–16, 220, 252
   Ferrara-Florence, Council of 13, 71–5, 77, 78, 79, 80–81, 82, 84, 86, 88, 89, 92, 113, 131, 136, 176, 178, 198, 207, 210, 211, 212, 213, 214, 216, 222, 226, 227
   Mantua, Council of 16, 143, 147, 181
Church of St Anthony of Chypriss 92–4
classical Greek 35, 45, 176, 257
classical literature 45, 174, 178–81, 183, 184, 208, 209
Comnenus dynasty 16, 22, 156, 160

Concordat of Vienna 14, 103, 217
Constantine XI Dragas Palaeologus, Emperor of Constantinople 12, 89, 210–12, 213
   accession to throne 107–8, 113–5
   as regent for Emperor John VIII 61
   death in battle 126, 129
   and Decree of Union 109, 113
   defence of Constantinople 111, 118–19, 120, 122
   Despot of Morea, role as 33, 100
   friendship with George Sphrantzes 29, 30
   relationship with Mehmed II 108
Constantinople 1, 2, 17, 210, 211, 212, 213, 214, 216, 223, 225, 226, 228, 230, 231, 232, 234, 235, 237, 238, 245, 248, 253, 256, 261, 262
   Bessarion, role in 44, 45, 49–51
   crusade for 134, 135–40, 144, 153, 168–70, 171
   decline of 44, 46–7, 54, 177
   Decree of Union, opposition to 78–80, 82, 89, 135
   defence of 111, 117–20, 121, 126, 246
   fall of 15, 16, 15, 23, 24, 27, 28, 30, 32, 34, 38, 40, 79,

100, 108, 120–5, 126, 127, 129, 135, 137, 141, 161, 162, 180, 182, 191, 195, 201, 205, 218, 227
foundation of   19
historians of   23–4
Isidore, role in   40, 43, 44, 45, 50, 108–11, 112, 113, 117–19, 120, 125, 127–8, 130, 132, 154
Kritovoulos, account of   36–7
Mehmed II and   104, 106, 120, 127
occupation by Latins (1204)   63–4, 71–2, 239–43
recovery under Mehmed II   174, 191–5
rivalry with Rome   20, 61–2
Russian aspirations   199–200
siege of 1422   58–9
siege of 1453, eve of   111–12
support from the West   70, 97, 144
Corfu   53, 77, 146, 147
Crete   15, 54, 128, 129, 148, 164, 180, 234, 236
Crusade   13, 14, 16, 17, 207, 208, 211, 219, 221, 223, 224, 238, 239, 240, 246, 257
  Calixtus III, Pope   139–40
  crusade to liberate the Morea   148
  efforts to raise a crusade against Turks   52, 72, 88, 92, 96, 97, 129, 149, 152, 155, 166, 182, 187, 199, 203
  Eugenius IV, Pope   97–101, 136
  Fourth crusade   40, 63–4, 71–2, 239–43
  Louis XI, King of France   172
  Nicholas V, Pope   136–9
  Paul II, Pope   160, 170–3
  Pius II, Pope   143–5, 150–1, 152–3
  Venetian participation in   97, 98, 99, 120, 124, 139, 148, 152–3, 155, 170, 171, 172, 181–2, 245

Decree of Union   8, 77, 78, 80, 82, 97, 117, 214
  eastern Europe, reaction to   83, 85, 86, 87, 88, 101
  implementation of   119, 120, 121, 132, 207
  Nicholas V, Pope   108–10
  opposition to   113–16, 153, 184, 195, 226, 227
Demetrius Palaeologus, Despot of the Morea   38, 107, 118, 141–6, 160, 212–13
Despotate of the Morea   22, 33, 61, 146, 211, 253
Dositheos, Bishop   44, 49, 73, 177
Doukas   24, 26–9, 30, 33, 105, 106, 112

Edirne see Adrianople
Euboea see Negroponte
Eugenicus, Bishop Mark of Ephesus   78–9, 80, 226–7
Eugenius IV, Pope   7, 14, 72, 88, 90, 93, 96–101, 103, 186, 214–16, 217, 220, 221, 224

challenges to papacy 74, 96
Council of Ferrara-Florence,
  role at 68–9, 73, 75, 82
crisis in Rome 67–69
crusade (1444) 97, 98, 109,
  136, 137
relationship with Bessarion 82,
  83, 89, 91–92, 96
relationship with Isidore 75,
  82, 83–84, 89

Federico, Duke of
  Montefeltro 171, 180, 182
Felix V, antipope 103, 216, 220
Ferrara 70, 74, 85, 169, 180,
  214
Fichet, Guillaume 167–9, 172
Filioque 226, 254, 261, 263
Florence 85, 87, 109, 170, 183,
  186, 212, 214, 215, 219, 223,
  254
  cooperation with
    Ottomans 155
  Decree of Union 78, 80
  funding of crusade 97
  Greek delegates in 74–5, 79,
    178
  Italic League, role in 136, 137
Forari, Doge Francesco 66, 71,
  97, 98, 128
Franciscan Order 92–4, 128,
  159, 222
Frederick III, Holy Roman
  Emperor 102, 103, 108,
  118, 140, 220

Galata *see* Pera
Gallipoli 58, 180

Gennadios, Patriarch of
  Constantinople *see also*
  Scholarios, George 37, 195–6
Genoa (Genoese) 26, 42, 99, 97,
  106, 107, 112, 120, 127, 128,
  129, 139, 154, 164, 170, 242,
  243
George of Trebizond 81, 183,
  192
Gibbon, Edward 23, 26
Golden Horn 19, 58, 121, 122,
  123, 129, 246
Greek manuscripts 129, 175,
  179–81
Gregory Mammas III, Patriarch
  of Constantinople 88, 108,
  110, 113, 132, 186, 187, 212
Grottaferrata, Abbey of 188–9,
  208
Guarino dei Guarini of
  Verona 45, 49

Hagia Sofia 46, 71, 114, 119,
  120, 126, 127, 128, 132, 191,
  192, 240, 243, 256
Hassan, Uzun 158–9, 160
Hellenes 19, 35, 160
Hellenic revival 28, 177, 179
Hellenism 178–9, 183, 257
Hellenist 36, 184
Hexamilion Wall 14, 100, 211
humanist 45, 133, 137, 176, 179,
  180, 183, 192, 216, 217, 220,
  222, 226
Hundred Years' War 96, 155
Hungary, kingdom of 15, 118,
  159, 170, 224, 227, 246
  crusade (1444) 95–9

Index

domestic challenges 97–8, 104
Isidore, role in 88
John VIII in 61, 64
Ottoman threat 85, 95–6, 103, 131, 158, 171, 204
Hunyadi, John 14, 97, 98–9, 107, 118, 140, 207, 227–8

icon 175, 184–5, 208, 243, 256
Antoniazzo Romano 20, 185–6
Bessarion's collection 175, 184–5, 187
destruction of 127
St Demetrios 19, 185
Isidore of Kiev, Cardinal 3, 4, 15, 210, 221, 223
acceptance of cardinalate 82
blamed for loss of Constantinople 154
career in Orthodox Church 50–1, 55, 65
Constantine XI, relationship with 114–15
Council of Basel, role in 53–4, 68–9
Council of Ferrara-Florence, role in 74, 75, 76, 77
crusade planning 101, 134, 135, 136, 138, 139, 140, 141, 143
defence of Constantinople 117–20
defence of the Morea 88, 147
early years 39–50
escape from Constantinople 127–28
George Scholarios, relationship with 113–14
Metropolitan of Kiev 70, 74
mission to Slavic lands 83–8
Pius II, relationship with 141–3, 144, 149, 150, 153
propaganda campaign 129–33
relationship with Eugenius IV 82, 83
resistance to Ottomans 38, 51, 173
sent to Constantinople by Nicholas V 108–13, 207
siege of Constantinople 120–7
Italic League 16, 136–7, 170, 258
Italy 20, 64, 94, 138, 168, 172, 215, 222, 226, 230, 231, 233, 236, 243, 257, 258
Bessarion's role in 42, 52, 83, 89, 184
diplomacy between Italian states 167, 169
doctrinal differences with Constantinople 154
efforts to raise crusade 171, 216
Greek delegates in 70, 72, 74, 78, 176, 179
Isidore's role in 39, 83, 88, 119
Order of St Basil 188, 208
Ottoman threat to 131, 166, 167, 173, 204
relationship with Byzantium 13, 111, 177, 235, 237

Ivan III (the Great), Grand Prince of Moscow   199, 200, 202
Ivan IV, Grand Prince of Moscow   202

janissaries   33, 138, 163, 165, 224, 225, 253, 258, 263
Jews   144, 225, 260
John IV Comnenus, Emperor of Trebizond   156, 157–8
John VIII, Emperor of Constantinople   11, 30, 97, 107, 109, 114, 210
  co-emperor with Manuel II   55–9
  Council of Ferrara-Florence   71, 77, 78–9, 80
  diplomacy with West   64
  relationship with Isidore and Bessarion   55, 66–8
  resistance to Ottomans   54, 56–9
  treatment of the Morea   61
  siege of Constantinople (1422)   59
  unification of Churches   64, 66, 136
Joseph, Patriarch of Constantinople   13, 64, 70, 71, 72–4, 76, 79, 80, 86, 109, 212, 213–14

Kiev   50, 200
  Decree of Union, reaction to   85, 87
  Metropolitan of   51, 70, 83, 86, 88, 125, 201

Kritovoulos, Michael   24, 25, 35–7, 142, 193

Latins   54, 94, 112, 189, 190, 194
  Church union   56, 69, 195, 214
  occupation of Constantinople   145, 240, 242, 243
  relationship with Greeks   64, 74
Lemnos   38, 53, 58, 118, 140, 162, 194, 226
Lesbos   26, 54, 107, 140, 194
Louis IX, King of France   159, 168, 169, 172
Ludovico da Bologna, Fra   159, 169

Manuel II, Emperor of Constantinople   29, 40, 44–5, 48, 55–7, 58, 198, 212, 213, 245–6
marriage alliances 41, 64, 65, 199, 200, 211, 243
  Cleope Malatesta, wife of Despot Theodore   63, 177
  Sophia of Montserrat, wife of John VIII   56, 64
Mehmed II, Sultan   14, 15, 25, 66, 108, 128, 130, 131, 135, 140, 144, 161, 166, 189, 206, 207, 212, 220, 225–6, 227, 228
  accession of   104
  conquest of Lesbos   26

Index

construction of Rumeli Hisarı 105–7
Fall of Constantinople 120–7
Fall of Negroponte 162–5
invasion of the Morea (1458) 141–3
invasion of the Morea (1464) 145–7
invasion of Trebizond 157–60
Laonikos Chalkokondyles on 33–4
Michael Kritovoulos on 25, 35–8
Orthodox Church 195–7, 203
siege of Belgrade (1456) 140
propaganda campaign against 130–3, 167
rule of Constantinople 174, 191–4
siege of Constantinople (1452) 112, 118
treaties with Christian nations 155
Xerxes the Great, comparison with 123, 133
Melissenos, Metropolitan Makarios of Monemvasia 30–1, 32
Milan 61, 70, 137, 143, 147, 152, 166, 170, 182
Mistra 48, 49, 50, 107, 141, 144, 146, 177, 212, 246
Monemvasia 30, 40, 45, 48–9, 145–6
Mongols 41, 197, 201, 241, 245, 246, 258, 260–1

Morea, the 13, 14, 16, 22, 29, 60, 170, 193, 197, 199, 205, 211, 212, 213
attacked by Ottomans 30, 101, 105, 141–2, 145
Bessarion, role of 49–50
centre of Byzantine resistance 56, 61, 148–9
defence of 100, 147
Isidore, role of 40, 44–5, 48, 49, 89
Moro, Doge Cristoforo of Venice 166, 171, 182
Moscow 85, 86, 87, 88, 197–203, 208, 228, 261
Murad II, Sultan 14, 15, 58–60, 64, 99, 100, 104, 211, 224–5
Mustafa, brother of Mehmed I 57–8
Mustafa, brother of Murad II 59

Naples 31, 68, 103, 112, 137, 139, 155, 166, 170, 171, 172, 182, 226
Negroponte (Euboea) 17, 53, 77, 171, 194, 242
fall of 17, 161, 162–6, 169
Nicaea 12, 51, 156, 241–2, 245, 261
Niccolo da Canale, Captain-General 163–5
Nicene Creed 76, 79, 254, 261
Nicholas V, Pope 7, 14, 15, 16, 115, 119–20, 140, 159, 170, 176, 180, 181, 216–18, 219, 220, 221, 223
Byzantine appeals 108
campaign for a crusade 136–9

challenges facing papacy 102–4
Fall of Constantinople 120, 136
implementation of Decree of Union 109, 113–14, 116, 207
Isidore's letters to 119, 120, 122, 130, 132, 133

Order of St Basil 47, 127, 168, 188, 208, 261–2
Oriental League 156–9
Orthodox Church 13, 14, 15, 210, 213, 214, 226, 227, 228, 230, 233, 239, 252, 253, 254, 255, 256, 257, 260, 261, 262, 263, 264
 defeats 56–7, 61, 98, 121–2, 140, 172
 doctrinal differences with Roman Catholics 76, 77, 79
 in Italy 188–9
 Ottomans 174, 195–7, 203
 Roman Catholic Church, relationship with 61, 62
 Rus', relationship with 87, 197–202, 208
 union with Roman Catholic Church 65, 81
Ottoman 12–17, 21, 24, 38, 210, 211, 212, 213, 224, 225, 226, 227, 245–6
 engineering 122–3, 145–6, 160
 expansion of territory 100, 108, 173, 204
 Hungary 85, 103
 internal division 57, 206
 Laonikos Chalkokondyles 32–3, 43
 Michael Kritovoulos 35–7

 Mustafa and challenges to throne 58–9
 religious tolerance 174, 193–7, 203
 Republic of Venice 60, 161–2, 181
 sack of Byzantine territories 60, 100, 126–127, 144, 152, 165, 173, 184, 191, 203
 Seljuk Turks 63, 158, 237, 243, 245
 threat to Christianity 104, 130, 131, 133–4, 135, 138, 166–7, 171, 173, 203–4
 vassalage treaties 41, 60, 100, 141

Palaeolinga, Zoe 199–200, 202
Palaeologus dynasty 142, 145, 155, 156
papacy 14, 216, 248
 Calixtus III 139, 219, 220
 challenges to 70, 102, 136, 215, 229
 Eugenius IV 67, 68, 215, 221
 Nicholas V 103, 217
 Orthodox Church, relationship with 62, 233, 243
 Paul II 222
 Sixtus IV 222–3
 Venice, relationship with 62, 162, 233, 243
Paul II, Pope 17, 155, 161, 167, 169–71, 221–2
Peloponnese 50, 53, 56, 57, 60, 61, 64, 118, 141, 142, 147, 211, 246

Index

Pera (Galata)   120, 122, 123, 127, 128, 162, 194
Philip III the Good, Duke of Burgundy   97, 143, 151, 158–9
Pius II, Pope   10, 17, 16, 17, 141, 143–6, 147, 148–53, 155, 159, 161, 162, 181, 186, 187, 207, 219–21
Pletho, Gemistus   50, 81, 177–9

relics   5, 19, 21, 46, 175, 186
   Ottomans, looting   127, 131, 173, 184, 203
   crusaders, looting   71–2, 240
   Apostle Andrew *see* Andrew, Apostle
   stauroteca of True Cross   5, 21, 186–7
rites   62, 85
   Byzantine Orthodox Greek   88, 184, 188, 256, 259, 264
   Latin   64, 86, 113, 256, 259
   Roman Catholic   13, 210, 214, 226, 229, 230, 233
   alliance with Greeks   54, 64, 81
   Bessarion, role of   81, 89, 92, 101
   church supremacy   93, 149
   doctrinal debates   75–8, 79
   Greek Orthodox Church, relationship with   61–2, 73
   Greek suspicion of   75, 113, 143
   inaction and complacency   133
   Isidore, role in   82, 86–7, 101
   missionary orders in Byzantium   93

Zoe Palaeologina, conversion of   199–200
Rome   15, 16, 17, 46, 54, 84, 88, 110, 111, 133, 137, 138, 143, 153, 155, 159, 166, 170, 176, 188, 199, 202–3, 213, 215, 216, 217, 218, 219, 220, 221, 222, 223, 226, 233, 239, 243, 256, 262–3, 264
   Bessarion, role in   92, 180, 182, 183, 184, 185
   church supremacy   62, 193, 149
   civic conflict   67–8, 206
   condition of   55
   Despot Thomas, arrival in   148, 149
   exile of papacy   68
   Nicholas V renovations   139
   split with East   20–1, 62
   translation of relic of St Andrew   148–51
Rumeli Hisarı   15, 105, 112
Runciman, Steven   23–4, 52
Rus'   39, 50, 51, 54, 74, 84, 86–8, 154, 200, 201, 228
Russia (Russians)   62, 88, 94, 190, 197, 201, 243, 261
   independence from Constantinople   87, 191, 198–9, 200, 202–3
   Isidore, role in   51, 70, 83, 153

SS Apostoli, Basilica di   92, 185
Scholarios, George *see also* Gennadios   37, 49, 79, 81, 111, 113–14, 196, 227
Sea of Marmara   58, 60, 112, 162
Serbia   15, 98, 107, 226, 238, 255

Sforza, Duke Francesco of Milan 137, 143, 152
Sixtus IV, Pope 16, 136, 171–3, 182, 200, 222–3
Soemmern, Henry 117, 127
Sphrantzes, George 24, 29–32, 33, 56
Strategicon adversus Turcos 138–9
Syropoulos, Sylvester 72–4

Tafur, Pero 47, 54
Tamerlane *see* Timur
Theodore I, Despot of the Morea 40, 48
Theodore II, Despot of the Morea 49, 56, 61, 64, 177, 211, 213
Thessalonica 39, 61, 63, 162, 180, 231, 234, 238, 241, 246
 siege of 59–60
Third Rome 191, 201, 202, 203, 208, 261
Thomas Palaeologus, Despot of the Morea 14, 16, 17, 29, 61, 89, 100, 107, 118, 141–3, 145–50, 155, 156, 199, 211, 212, 213
Timur (Tamerlane) 13, 157, 246
Topkapı Palace 35, 42, 192–3, 225
Treaty of Lodi 137, 170
Trebizond 16, 22, 40–3, 44, 49, 54 94, 118, 119, 156–60, 161, 197, 205, 226, 241

Varna, battle of 14, 99–100, 104, 136, 207, 224
vassalage under Ottomans 12, 38, 41, 64, 102, 211, 245, 246, 264, 265
Vassily Vasil'evich, Grand Prince of Moscow 74, 84, 86–7, 88 198, 201, 228
Venice (Venetian) 58, 61, 63, 64, 78, 88, 106, 137, 200, 239, 240, 242, 243, 249, 253, 265
 Bessarion's donations to 180–2, 186–7
 Constantinople, defence of 111, 119–20, 121–2, 129
 crusade 97, 98, 99, 120, 124, 139, 152–3, 155, 170, 172, 181, 245, 139, 148
 Greeks in 71, 182
 Isidore 119
 Monemvasia, defence of 146–7
 Negroponte, defence of 161–6
 Ottoman-Venetian war 17, 162
 papacy, relationship with 137, 170–1, 214, 221
 sack of Constantinople (1204) 239–40, 242
 Thessalonica, defence of 13, 59, 60
 treaties with Sultan 154–5
Vladislaus, King of Poland and Hungary 97, 98, 99